Promoting the Values & Virtues of Classical Education ✦

The Thales Canon

Volume I: The Bronze Age

Thales Press   Raleigh, North Carolina

This book is the property of:

....

....

....

....

Thales Canon: Volumes I-III

Volume I: The Bronze Age

Copyright 2023 by Thales Press. Text written by Winston Brady with editing provided by Wesley Hoag, Will Begley, and Keller Moore.

For tests, answer keys, and supplementary materials, please email us at thalespress@thalesacademy.org.

Cover photo is of the Standard of Ur, a Sumerian-era artifact made circa 2,600 BC; the photo is available in the public domain. The photo in the Table of Contents is of Karnak Temple and was taken by Diego Delso. Text and references from the Old Testament are taken from the World English Bible, available in the public domain.

For an answer key, assessments, and other supplementary resources, please email thalespress@thalesacademy.org.

Table of Contents

Section I
The Beginnings

LIBRARY AT WELLS CATHEDRAL / GREAT BRITAIN

Photo by Annie Spratt

1

CHAPTER

The Study of History

ROADMAP

✦ Learn what history is, why history is so important to your education, and history's place within the *liberal arts*.

✦ Learn about primary and secondary sources, archaeological remains, and more.

✦ Read a selection from Herodotus and the introduction to his great work, *The Histories*.

✦ Practice our knowledge of maps and chronology, as well as our writing skills through reading comprehension questions and an essay.

✦ Conduct historical research of your own by interviewing family members and consulting family records.

THALES
OUTCOME
N⁰ 4

A **Truth Seeker** *critiques a variety of truth statements and/or observations through research and scientific methodology.*

History is ultimately the study of the past, and we study history because it is both a fascinating subject and helps us become better individuals. We study the choices of great men and women long ago and imagine what difficulties they must have faced in hopes that we too may make better, more meaningful choices in the present.

The Student Historian / The Beginnings

HISTORY SHOULD MAKE US HAPPY. The study of past events—that's what history is, after all—should be one of the happiest classes we take in school because in history, we're learning about the past, and many amazing things have happened there. In fact, anything amazing that has ever happened has happened in the past. In the past, we have stories of great figures, people who either did great things or stopped terrible things from happening: the Pericleses, the Ciceroes, the Alfreds, the Franklins, the Tubmans, to name a few. We will also learn about those people who did terrible things, although we do not want to imitate their character or their actions. Importantly, we will also learn about those ordinary people, people far more like us who did their best with the time that was given to them.

Given the importance of knowing about what happened in the past, the large and the small, the Roman senator and philosopher Cicero (106-43 BC) remarked that to not "know what happened before you were born is to remain a child forever." For the more we learn from such individuals and why they made the choices that they made, the more strategies and insights we gain in making our own choices and overcoming our own struggles. The study of history is, in part, just a part of growing up.

Thankfully, the study of history is one of the best parts of growing up. History, as the name implies, is a story, and good history, at its best, can be one of the most engaging and exhilarating stories we read. History is a story told about the past that contains meaningful insights for our present day, insights that, if we learn them now, can provide for a better future later. After all, the world in which we live seems a little crazy, but the more we know about past events, the more we can make sense of what is happening in the world. That's because history is, at heart, the story of people and how they overcame all kinds of challenges that the world offers, and people are some of the most amazing creatures living in the world. People may not be fast like cheetahs or strong like lions, but people do have one ability that all other creatures lack: the ability to make meaningful choices.

People are indeed the only creatures capable of making choices. That is, we may have two options, both of which seem pretty good, and individuals can choose from one of those two options. We could go left, but we decide to go right; up instead of down; forward instead

BIG IDEA

History is the study of individuals who lived in the past, the challenges those individuals faced, and the choices they made to take on those challenges. We study history because it is a subject worthwhile to study for its own sake, because the knowledge of the past helps bring us joy, and because studying the choices of men and women across the historical ages helps us to make better choices now and in the future.

of home. The Sumerians could have looked for a better spot than the Tigris and Euphrates Rivers to settle, but then we might not have gotten the wheel (not every civilization had the wheel, after all). Hannibal could have crossed the Straits of Messina, but he crossed the Alps instead. Romulus could have cooperated with his brother Remus in building a set of walls, but then we might be studying the Reman Empire instead of the much-better named Roman Empire. At any point in time, things could have been different, and to understand why things happened the way they did and what became of such choices lies at the heart of history. The Greeks found history to be so meaningful that they even gave the study and practice of history its own Muse, Clio, whose name came from the Greek verb *to recount*, *to celebrate*, and *to make famous*. That is, after all, what history does: history recounts past human events and makes them, at least, famous enough that we would not forget them.

In taking all of these points into consideration, why should we study history? Well, why should we study anything at all? Why study math or science, Latin or literature, coding or engineering? Some subjects we study because of their practical utility–that is, the subject is useful to us, and helps us develop practical skills we can use to get a job. History does teach writing and communication skills even if it does not have the same sort of practical utility that coding or engineering may have. Instead, like the other liberal arts, the study of history brings a certain joy that comes through learning something for its own sake. The joy of learning is the true meaning of the word *liberal* in *liberal arts,* with the word *liberal* derived from the Latin *libertas*, meaning "freedom" or "liberty." The liberal arts are those subjects that began with the *trivium* (grammar, logic, and rhetoric), and continue with the *quadrivium* (geometry, arithmetic, music, and astronomy). Today, the idea of the liberal arts typically includes all those disciplines like history, literature, and philosophy that may not yield immedi-

THE GREEK WORLD

Marten van Heemskerck, Abduction of Helen amidst the Wonders of the Ancient World (1535)

ate practical benefits (like coding) but are crucial to the development of our character. Indeed, the liberal arts are studied for their own sake and not for the sake of something else. Moreover, the liberal arts are so-named because they free individuals like us from ignorance, and we study the liberal arts because they free us from the ignorance that comes from not knowing anything about the world.

In summary, we study history because the past contains stories of human endeavor worth studying. Sometimes, the past is described as a foreign country, but it is a country not unlike our own. The inhabitants of that country, at times, faced terrible things: famines, plagues, warfare, barbarian invasions, and many other kinds of hardships from without and from within the lands these peoples called home. Some tribes, nations, and groups of people endured. Others were swept away in events too large and monumental for them to withstand. The way that they responded to these challenges holds immense opportunities for us as aspiring student historians to learn what makes life meaningful. In history, we build from the mere knowledge of dates, facts, and places to understanding the intricate relationship between historical events and the significance of these events to our lives.

The more we know about the past, the more equipped we are to make better, more informed choices in the present, an understanding that we hope would equip us to contribute to a better future. The individuals whom we will study faced circumstances not unlike our own, and they responded to these challenges the best way they saw fit. Did their choices play out the way they anticipated? How should we judge their motives, their aspirations, and their convictions? How may we learn from them to cultivate the kind of character needed to make good decisions, withstand hardship and suffering, and make our own small corner of the world a better place? At its core, history is the study of people, and this study helps us understand not only how our world came to be but also our place in the world. So where do we get started?

THE SEVEN LIBERAL ARTS

Hortus deliciarum, Herrad of Landsberg (12th century)

✦✦ **Reading Comprehension Questions**

What exactly is history?

....

....

....

....

....

Why do we study history?

....

....

....

....

Why is it important to study the good and the bad, the ordinary and the extraordinary, when studying history?

....

....

....

How are human beings the most unique of all the creatures in the world?

....

....

....

The Tools of the Historian

LET'S GET STARTED with the tools we aspiring student historians need to investigate the past and learn about its inhabitants. Here are some of those tools.

Primary Sources

Primary sources are sources of information created at or very near the time of the event under investigation. They are a record created around the time of the event the historian is studying, and they can include the chronicles of great kings, letters, poems, songs, diaries, historical artifacts, and even paintings. If you keep a diary, that diary could become a primary source for someone studying what life was like at or near the writing of this book, one day far off into the future.

Secondary Sources

Secondary sources are sources of information created later by someone who did not experience first-hand the events they write about. That is, the authors of secondary sources did not live at or near the time of the events they are writing about. Instead, their authors are separated from such events by great lengths of time and distance. At times, this gap can work in their favor. The increased time brings perspective, a greater multitude of primary sources, archaeological finds, and other similar discoveries that give the authors of secondary sources advantages they would not have if they wrote about events in their own day and time. Moreover, the authors of secondary sources are employing the same sort of historical tools we will develop in this class.

Such secondary sources include any books written about a time period that is separated from the author's own time period. These works include history textbooks like this one, and works of ancient, medieval, and modern history that attempt to explain past events.

Myths & Legends

A myth or a legend is an idea or story that many people believe, but is (at times) not entirely accurate. Often, myths may explain something important a particular culture wants to remember, but they may have forgotten or embellished some of the finer details. Myths almost always start with a "grain" of truth but change over time as individuals tell and retell the myth around a fire, in a palace, or at some large public ceremony.

In telling these myths, these storytellers often change certain details in the story to communicate a moral

BIG IDEA

Historians have a variety of tools at their disposal include primary and secondary sources, archaeological artifacts, and other kinds of evidence that a culture leaves behind, but the most important tool is the historical imagination, the ability to imagine what it was like to live in the period under study.

Vocabulary

Write down this vocabulary in your notebook. These terms will help you better learn and understand the material in this chapter.

History

Derived from the Greek word for story, "history" is the study of individuals who lived in the past, the challenges those individuals faced, and the choices they made to take on those challenges.

Primary Sources

A primary source is an account of a past event written at or very near the time in which the event occurred; primary sources include diaries, journals, chronicles, and other similar types of source material.

Secondary Sources

These are sources of information created later by someone who did not experience first-hand or participate in the events or conditions of which they are writing; they are typically separated from these events by a long period of time.

Material Culture

The physical artifacts that a people leave behind, which historians and archaeologists can later study.

Strata

A layer at an archaeological site; lower stratas are typically from an earlier period than those strata closer to the top.

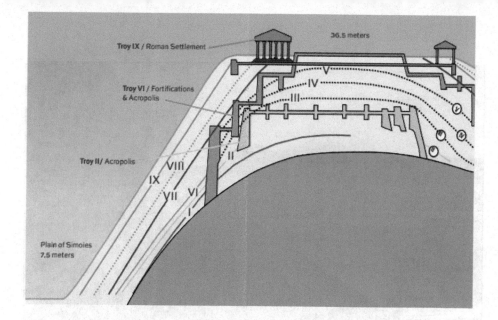

DIAGRAM OF ANCIENT TROY / ARCHAEOLOGICAL SITE
This map is of the ruins of what could be the city of Troy, with each "layer" being a different period of settlement at the site.

lesson to their listeners or pass on some important information from one generation to another. While these myths may not necessarily be true, they do tell us many things about that society and the sorts of things that they valued. The details that change from the "reality" to the "story" often communicate profound truths about human nature, morality, and the nature of the world around us.

Material Culture

Material culture is all the stuff that a people left behind. We'll use the words *material culture, archaeological artifacts, archaeological remains,* and similar words to refer to the physical stuff left behind by a particular culture we can study today. These artifacts may include whole buildings as grand and majestic as the soaring ruins of the Roman Colosseum or the ziggurats that still dot the deserts of Iraq. Material culture may also include the homes of ordinary individuals alongside the tools, pottery, and weapons they used day-to-day, or even in their garbage. In fact, we can learn a lot about ancient peoples by studying their garbage.

To date objects found at an archaeological site, archaeologists carefully record the placement of objects within each **strata** or layer of the excavation site under investigations. They date objects found in a lower strata (layer) earlier than those from a strata closer to the surface of the earth, as the lower levels are under more historical "stuff" and thus implies those levels are older. At times, we may have evidence of an earthquake that mixes the layers and makes it even harder to determine a year or a decade or even a century for that particular layer.

‖ **MOUNT VESUVIUS & THE RUINS OF POMPEII**

Vocabulary

Historiography
The study of historical writing and of the choices historians make in the presentation of their material.

Geography
The study and knowledge of natural, physical features such as mountains, rivers, oceans, and other natural features.

Chronology
The arrangement of dates and events according to a rational, normally linear fashion.

Periodization
The process of dividing history into periods with certain beginning and end dates.

Recent scientific advances have also provided historians with additional methods and technologies to help date artifacts from the ancient world. These include radiocarbon dating (sometimes called carbon-14 dating), dendrochronology (tree ring dating), and fission-track dating (uranium isotope dating).

As an example, consider the towns of Pompeii and Herculaneum in southern Italy (above). When Mount Vesuvius erupted in AD 79, these towns were buried in volcanic ash that effectively preserved everything in them for later historians to study. That included its temples and grand public buildings, but also its houses and restaurants, even its pets. Historians and archaeologists have made unprecedented discoveries about the ancient world from studying not only the grand civic life but also the garbage and the decorations in the households at these sites.

Historical Imagination

The most important tool we student historians have is our imagination. As historians, we want to try and understand key events in world history, the influences that brought about these events, and the impact that such events had on the events that followed after. We also hope to understand the way of life, the convictions, and the aspirations of the real living, breathing human beings who made those choices and why they did the deeds they did. That requires us to think deeply about the events we study and imagine ourselves as if we, in a meaningful way, were participating in those events.

In this way, history is a uniquely human enterprise. History, as the name implies, is a story, and good history, at its best, is the most engaging and exhilarating story set in the great landscape of the past. Indeed, the past is a foreign country, one that is interesting to visit and study for its own sake through investigating why humans acted the way they did. History may be best studied by visiting the ruins or the battlefields where these great events took place—but first-hand experience is often impossible. As a result, we have to use our imagination and create in our minds a picture of what the world may have looked so long ago.

To study and understand history, we have to use our uniquely human ability to tell stories and use those stories to understand the world and the challenges we might face over the course of our lives. We should remember dates and events as best we can, but the goal of history is to gain a better understanding of the past for its own sake. We want to better understand ourselves and our place in the world by learning about the world before we were born. As such, history may be best studied not in field trips but in libraries, poring over books and manuscripts and wondering what the world was like when those books were written and the deeds they describe done.

Conclusion

We student historians have a number of tools at their disposal to understand the past. We have the stories that people tell about themselves and how they understood the past and their place in it. We also have the remains of different cultures and peoples in the ruins and the artifacts that they leave behind. Lastly, we have our imagination and our unique ability to tell stories about the world. That historical imagination may be the most important tool we have, because we have to imagine what it was like to live through such monumental events in a world seemingly so different from the world we live in today.

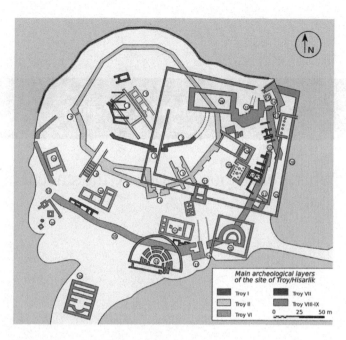

ARCHAEOLOGICAL PLAN / TROY
Image created by Bibi Sant-Pol

As a result, the study of history holds a particularly important role in classical education. History teachers offer up the very best examples of human achievement for students to study as a means of making better choices for the future. A classical education takes students through the very best books and the very best examples of human character in hopes that our students may be their very best.

History, at its best, is the story of people and how they overcame the myriad challenges that this world offers. History teaches how the world of the present came to exist. The past may be a foreign country, but it is a country not unlike our own, and the inhabitants of that country faced famines, plagues, warfare, barbarian invasions, and many hardships from without and from within the lands these peoples called home. Some tribes, tongues, and nations endured. Others were swept away in events too large and monumental to withstand, but the way in which these individuals responded to these challenges holds immense opportunities for students and historians to learn what makes life meaningful. By studying the choices they made, we hope to cultivate the kind of character needed to withstand the challenges of the present.

What are the tools available to the student historian? What may be the most important tool?

....

....

....

....

....

....

Why is geography so important to the study of history?

....

....

....

....

....

....

What is *material culture* and why is it important to the study of history?

Why is it so difficult to study history?

Primary Source Analysis / Herodotus' *Histories*

Recall that primary sources are documents (or similar artifacts) created at or very near the time of the event under investigation. They are a record created around the time of the event the historian is studying, and they can include the chronicles of great kings, letters, poems, songs, diaries, historical artifacts, even paintings. We will examine primary sources of various lengths this year, with reading comprehension questions to follow after.

Title: Herodotus' *Histories,* a sprawling work that chronicles the Persian Wars (499-449 BC).

Date: 430 BC, shortly after the Persian Wars (but enough time for Herodotus to gather his source material and write his narrative).

Location: Herodotus is from Halicarnassus in Asia Minor, but his historical research includes Persia, Babylon, Egypt, the Greek city-states, even the Scythians of Central Asia.

Description: The *Histories* is the earliest example of what we would consider historical narrative, so much so that Herodotus has been described as the "father of history."

HERODOTUS OF HALICARNASSUS / 484 - 425 BC
The author of the Histories; *nicknamed the* Father of History.

⁰¹ Book 1: Herodotus' *Histories*

01 Thus Herodotus of Halicarnassos begins his inquiry, to the end that neither the deeds of men may be forgotten by lapse of time nor works great and marvellous, deeds having been produced by the Greeks and others by the barbarians, lose their renown; and especially that the causes may be remembered for which these waged war with one another.

HERODOTUS' *HISTORIES*
Translated by Lorenzo Valla (AD 1494)

Why did Herodotus write his history?

What exactly will Herodotus investigate in his work of history? Why is his introduction important to the historian?

What did Herodotus have to do to write this particular work of history?

A Closer Look at Maps

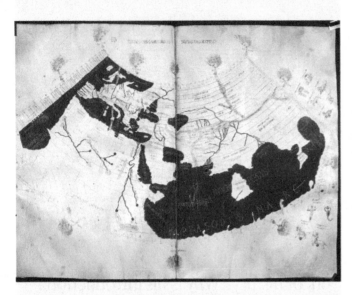

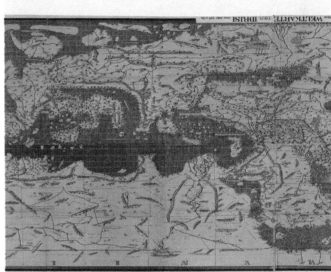

‖ PTOLEMY'S WORLD MAP / CIRCA 150 BC
‖ GREEK ASTRONOMER AND CARTOGRAPHER

‖ MUHAMMAD AL-IDRISI'S WORLD MAP / AD 1154
‖ ISLAMIC GEOGRAPHER AND CARTOGRAPHER

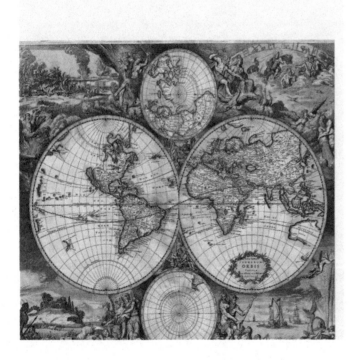

‖ GERARD VAN SCHAGEN'S MAP / AD 1689
‖ DUTCH ENGRAVER AND CARTOGRAPHER

‖ CIA WORLD FACTBOOK / AD 2016

Why is it so difficult to make a map?

....

....

....

....

....

....

....

What kinds of activities have the greatest need for maps and mapmakers?

....

....

....

....

....

....

....

Writing Prompt

Writing is thinking, so we will spend considerable time this year writing and thinking about history. In the space provided, write a short essay answering the question: *Why exactly should we study history? What do we gain by our study of the past?*

Direct Instruction Review

The hardest part about history is memorizing all those facts, dates, and events. To make this process easier, we have included this short section called *Direct Instruction Review*. Direct Instruction (or DI) is a powerful pedagogical tools whereby teachers ask students a series of *call-and-response* questions, and students respond back with the aim of learning this material to *mastery*. Teacher's lines are in **bold**; student's lines in *italics*.

What is history? *History is the study of the past, of past events and the reasons why people made the choices that they did.*

What do we learn about when we study history? *We learn about the individuals who lived in the past, the challenges those individuals faced, and the choices they made to take on those challenges.*

Where does the word history come from? *History from the Greek word* istoria *for "story" since history is, after all, a story of real people living in a real time and place.*

What do we need to study the past? *We need primary and secondary sources, artifacts from the time period we're studying, and historical imagination to picture what life was like back then.*

What about geography and chronology? *We need to know geography and chronology so that we can know where things happened and when they happened.*

What is the study of geography? *Geography is the study of physical locations on the earth such as oceans, mountains, and rivers, as well as plants and animals, and how they influence human events, and its object of focus is the map.*

And the study of chronology? *Chronology is the study of time, and its object of focus is a timeline that shows a sequence of events, one happening after another.*

What about those BC and AD designations? *All cultures date historical events differently and since the Middle Ages, the Western world dated events in regards to the life of Jesus of Nazareth.*

What does BC and AD mean then? *Before Christ (BC) and Anno Domini, "in the year of our Lord" (AD).*

And what about BCE and CE? *Since the Scientific Revolution, the abbreviation BCE and CE have stood for Before Common Era and Common Era, respectively.*

Does BC and AD and BCE and CE refer to the same dates? *Yes, these abbreviations refer to the same date; the only change is in the abbreviation itself.*

Why do we study history? *We study history because the past is worthwhile to study for its own sake, it helps us make better choices in the present, and the better we understand the past, the more we can contribute to a meaningful and wonderful future.*

Timeline Practice / The Ancient World

The hardest part about history is memorizing all those facts, dates, and events. To make this process easier, check out the timeline below—well, technically, there are *two* timelines. Some entries are missing dates, and others are missing the event that occurred on that date. With the information available from both timelines, fill in the missing blanks to get a better sense of the timeline for this chapter.

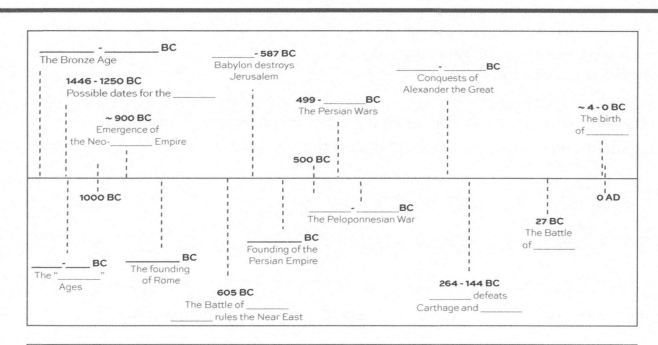

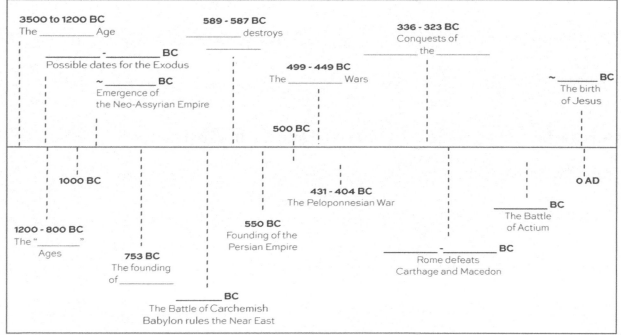

Family History Research

History is a uniquely human enterprise, one where we investigate the world and what it was like before we were born. So, what was that world like before you were born?

Use this page to organize the history of your own family and what makes your family unique. In doing this exercise, you will need to speak with family members—parents, grandparents, aunts and uncles, friends and well-wishers—anyone who may serve as a guardian of your family's past and background.

For teachers and teaching parents, this activity may merit more time than would be alloted to a normal opening activity. Consider making this activity a classroom presentation or a writing assignment.

In researching, try to find stories that help answer the following questions:

If you wanted to find out more about your great-grandparents and great-great grandparents, how would you go about discovering that information?

In conducting your research, how far back could you go in your family history?

What was the best, most noble story you could find out in your research?

ACTIVITY

Map Practice: The World's Continents & Oceans

Instructions: Carefully look over the map below, which provides the oceans and continents of the world. Write in the correct continent or ocean in the blank spaces below.

The World's Continents & Oceans: Continents such as North America, South America, Asia, Australia, Africa, and Europe; and oceans such as the Indian, the Pacific, the Atlantic, and the Arctic.

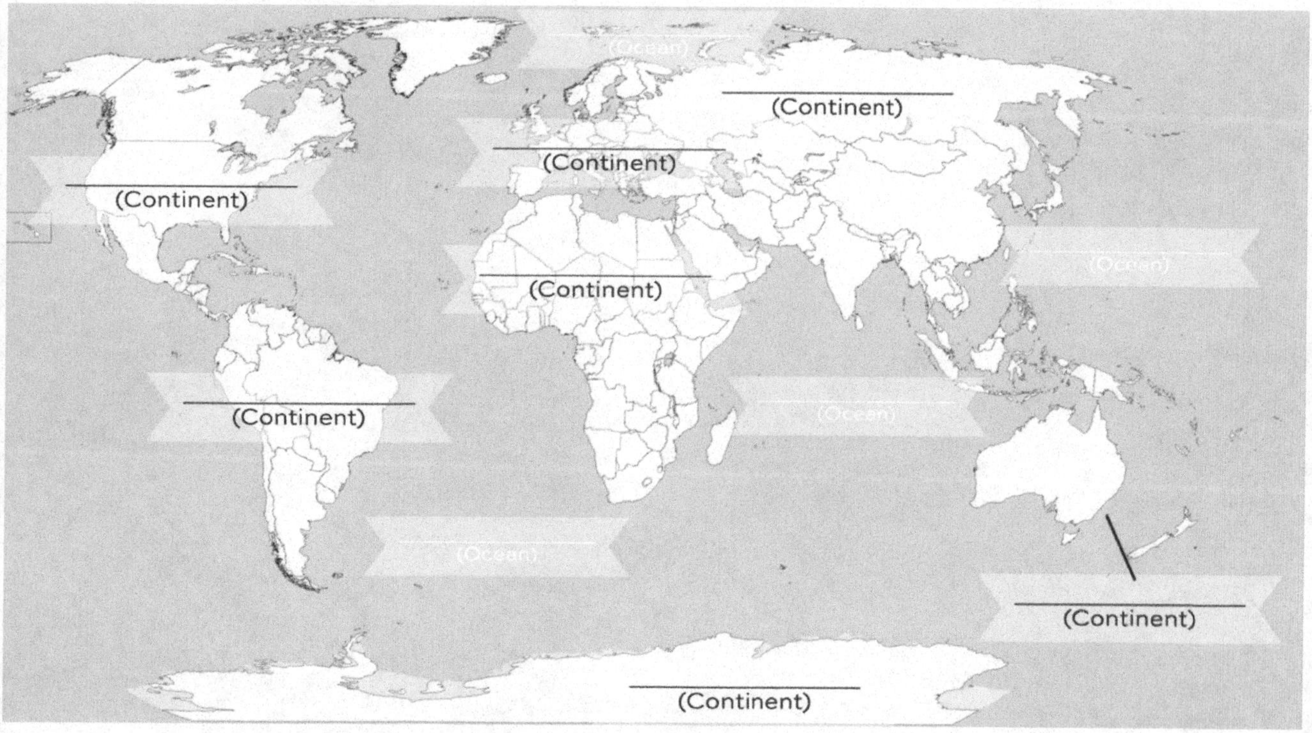

(Ocean)

(Continent)

(Continent)

(Continent)

(Ocean)

(Continent)

(Continent)

(Ocean)

(Continent)

(Ocean)

(Continent)

(Continent)

CHAPTER

The Neolithic Revolution

ROADMAP

✦ Learn about the Paleolithic era and the lifestyle of hunting and gathering.

✦ Read about the Neolithic Revolution and the transition from hunting and gathering to farming and herding.

✦ Study the Cave Paintings at Lascaux, France and what they can tell us about human beings and life during the Neolithic era.

✦ Practice our knowledge of maps and chronology, as well as our writing skills through reading comprehension questions and an essay.

THALES
OUTCOME

№ 3

*Someone with **Self-Reliance** evaluates his/her interdependence, independence, and dependence to local, national, and global communities in relation to oneself.*

The prospect of finding food is exceedingly difficult, and around 12,000 years ago, human beings transitioned from a lifestyle of hunting and gathering to a sedentary lifestyle marked by farming. From this point forward, human beings no longer relied on the environment, but on themselves and their labor to secure the food they need to survive.

You and your tribe, a group of people with black hair and big dreams, have been wandering across a vast and empty wilderness for what seems like forever. What might convince you to stop and settle down some place?

The Starting Line / Hunters & Gatherers

EACH CHAPTER, WE WILL STUDY different groups of people and how they got along with their neighbors. The Sumerians (the people with "black hair and big dreams," mentioned above), the Egyptians, the Phoenicians, and the Israelites are just a few of the groups of people we'll encounter through our study of the ancient world. At times, we will begin a chapter with that culture's story of what they believed about human beings—how human beings were created, and from where they believed we human beings came. That way, we can evaluate how such ancient peoples viewed mankind and the kinds of ends for which they believed mankind should live. Those stories may help to explain many of the historical occurrences during that particular historical period and amongst that particular group of people. This chapter is different because we are at the very beginning of it all—*the starting line*, as it were. We will not begin with a group of people but with a lifestyle, a lifestyle known as **hunting and gathering**, and the people who practiced that lifestyle known as **hunter-gatherers**.

The period that some historians call the Paleolithic period *did not leave behind any written, historical sources, making our task as historians nearly impossible. We can make inferences based on archaeological evidence, but we have to wait until the advent of writing before we do the hard work of historical investigation and study.*

Vocabulary

Write down this vocabulary in your notebook. These terms will help you better learn and understand the material in this chapter.

Paleolithic Period

Derived from the Greek words for *stone* and *old*, the "Stone Age" was characterized by its use of stone tools.

Hunting and Gathering

A lifestyle, exercised by early human cultures, consisting of following animals and supplementing one's diet with crops found naturally in the wild.

Hunter-Gatherers

The earliest groups of human beings migrated across vast distances in search of food and game.

Sedentary

A lifestyle marked by "sitting"; this is the period when human beings settled down, focused on farming and raising livestock, and lived in towns and villages that would eventually become cities.

NEOLITHIC TOOLS

Tools located in the Museum of Toulouse; photo by Didier Descouens.

So if we are to begin at the beginning, we begin with the Stone Age. That time was so long ago that no one is quite sure how long ago it was, perhaps somewhere on the order of around 50,000 BC to as relatively-late as 12,000 BC. We do not know for sure the exact year because no one at that time was writing anything down. We have only archaeological remains—that is, artifacts. Today, historians and archaeologists call this period the **Paleolithic Period**, based on the kinds of tools and objects they have found at archaeological sites. The term Paleolithic period comes from the Greek word *lithos* for "stone" and *paleo* for "old," so that *Paleolithic* means the "Old Stone Age." Historians and archaelogists use the term *Stone Age* to refer to this period because people used stone to build tools or make weapons, stones or glass like flint and obsidian. These materials are hard and brittle, but bits of it can be broken off to make a suitable tool. Historians and archaeologists estimate that this period lasted somewhere on the order of 50,000 to 12,000 BC.

Before we talk anymore about the Paleolithic period, let's spend some time talking about historical periodization. Historical periods are historical eras with shared characteristics and cultural traits. There is also a long tradition of dividing up historical periods according to the materials that people worked with. Our own age is the "Information Age," since information and data is the most valuable currency in use today. This method derived from Greek mythology, wherein the ages of man are described as having descended from a wonderful Golden Age, followed by a Silver Age that was not as good, then the Bronze Age that was an age of heroes, and at last, the very worst age of all, the Iron Age. The Iron Age was so bad because during that age, man learned how to make new and terrifying weapons from iron. With these new weapons, human beings brought down great anguish and suffering upon themselves. While the Golden and Silver Age are not recognizable in the archaeological record, the Bronze Age and the Iron Age were are real discernible, historical periods. The Bronze Age lasts from approximately 4,000 BC to 1,200 BC, and the Iron Age begins at around 1,200 BC. The Bronze Age and Iron Age begin and end at different times in different places, depending on when the people living in that place came to use bronze or iron.

But what about the people living during the Paleolithic period? Again, unfortunately, we cannot know for sure who these people who were. They did not write anything down, so we can only make educated guesses about their lives based on grave sites and archaeological sites like caves (although some of those caves have beautiful paintings in them). We do know about their lifestyle, a lifestyle marked by hunting and gathering so that the people who practiced that lifestyle are known as hunter-gatherers. Certainly, the term *hunter-gatherer* says a lot about the kind of lifestyle these people were involved in. They *hunted* wild animals and *gathered* fruits, berries, and other edible foods they could find in the areas they lived. They were therefore finders of food and foragers of food, not producers of food. Hunter-gatherers lived kind of like birds: in the winter, we see thousands of birds migrating from the northern hemisphere, where it is cold and there is little food, to the southern hemisphere, where it is warm and has food. If the birds could produce shelter to protect them from the cold, or force the ground to produce enough worms in the winter, then the birds would not need to migrate.

Before human beings learned how to protect themselves from the elements and either produce or store enough food in the winter, they also had to move. Hunter-gatherers were not a **sedentary people**–that

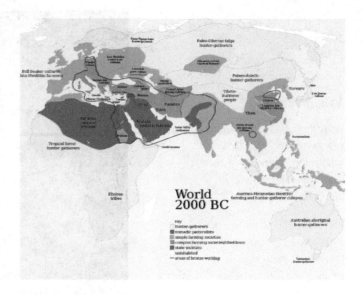

HUNTER-GATHERERS / CIRCA 2,000 BC

This map shows the distribution of hunter-gatherer societies circa 2,0000 BC.
Hunter-gatherer tribes are shown on the map above in yellow.

is, they did not sit down in one settled, established place (*sedentary* comes from a Latin word that means *to sit*). Instead, these hunter-gatherers traveled across large tracts of land following herds of game. They ate fruits, berries, and grains as they came upon them, and they did not stay in one place long enough to build the things that we would associate with civilization. Their movements were likely tied to the migrational patterns of the animals they hunted and the growing periods of the foods they gathered.

Paleolithic societies of hunter-gatherers were small, with groups likely numbering between twenty-five and fifty people. Hunter-gatherers also did not write anything down, so we do not have any written historical records we could use to study these people and how they lived. (If hunter-gatherers maintained little to no private property and owned only what they could carry with them, there was no real need for written records.) The lifestyle of hunter-gatherers changed, however, as tribes figured out how to grow food and store it, as well as how to build settlements that could withstand the elements. That surplus of food allowed these groups of hunter-gatherers to settle down into the world's first towns and cities. This period of settling down came in at around 12,000 BC at the start of the Neolithic Revolution.

How do historians group together early historical periods? From where did the term Paleolithic come?

Who are hunter-gatherers? How did they live? What makes them unique?

Why do we know so little about hunter-gatherers?

The Neolithic Revolution

THE TERM *NEOLITHIC* IN Neolithic Revolution derives from two Greek words: *neo* meaning "new" and *lithos* meaning "stone." Thus neolithic means *new stone* and refers to the *New Stone Age*, one where we can see changes between how people lived in the Paleolithic Age and how people lived after this Neolithic Revolution. A revolution is a period of immense, sometimes violent, but always significant changes that take place in a relatively-short span of time, and the Neolithic Revolution was the world's first historically verifiable revolution, a revolution that took place first in agriculture. Agriculture refers to the practice of farming and the ways we produce food, activities you may not associate with being part of a revolution. The Neolithic Revolution, however, may be the most important event we study this year because of the way it transformed human life from that point forward. In the Neolithic Revolution, many groups of people moved from a lifestyle of hunting and gathering to one of farming and settlements.

All of the advancements and creature comforts that we associate with living in society derives from the fact that we have settled down. That is, we sat down in one place and started building up the things we need to make life in this world more comfortable. Civilization and everything we know about it cannot take root if that civilization is made up only of the items one can carry with one's tribe over long distances. Later, as these settled populations grew, they became cities and city-states.

Soon, people got so good at growing food that not everyone had to spend their days working fields or minding sheep. That is, a small portion of the population could spend their days farming while other people could do other things that the farmers and other members of society also needed. This process is called the division of labor and is another key component of civilization as we know it. The term *division of labor* can be used synonymously with terms like *job specialization* and other similar terms.

Today, relatively few people are engaged in farming and agriculture. Agriculture refers to the purposeful cultivation of certain foods solely for human consumption and flourishing. Today, our farming methods are so efficient that an incredibly small segment of the population can produce enough food to feed themselves and almost everyone else, and now everyone else is freed up to become doctors, lawyers, teachers, astronauts, police

BIG IDEA

The Neolithic Revolution is one of the most significant events in human history: from this point forward, human beings no longer relied solely on the environment but on themselves and their labor to secure the food they need to survive. The practice of farming would lead to the build-up of a surplus of food that could help communities survive in times of famine and hardship, increase the division of labor, allow for larger populations, and assist in creating cities.

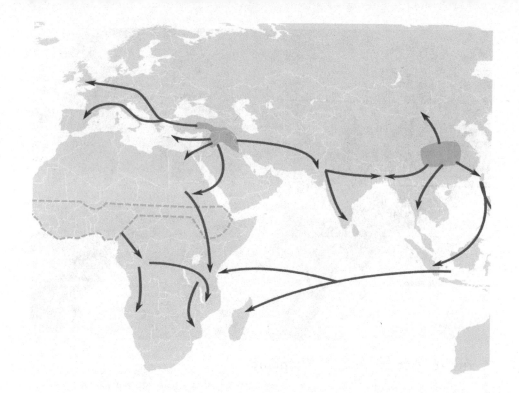

Vocabulary

Write down this vocabulary in your notebook. These terms will help you better learn and understand the material in this chapter.

Neolithic Revolution

A point around 12,000 years ago when human beings learned how to grow their own food, as well as live in cities and established communities.

Neolithic

The word *neolithic* comes from the Greek words *neo*, meaning "new" and *lithos*, meaning "stone." The term *neolithic* means "new stone."

Revolution

A period of immense, sometimes violent, but always significant changes taking place in a relatively short span of time.

Agriculture

The purposeful cultivation of certain foods solely for human consumption and flourishing.

Division of Labor / Job Specialization

As communities grow in population, less people need to be directly engaged in farming and agriculture. More food means more people, and more people means more "activities" can be done that are directly related to farming.

Staple

A food like wheat or rice that forms a substantial part of the diet of a large group of people.

|| **THE BEGINNINGS & SPREAD OF AGRICULTURE**

officers, firefighters, and other jobs we need for society to function properly. More people doing more jobs than simply farming allowed society as a whole to take root and flourish. But how did the process of farming begin? How did we figure out how to grow and store our own food in such large quantities that settlements could grow larger and larger and survive famines and whatever hardships that befell them?

Certainly, the large, navigable rivers upon which these farming communities depended played a large role. We could do a thought experiment and imagine a tribe of hunter-gatherers coming upon a field of tall, wild grasses. These would be the kinds of plants we know today as wheat, barley, and other staple grains. The term **staple** refers not to a small metal piece that holds paper together but to a food that is eaten in large quantities by such a large number of people that it forms a substantial part of their diet. That transition from a hunting and gathering lifestyle to one of farming and **domesticating** animals happened slowly, bit by bit. The term domesticate means to make some wild animal or some wild plant fit to live in or near one's house. If you have a dog or a cat, that pet is a domesticated animal, one fit to live in a domicile like your house (although the learning curve with puppies is quite long).

At one point, all animals were wild and undomesticated. But slowly, people learned how to domesticate animals which seemed like they would be useful to us: animals like sheep for their wool or dogs for their companionship. Once one group of people figured out how to domesticate an animal like sheep or grow a wild grain like wheat, that information spread to other groups of people living nearby. Not every plant or animal is a good candidate for do-

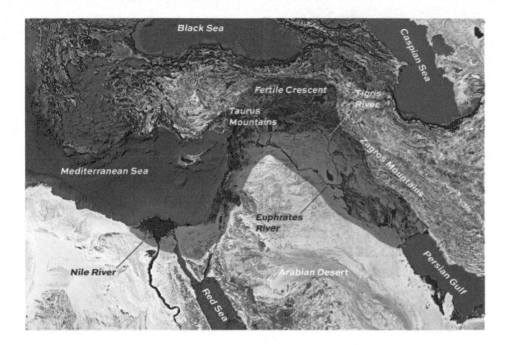

THE FERTILE CRESCENT / 12,000 BC

Intensive agriculture first began here in the Fertile Crescent, a region that included Egypt and ancient Sumer.

Vocabulary

Domestication
A way of taking wild plants and animals and bringing them under human control to help with human flourishing.

The Fertile Crescent
A crescent moon-shaped region that includes the river valleys of the Tigris, the Euphrates, and the Nile where peoples first learned to practice intensive agriculture.

mestication; a plant has to be pretty easy to grow. And, that plant has to produce enough food to make that plant worth the trouble growing it. Nor is every animal a good candidate for domestication: animals have to be gentle enough to live with human beings. For example, we know horses can be domesticated, but zebras have the terrible habit of biting zookeepers. Animals should also produce enough offspring so that the animal is, again, worth the time to domesticate that animal. Elephants can be tamed, but they produce so few calves that it is not worth it to raise elephants on a farm (see Diamond's *Guns, Germs, and Steel*).

This process of domesticating plants and animals occurred the earliest in a place called the Fertile Crescent. **The Fertile Crescent** is a stretch of territory shaped like a crescent moon that includes the river valleys of the Tigris and the Euphrates in the east, the Nile River in the west, and the fertile regions in between that include modern-day countries like Israel, Syria, and eastern Turkey. The Neolithic Revolution is centered on farming, and that farming-revolution took root in the Fertile Crescent first for the following reasons. The Fertile Crescent has a relatively-warm, dry climate that makes farming easier, and it includes three of the world's most impressive river systems: the Tigris and the Euphrates in ancient Sumer and the Nile in ancient Egypt. Farming is difficult, but these rivers made that process easier by irrigating crops and carrying loads of silt that could be used as fertilizer.

In addition, the Fertile Crescent could grow both wheat and barley. Wheat and barley are great plants to domesticate since they are easy to store and, once processed into flour, can last a long time. That way, if there is a famine or a bad harvest, a settlement can tap into its storehouses of grain to survive. A field planted with wheat or barley will generally produce a large harvest, and these crops are hardy enough to withstand the extreme temperatures experienced in the area. Then, of the 150 (or so) possible candidates for domesticated animals, 14 of them are found in the Fertile Crescent. Even the ones that aren't available nearby—such as the horse—are domesticated in Central Asia and are accessible to the Fertile Crescent by long, overland trade routes.

Sometime around 4,000 BC, in an event that happened in some areas earlier than others, the world entered the Bronze Age. Bronze is an alloy made from a combination of about 12% tin and 88-90% copper; copper may be brittle and tin has the consistency of cream cheese, but, when combined together, they become strong enough to form tools and weapons. The technology to make bronze first appeared in ancient Sumer, the cradle of civilization, and that technology spread via trade networks, for any civilization that did not adapt and learn to make its own bronze would be easily destroyed by civilizations that did. The knowledge of bronze-making took significant time to diffuse across the world, so much so that the "Bronze Age" begins in some areas far earlier than others and ends in other areas at far later periods in time. The need to make bronze also brought about the growth of far-flung trade routes across the ancient world since no single location had access to both tin and copper.

To summarize, the earliest groups of people lived lives of hunting and gathering. Then, around 12,000 years ago, different settlements at different places around the world made the slow, bit-by-bit transition from hunting and gathering to a settled lifestyle of farming and tending animals. This process first occurred in the Fertile Crescent, a crescent-moon-shaped region that included the Tigris and Euphrates river valleys in ancient Sumer and the Nile River in Egypt. These rivers made the process of farming much easier since it irrigated and fertilized farmland, and it is the civilizations that arose on the banks of these rivers we turn to next.

What was the *Neolithic Revolution*?

What animal do you think was the easiest to domesticate? What animal do you think was the hardest to domesticate?

What features of the Fertile Crescent made it an ideal location for the beginnings of agriculture?

If you had lived your whole life as a hunter-gatherer, would you embrace a lifestyle of farming and herding? Why or why not?

Primary Source Analysis / Lascaux Caves

Recall that primary sources are documents (or similar artifacts) created at or very near the time of the event under investigation. They are a record created around the time of the event the historian is studying, and they can include the chronicles of great kings, letters, poems, songs, diaries, historical artifacts, even paintings.

Title: The Cave Paintings at Lascaux, France

Date: 17,000 - 15,000 BC, during the Paleolithic Era

Location: Lascaux, France

Description: The caves in Lascaux, France contain over 600 paintings, mostly of animals, scattered throughout the cave system. Four French boys serendipitously discovered the caves and these beautiful works in 1940.

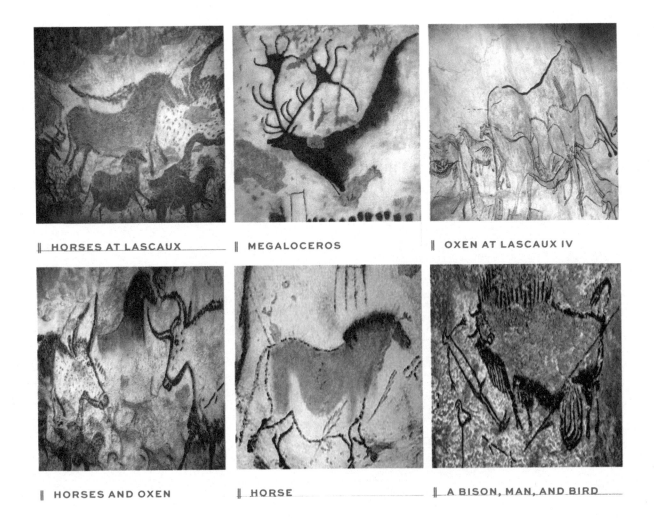

‖ HORSES AT LASCAUX   ‖ MEGALOCEROS   ‖ OXEN AT LASCAUX IV

‖ HORSES AND OXEN   ‖ HORSE   ‖ A BISON, MAN, AND BIRD

What do these paintings show us about life during the period of the Paleolithic Era, when people lived as hunter-gatherers?

What purpose did these paintings serve?

What do these paintings tell us about human nature?

Writing Prompt

Writing is thinking, so we will spend considerable time this year writing and thinking about history. In the space provided, write a short essay answering the question: *Why might the Neolithic Revolution be the most significant period we study in history?*

Direct Instruction Review

The hardest part about history is memorizing all those facts, dates, and events. To make this process easier, we have included this short section called *Direct Instruction Review*. Direct Instruction (or DI) is a powerful pedagogical tool whereby teachers ask students a series of *call-and-response* questions, and students respond back with the aim of learning this material to *mastery*. Teacher's lines are in **bold**; student's lines in *italics*.

What was the Paleolithic era? *The Old Stone Age.*

And how did people live during this Old Stone Age? *They lived as hunter gatherers.*

And how did hunter gatherers live? *They hunted wild animals and gathered fruits, berries, roots, and other foods that they could find where they lived.*

Did hunter-gatherers stay settled in one place? *No, they migrated across large stretches of territory, following herds of game.*

And when did everything start to change? *The Neolithic Revolution, circa 12,000 BC.*

What does Neolithic mean? *The New Stone Age.*

And how did people live during this New Stone Age? *People slowly learned how to farm, and farming allowed them to stay in one place.*

What kind of a lifestyle do we call this? *A sedentary lifestyle, a lifestyle where you sit down and stay in one place.*

What did those early people have to learn, if they were to stay in one place? *They had to learn how to farm and how to domesticate wild plants and animals.*

What does it mean to domesticate a wild plant or animal? *To make it "fit" to live in a household, near human beings.*

What were some of the first plants to be domesticated? *Wheat and barley!*

And from all those people living in one place, what do they have to learn? *They have to learn how to work together–how to govern themselves, how to build houses and public buildings, and how to trade for the goods and services they need through a series of exchanges.*

And when all those people are living in one place, what do we call this? *A city!*

And where did all these processes, from farming and trading and city-building, first take place? *The Fertile Crescent!*

Timeline Practice / The Neolithic Revolution

The hardest part about history is memorizing all those facts, dates, and events. To make this process easier, check out the timeline below—well, technically, there are *two* timelines. Some entries are missing dates, and others are missing the event that occurred on that date. With the information available from both timelines, fill in the missing blanks to get a better sense of the timeline for this chapter.

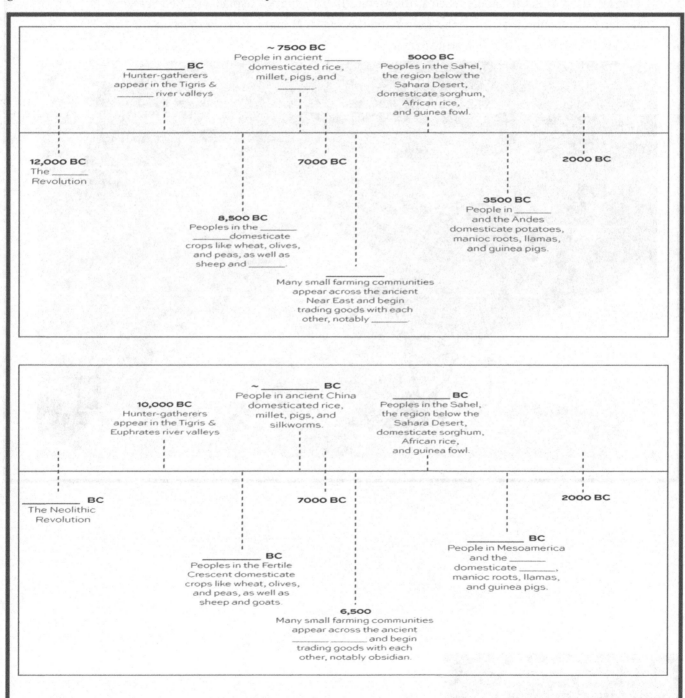

Map Practice: The Fertile Crescent

Instructions: Carefully look over the maps below, which are identical to maps provided in the rest of this chapter aside from one crucial difference—they have blanks in the place of the name of a sea, region, or site. Fill in the appropriate blank with the term list provided above each map.

The Fertile Crescent: Bodies such as the Mediterranean, Black, Caspian, and Red Seas and the Persian Gulf; mountains such as the Taurus and the Zagros Mountains; rivers such as the Nile, Tigris, and Euphrates Rivers; and the Fertile Crescent.

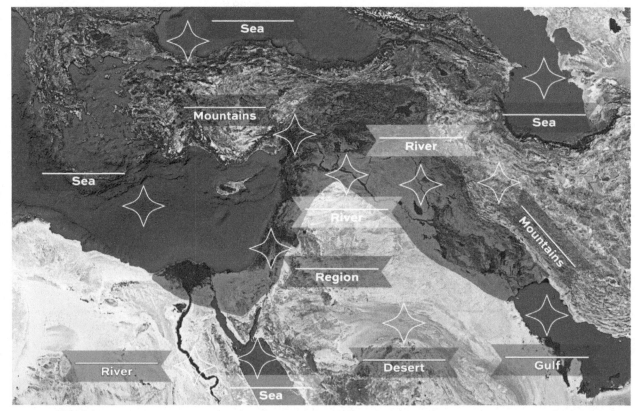

Want to study this map online? Type in the link below or scan the QR code to access an interactive diagram: https://bit.ly/3okSogF

Section II
Sumer & Egypt

THE STANDARD OF UR / PEACE SIDE

Created around 2,600 BC, the Standard of Ur was discovered in the royal tomb in the Sumerian city of Ur.

CHAPTER

Ancient Sumer

ROADMAP

- Read the *Atrahasis Epic*, a Sumerian myth about the creation (and purpose) of human beings.

- Study the ancient Sumerians and the civilization they built on the banks of the Tigris and the Euphrates Rivers.

- Understand about the challenges the first Sumerians faced in building a network of city-states scattered across the Tigris and Euphrates river valleys.

- Study Sumerian cuneiform, Sumerian ziggurats, and other artifacts from ancient Sumer including the Warka Vase.

- Practice our knowledge of maps and chronology, as well as our writing skills through reading comprehension questions and an essay.

THALES OUTCOME

Nº 11

Someone with **Dreams & Aspirations to Change the World** *produces plans to accomplish personal and educational aspirations.*

In this chapter, we begin our study of the world's first civilization, the Sumerians. They are the people with "black hair" and "big dreams" referenced in the opening question in the previous chapter. We are indebted to the Sumerians for inventing or developing many of the elements we associate with civilization including writing, intensive agriculture, and city-life.

Could civilization only have started in the Fertile Crescent? Why or why not?

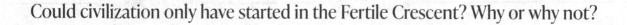

The Atrahasis Epic / Unknown author, 18th c. BC

IN THE BEGINNING, there were two ranks of gods— the seven great Anunna-gods, who ruled, and the Igigi-gods, who worked. And the Igigi did every-thing–they carved the very pathways of the Tigris and the Euphrates rivers. They dug canals and wells and heaped up high mountains to the east. The Anunna ruled while the Igigi did everything else, years of hard work and labor, toil and hardship. Finally, the Igigi could not take it anymore.

"Enlil," all of the Igigi gods cried out together, "is a hard master, cruel, mean, and unyielding. But we will rebel against him and demand that Enlil, god of the winds, lighten our burden and take all this hard work from us! Our time as servants is over!"

So the Igigi rose up and attacked the house of Enlil. Once they subdued the god of the winds, the Igigi demanded that he and the other Anunna gods do something about their toil. Then the Anunna-gods, gods like Enlil, the god of the winds, and Enki, the god of water, knowledge, and crafts, talked with each other and debated what to do.

Finally, they decided: "Let us make a new thing, a new creature, to bear the burdens the Igigi no longer wish to carry. Let us make man to maintain the canals, to dig the water courses, and to bear the toil. Let man do the hard work from now and forever more!"

THE TEXT ABOVE comes from *the Atrahasis Epic*, a Sumerian and Akkadian creation myth written in and around the 18th century BC. In this myth, man was created to serve the gods of the Sumerian pantheon. Indeed, man was created to be a servant and do the hard work the gods themselves were no longer willing to do. But who were the Sumerians, and what did they accomplish? On the following page, answer the questions based on the text of *the Atrahasis Epic*. Then, we will move into learning more about the ancient Sumerians and what makes their civilization so unique.

Summarize the plot and, in your opinion, the moral of the *Atrahasis Epic*.

Based on this creation story, the story that these people tell themselves about the creation of the world and man's purposes within it, what do you think life will be like in ancient Sumer?

Based on this brief reading, what seems to be man's purpose? What was he created for? Does this purpose seem sad, bleak, hopeless? Why or why not?

Land of the Black-Hair Kings ... / Ancient Sumer

THE ANCIENT SUMERIANS are the first recognizable people we can study from history. They built their civilization on the banks of the **Tigris** and the **Euphrates** rivers, in the very center of the Fertile Crescent. We don't know exactly who the Sumerians were or even where they came from–only that they migrated into the Tigris and Euphrates river valleys sometime around 4,000 BC. The **Sumerians**, though, called themselves *the black-haired ones* and called the land of Sumer where they lived *the land of the noble ones or noble kings*. And so these black-haired ones built a civilization that lasted for two thousand years from around 4,000 BC to 2,000 BC.

After 2,000 BC, names like **Babylon** or **Assyria** are used instead of ancient Sumer. Babylon was a powerful city in the south of what once was ancient Sumer, and Assyria a powerful city in the north. In the Iron Age, beginning around 900 BC, Assyria and Babylon would become the world's first empires and came to rule over almost all of the ancient Near East. Later, the Greeks would call this region **Mesopotamia**, Greek for *the land between the rivers*, those rivers being the Tigris and the Euphrates. Today, the land of ancient Sumer includes the modern-day countries of Iraq and some parts of eastern Syria and western Iran. But let us focus on the Sumerians and the civilization they built between the rivers, a civilization that spanned dozens of city-states up and down the Tigris and Euphrates.

The importance of these rivers cannot be underestimated. The Tigris and the Euphrates made the difficult practice of farming much easier for the Sumerians who lived along the banks of these rivers. The Tigris and the Euphrates carried nutrient-rich topsoil and silt, which it deposited along its banks at certain bends in the river. As a result, these rivers provided water for their crops but also fertilizer to help these crops grow. While these rivers were wild, unpredictable, and prone to dangerous flooding, they also helped the Sumerians produce bountiful crop harvests each year and supported cities with tens of thousands of people living in them. Let's look at Sumerian cities now and the things they did that helped these cities grow to such large populations.

Sumerian City-States

A **city-state** is a place that serves as a safe, convenient place for many people to live and work. That city might be in a good location that is both easy to defend and convenient for trading goods and services. Think of a city like the human body: the human body is composed of many parts, each of which has a very important

BIG IDEA

The world's first civilization arose on the shores of the Tigris and Euphrates Rivers, founded by a mysterious group of people known as the "Sumerians." The Tigris and the Euphrates carried nutrient rich silt and topsoil it deposited along its banks, which fertilized the land and made it much easier for the Sumerians to farm.

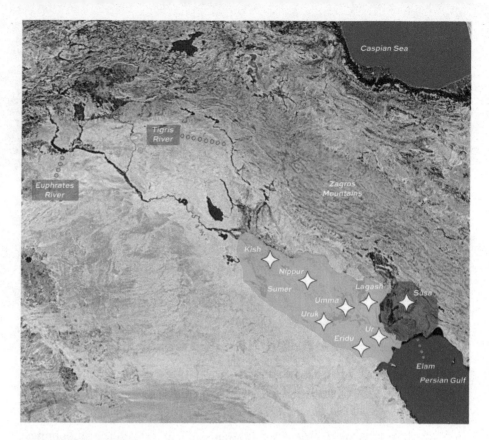

‖ **MAP OF ANCIENT SUMER**

function. We have eyes to see and ears to hear, and in the same way, cities have groups of people working at the same job to improve the quality of life for the people who live there. At times, we call large groups of people working together at the same function an **institution**. Those institutions might include markets with merchants, courts with judges, palaces with kings, and temples with priests. Such institutions can help cities with large numbers of people live and work together, and we find many of the *first* of such institutions in Sumer.

In Sumer, the largest and most important institution was the **ziggurat**, a massive step pyramid located in the center of each Sumerian city. These ziggurats served a number of important functions: they were the *home* of gods like In-anna and Enlil or another deity in the Sumerian gods; they were the residence of a class of well-educated priests who helped manage the Sumerian economy; and they were convenient places to trade goods and do business for the people living within and without a Sumerian city. In Sumer, the largest and most important city-states included the cities of Uruk, Ur, Umma, Lagash, Nippur, and Kish. Later, the city of Akkad and its inhabitants, the Akkadians, who took over the rest of Sumer under the leadership of Sargon of Akkad.

Sumerians are credited with making the world's first city-states. A city-state is a city, but it is independent of any other political entity. A city-state is responsible for its own laws and building projects, and even maintains its own army. City-states also flourished in ancient Greece and in Renaissance Italy. Indeed, some of the world's deadliest wars came about as a result of the rivalry between

CYLINDER SEAL / CIRCA 3,100 BC

The Sumerians used seals like this one to authenticate important documents. The above seal was from ancient Uruk and is now in the Louvre.

city-states, such as the rivalry between Athens and Sparta and the Peloponnesian War. But they may also produce some of the world's most beautiful art and architecture, as in the Italian cities of Florence, Milan, and Rome. Today, there are only two city-states left–Singapore in Southeast Asia and Vatican City in Italy. But the first city-states that appeared in history arose between the rivers in the land of ancient Sumer.

Since cities can't grow enough food to feed their inhabitants, a city-state also includes farmland outside the city. This inclusion of farmland was the case with ancient Sumer as with other civilizations where people lived in city-states. The people who lived and worked on those farms bring their crops to the city, where those farmers trade goods they have in abundance. In Sumer, such goods included wheat, barley, wool, and others, for goods that only people in the city can make, like tools, clothing, or baskets. Large groups of people engaging in many different tasks such as making clothes or making tools or making anything else people need to improve their lives is called the **division of labor**. Typically, a city-state is one organic unit, with the city and the countryside knit together by these economic and cultural ties.

Still, one city-state is independent from other nearby city-states. Those city-states may speak the same language and share the same customs, but they are not on the same team. They may even fight each other for resources. Often, city-states are in competition with one another to be the best, the most powerful, or have the most beautiful buildings. If one city-state invents some new technique or builds some towering new ziggurat, other nearby city-states race to catch up. Or, they simply fight over resources they need to survive, even if it is just a field or a vineyard. As

Vocabulary

Ziggurats
The step pyramids built by the ancient Sumerians that served as the "home" for the patron deity of a particular Sumerian city.

Division of Labor / Job Specialization
As communities grow in population, less people need to be directly engaged in farming and agriculture. More food means more people, and more people means more "activities" can be done that are directly related to farming.

Shadoof
A shadoof is a tool used for irrigating fields, first used in ancient Sumer and commonly used throughout the world today.

King
A king is someone who has been given the right to rule over a group of people.

Priests
Priests are relatively well-educated individuals who have a special relationship with the gods and know how to keep them happy.

Cuneiform
A Latin word meaning "wedge-shaped writing" invented by the ancient Sumerians, made upon wet, clay tablets.

a result, city-states often produce beautiful monuments or works of literature, or produce new technological innovations that helped that civilization to thrive. Or, as in the case of the Sumerians, they fight with each other until they are all conquered by a larger and more powerful city-state.

Farmers, Priests, and Kings

And to build those cities must have been very difficult. First, the Sumerians were the first civilization, so they didn't have the benefit of history as we do. They had no other civilizations to read about and learn from their mistakes. Two, the Sumerians had to invent many of the implements so crucial to civilization. That included practices like farming and tending animals and inventions like the wheel and writing, and even the calendar. Three, the land of ancient Sumer–the land of the Tigris and the Euphrates river valley may be fertile, but those rivers flood easily. Really, the land of the Tigris and Euphrates is somewhat terrifying: hailstorms, flooding, and without any real natural barriers, barbarian tribes could invade and destroy Sumerian civilization easily. The Sumerians may have built a civilization, but their world could come crashing down at a moment's notice.

Yet, the Tigris and the Euphrates helped the Sumerians immensely. Aside from these mighty rivers, ancient Sumer was a desert. The Tigris and the Euphrates supplied fresh drinking water and also helped to fertilize the fields that the Sumerians planted with wheat or barley. You see, as the rivers flowed from their source in the Taurus Mountains, the rivers carried something called silt. Silt is sand or dirt that contains nutrients plants need to grow, like the fertilizer used in gardens at home. The Tigris and Euphrates would carry this silt and deposit it along the riverbanks, making it possible for farmers living near the rivers to grow more crops with less effort. After all, those early farmers may not have understood at first all the little, gritty details about

SHADOOF

A shadoof is pulley system to lift water from a canal or a stream.

farming and fertilizing, but the Tigris and the Euphrates took care of this process for them.

To help increase the amount of land they could farm, the Sumerians built a system of canals. A canal is essentially a man-made waterway, like a creek or a river dug by human hands. Then, to get water exactly where they needed it, the Sumerians used an invention called a **shadoof**; essentially, a shadoof is a bucket on a lever that could carry water from a lower level and pour it onto a higher level. One can only imagine how difficult it would be to keep the canals from overflowing or to lift enough water to irrigate an entire field. The Tigris and Euphrates flowed through the deserts of what is today Iraq, so the rivers changed courses frequently, flooded villages, and destroyed canals. As a result, Sumerian civilization required constant upkeep and maintenance. No wonder, then, that in the creation myth referenced above, man is created just to maintain the canals and perform the other difficult tasks needed to keep civilization going.

The world of ancient Sumer was unpredictable and full of hardships. To help prevent Sumerian cities from literally being washed away in a flood, the Sumerians were ruled by both **kings**–black-haired kings–and **priests** who spoke for the gods. A king is an individual who has been given significant authority to rule over a group of people who speak the same language or follow the same laws, like a city, or a large geographical area.

That king may have proven himself in battle as a great warrior, one capable of leading his soldiers to future victories. Or, he may have distinguished himself as a wise ruler capable of solving complex problems. When the king dies, the people he has ruled over have to decide who will become king after him, a problem that different societies solve in different ways. That society's best citizens may vote on a new king or accept the son of the previous king as their new ruler. But in all regard, they believe that the decisions of the king are somehow different than the decisions reached by everyone—they are, in fact, better, and everyone else ought to follow them.

The priests, meanwhile, are a class of leaders who have a special relationship with the gods. They know the complex series of rituals needed to keep the gods happy, and they can deal with the gods on behalf of the people. Those gods could make life very difficult for the people of Sumer, so whatever the priests said was treated as if it came directly from the gods. To help withstand possible floods, a canal breaking down, or barbarian invasions, strong, powerful kings had to emerge to tell the people exactly what to do and prevent chaos from ripping Sumer apart. These kings, supported by the priests, would form a monarchy in the simplest sense of the world, the rule of one person. The rule of that king and of the priestly class of Sumer could not be questioned since a hailstorm or a swift turn of the Tigris might wipe out years of hard work. Sumerian kings needed lots of people to know their role and do their jobs tending crops and irrigating fields.

To help them govern their cities and the surrounding farmland, the kings relied on that class of well-educated priests. These individuals lived at the ziggurat and, because food was brought to the temple each day, could afford to spend the time needed to learn the complicated writing system known as **cuneiform**. Cuneiform

NECKLACE OF SUMERIAN PRIESTESS
Reconstruction from the British Museum

comes from the Latin words meaning "wedge-shaped" and was a form of writing developed by the ancient Sumerians. Cuneiform may be the most significant of all the advancements made by the ancient Sumerians, for it is with writing that the process of building a civilization can truly begin. With writing, a group of people can pass on a record of what their world was like to the next generation, who can then build on their accomplishments. Moreover, we student historians need their writings to understand what their world was like and the challenges they faced.

To get a better sense of how Sumerian society operated, let's take a *closer look* at the Warka Vase, created around 3200 BC. The Warka Vase tells a unique story about Sumer's priests, gods, and residents, and how Sumerian society functioned to withstand the challenges that struck the land between the rivers of the Tigris and the Euphrates. The meaning of the Warka Vase carries the same message embedded in the *Atrahasis Epic*. Once this message is understood, the student historian should pause and wonder about the kinds of assumptions and understandings of human beings upon which a society operates, for those assumptions would help us better understand the workings of Sumerian society in general and indeed, the nature of the good life and the kinds of values that contribute to human flourishing.

Who exactly were the Sumerians?

....

....

....

....

Why did the world's first civilization develop in the Tigris and the Euphrates River valleys?

....

....

....

....

What other names do we use to refer to the land of the Tigris and the Euphrates River valleys?

....

....

....

....

What is a ziggurat? What functions did it serve in ancient Sumer?

....

....

....

....

Primary Source Analysis / **Warka Vase**

RECALL THAT PRIMARY SOURCES are documents (or similar artifacts) created at or very near the time of the event under investigation. They are a record created around the time of the event the historian is studying, and they can include the chronicles of great kings, letters, poems, songs, diaries, historical artifacts, even paintings.

Look carefully at the images below depicting the Warka Vase, a beautiful vase created circa 3,200 BC in Uruk, the world's first city. Try to guess who each of the figures might be—gods or goddesses, priests and kings, or normal, everyday residents of Uruk and of the surrounding countryside. Then, answer the questions on the following page.

Title: The Warka Vase

Date: Circa 3200 BC

Location: The mighty city of Uruk, the first Sumerian city to emerge from the Tigris and the Euphrates River valleys.

Description: The figures on this alabaster vase were carved in relief, meaning that the figures emerged as material is removed from a flat surface.

WARKA VASE / 3,200 BC
Worshippers bringing their offerings to Inanna; Photo by Osama Shukir Muhammed Amin.

ILLUSTRATION OF THE WARKA VASE
Illustration by Jennifer Mei

Who is at the center of the scene?

....

....

....

....

Who are the other figures in this scene?

....

....

....

....

What might this scene be depicting?

....

....

....

For teachers and teaching parents: The scene depicted on the Warka vase is that of the priest in charge of the temple of Inanna in ancient Uruk. The goddess Inanna, the Sumerian equivalent of Venus or Aphrodite, stands on the top row, while the priest directs the worshipers who are also conveniently bringing their goods as an offering to the goddess. More information is available on the following page.

Primary Source Analysis / Warka Vase

IN THE *ATRAHASIS EPIC*, the gods create mankind to do the kind of hard, manual labor the other gods refused to do any longer. The lower-ranking gods wanted to be released from their toil, and so mankind was created as the servant of the gods to maintain the temples, repair the canals, and perform the kind of toil the gods refused to do any longer. If you were an uneducated resident of a city like Uruk or Eridu, it may be hard to get out of your daily obligations maintaining the canals or irrigating fields since, after all, these jobs were what mankind was *created* to do.

The story depicted on the Warka Vase seems to support this interpretation gleaned from the *Atrahasis Epic*. The bottom tiers on the vase feature local farmers and herders, bringing their gifts to the local ziggurat. They bear gifts to the goddess Inanna on the top row, whose divinity is identified by the reed-like shapes immediately

behind her. The other central figure is the well-educated priest, capable of reading and writing cuneiform, who directs the worshipers and their offerings to the appropriate spot. The priest, subsequently, is in charge of the procession, and he decides how these resources will be meted out on behalf of the goddess Inanna.

And it is the priests who wrote the *Atrahasis Epic*, weaving the story of man's creation with man's purpose: that of serving of gods and also, indirectly, serving the priests in charge of the local ziggurat. The Warka Vase and the *Atrahasis Epic* serve as powerful reminders for the idea of the *Imago Dei*, that of mankind being created in God's image and thereby endowed with great dignity and value. The alternative to this message typically degrades human beings to an instrument, serving the needs of the elites, as is depicted in the image below.

The Goddess Inanna
The Warka Vase was found in Uruk, home to a massive ziggurat dedicated to Inanna, goddess of love and desire.

The Priests
In ancient Sumer, the priests were a well-educated class of scribes and bureaucrats, each of whom could read and write in cuneiform. As a result, they tended to direct many of the day-to-day functions of the economy.

His status is represented via his size, which is noticably larger than other figures in the vase, as well as the servant carrying the train of his robe.

The Worshippers
Here, a procession of worshippers willingly bring their offerings to the local ziggurat as part of their worship of the goddess Inanna. In this way, the local ziggurat served as a center for trade and commerce, since people living within and without the city willingly came to the temple with goods for the goddess.

The Offerings
The sceen features goats and sheep, animals raised in ancient Sumer for their milk, meat, and wool.

Cuneiform & Ziggurats / Eridu & Uruk

THE SUMERIAN KINGLIST, a chronicle of Sumerian history, says the first city the Sumerians built was named Eridu. Eridu was the place where "after the kingship descended from heaven, the kingship was in Eridu"–that is, the first real, noticeable place where something like civilization first appeared. Eridu is a real historical site, one founded sometime around 5,400 BC. The city is located near the much larger Sumerian city of Ur in what is today southern Iraq.

Eridu was also the home of the Sumerian god Enki, the god of water, knowledge, and crafts. Enki is a god like Loki in Norse mythology or Prometheus in Greek mythology, one responsible for giving the Sumerians all the crafts and inventions they needed to build civilization. These inventions that are at least attributed to the Sumerians include the wheel (no small feat), sailboats, pottery, basket weaving, the sail, beer brewing, bronze-making (also called metallurgy), the plow, and of course, cuneiform, a Latin word that means "wedge-shaped writing." Cuneiform, the world's first written language, is perhaps the greatest gift that the Sumerians gave to subsequent generations. So how did they come up with it?

First, cuneiform arose out of the need to record stuff, all kinds of stuff but especially business stuff. It sounds boring, but a civilization cannot last long if it does not maintain accurate records. The first writing emerged from the simple need to record the sale of a field or the loss of a herd of sheep, with simple pictures representing physical objects and symbols to represent the numbers of things being bought or sold, gained or lost. The Sumerians had writing material in great abundance in the Tigris and Euphrates river valleys in the form of, well, mud. That's right–mud, mud used for making clay tablets, as well as reeds that could be used as a pen-like instrument called a stylus for making swift, wedge-like impressions in the clay. (As you can see, we have come so far from the Sumerians, for you may be reading this book on a tablet and making annotations with a stylus.)

At first, those wedge-shaped impressions looked like the physical objects they represented. These images were called pictograms, as they were essentially pictures that resembled the ideas or things they represented. But over time, these symbols became a complicated series of strokes and wedges (cuneiform means wedge-shaped writing, after all) representing various things in the world. To us, these pictograms appear almost incomprehensible, and they were to most Sumerians too. Only

BIG IDEA

The Sumerians were the first people to practice intensive agriculture, or the act of growing wheat and other crops in such abundance to support cities with tens of thousands of people living in them. The Sumerians developed many of the elements we associate with civilization, including the world's first writing system, known as cuneiform, the world's first calendar, and even the wheel.

ADDA SEAL (LEFT, 2,300 BC) / ZIGGURAT OF UR (RIGHT, 2,100 BC)
The Adda Seal, featuring the Sumerian gods Inanna, Utu, and Enki, was a cylinder that was rolled across important documents to signify their authenticity; the Ziggurat of Ur was built by King Ur-Nammu of Ur.

the well-educated class of priests, known collectively as **bureaucrats**, had the time needed to learn the complicated system of cuneiform. In time, the priests became a class of well-educated, literate bureaucrats who not only performed priestly functions but also kept records and wrote books.

To help maintain those records, the Sumerians invented the 60-second minute and 60-minute hour, known to us today as the **sexegesimal system**. The Sumerians devised this base-60 system based on a method for making quick calculations: if you count the knuckles on your pinky, index, middle, and pointer finger, you'll find you have twelve knuckles. Twelve knuckles multiplied by five fingers on each hand gives sixty. Some historians argue that a counting system based on knuckles and fingers plus the sheer number of multiples in the number 60—1, 2, 3, 4, 5, 6, 10, 12, 15, 20, 30—made the sexegesimal system a convenient way to make advanced, rapid calculations. One can imagine a Sumerian bureaucrat in a field predicting the upcoming harvest by counting on his knuckles and fingers.

The Sumerians also divided the day into 12-hour parts, with each hour composed of 60 minutes and each minute composed of 60 seconds. The Sumerians and their successor civilizations in ancient Babylon and Persia were also dedicated astronomers and stargazers, all of which combined to give us the first calendar.

Civilization may have begun at Eridu, but it took off at nearby **Uruk**. Uruk is arguably the world's first city–not just a settlement or a large village but a real, big city. Uruk was founded sometime between 4,000 and 3,000 BC and at its height, the city of Uruk was around 250 square acres in size with a population of around 50,000 to 80,000 people. For comparison, later Sumerian cities averaged about 25 square acres.

One thing that helped Uruk grow was its location at the center of several different ecosystems, and each ecosystem produced some kind of food in abundance. An ecosystem is like a city, in that an ecosystem has different plants, animals, and other living creatures interacting with each other. Nearby pasturelands were great for raising sheep, the rivers had fish and water birds, and the riverbanks were used for growing wheat and barley.

Uruk was near the Persian Gulf, so that it could trade with settlements as far as the Indus River valley (more on the civilization of ancient Harappa later). And the Tigris and Euphrates Rivers could be used to transport goods to other cities along the riverbanks. A network for trading and shipping goods soon sprang up throughout the region, with mighty Uruk at the center. Merchants from Uruk brought not only goods but also the knowledge of cuneiform throughout ancient Sumer.

We start with Eridu and especially Uruk because these cities set the standard for other Sumerian cities that would follow. For example, most Sumerian cities had a towering ziggurat at the center of their city. A ziggurat is a massive step pyramid, a temple that serves as the home for the god or goddess sacred to the city. Uruk was no different in this regard, except Uruk had two temple districts: one dedicated to the goddess Inanna, the goddess of love and war, known more widely by her Babylonian name, Ishtar. For comparison, Inanna is something of a counterpart to Aphrodite and Venus, the Greek and Roman goddess of love, respectively. The other ziggurat was dedicated to Anu, the god of the heavens.

Sumerians living outside of Uruk came to the ziggurats to Inanna and Anu not only to worship these gods but also to barter for goods. Uruk's people would bring

	SUMERIAN (Vertical)	SUMERIAN (Rotated)	EARLY BABYLONIAN	LATE BABYLONIAN	ASSYRIAN
star					
sun					
month					
man					
king					
son					
head					
lord					
his					
reed					
power					
mouth					
ox					
bird					
destiny					
fish					
gardener					
habitation					
Nineveh					
night					

CUNEIFORM STYLES / SUMER TO ASSYRIA

The development of cuneiform across civilizations

"offerings" to the goddess Ishtar, which the priests would either take for themselves or redistribute to the temple "dependents," who lived and literally depended on the priests for their daily bread (Mieroop 30). The ziggurat became as much a commercial center—a place for buying and selling—as much as it was a religious center—a place for worshiping the gods like Inanna and Anu, amongst others. The priests living at these ziggurats kept records of whatever was bought or sold. Their knowledge of cuneiform gave them great power and influence.

But Uruk was not the only Sumerian city-state. Other city-states appeared along the banks of the Tigris and Euphrates and, as they grew in size and population, they fought against each other for resources. It is to that period in Sumerian history we next turn.

Describe Sumerian cuneiform. How did it develop, why did they need it, and what was it like?

What factors made life in ancient Sumer so difficult?

For what other innovations were the Sumerians responsible?

What is a ziggurat? What functions did it serve in ancient Sumer?

A Closer Look at Cuneiform

LET US TAKE A CLOSER LOOK at cuneiform, the wedge-shaped writing of the Sumerians. Initially, writing arose in ancient Sumer for the purposes of keeping records of commercial transactions, a means of helping the "king-priest", the figure in charge of the local ziggurat, know how much food was on hand and could be expected at the next harvest.

Writing was thus the privileged technology of the bureaucratic elites in ancient Sumer, and they were a very, very low percentage of the population who were well-educated enough to read in this difficult script. Over time, these well-educated priests would adapt cuneiform writing for writing works of literature and history in addition to record-keeping. Today, the system of cuneiform looks incomprehensible. It seems beyond our comprehension how anyone could use this system of wedges and brushstrokes to communicate.

Yet, if we were to trace the changes in cuneiform from the objects these symbols represented to the wedges they gradually became, Sumerian writing becomes a bit easier to understand and more straightforward. So, let us take a moment to do just that—examine cuneiform writing from the objects they represent to the wedges and strokes they eventually became.

Below is an illustration of various cuneiform pictograms and the objects they represent to help draw the connection between the *symbol* and the thing *symbolized*. In the space provided, write an explanation of what this cuneiform symbol could have symbolized. The first symbol for *bread* has been done for you as an example.

Cuneiform Symbols

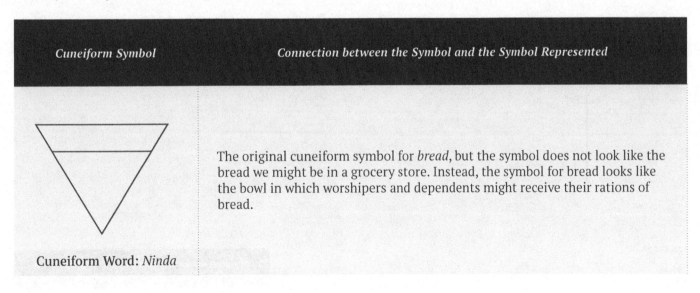

Cuneiform Symbol	Connection between the Symbol and the Symbol Represented
Cuneiform Word: *Ninda*	The original cuneiform symbol for *bread*, but the symbol does not look like the bread we might be in a grocery store. Instead, the symbol for bread looks like the bowl in which worshipers and dependents might receive their rations of bread.

Cuneiform Symbols (Cont.)

Cuneiform Symbol	Connection between the Symbol and the Symbol Represented

Cuneiform and its Development

Instructions: Below is a diagram containing a series of cuneiform symbols presented in a grid pattern. The left-hand column contains the name, in English, of each symbol, whereas the top column identifies as symbol as being from ancient Sumer and the later variations of cuneiform writing. The goal here is to trace the more complicated symbols in the Babylonian and Assyrian script to what those symbols originally looked like which, as the diagram suggests, looked remarkably like the real-world objects each cuneiform symbol represented. The answer key is available on the following page, with the missing cuneiform symbols circled.

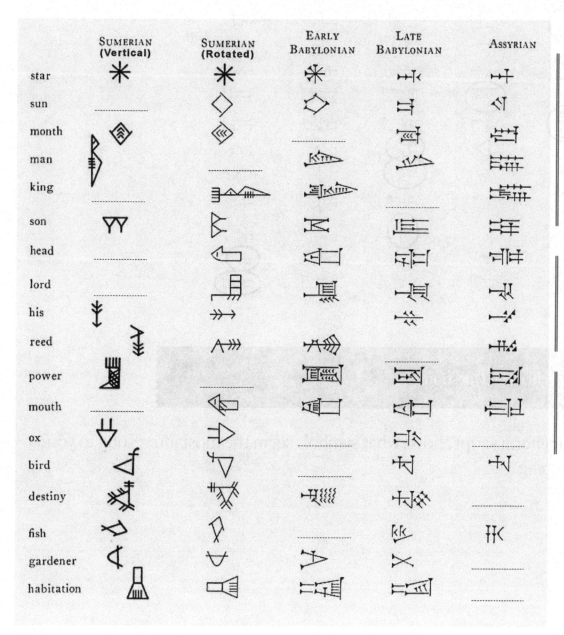

CUNEIFORM SCRIPT

Take a look at the similarities and differences of Sumerian writing compared to later versions of cuneiform.

What kinds of patterns do you notice?

CUNEIFORM SCRIPT

Why do you think some symbols look more like the objects they represent than others?

NOTE

The line marks where no cuneiform symbol existed or has been found.

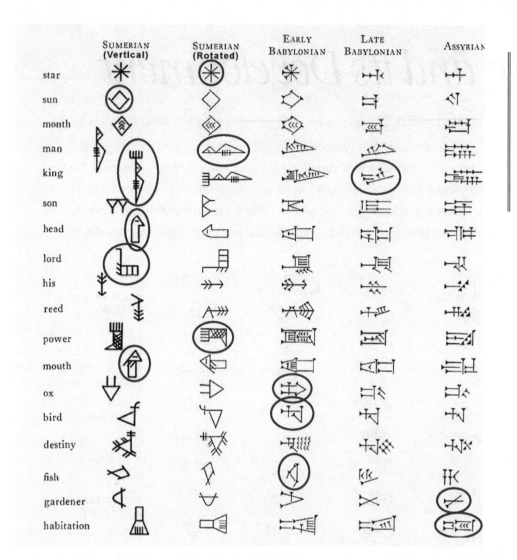

Take a look at the similarities and differences of Sumerian writing compared to later versions of cuneiform.

How similar (or dissimilar) were your guesses, compared to what the circled symbols actually looked like?

✦ ✦ Reading Comprehension Questions

Looking at the cuneiform script above, what symbols seem the most interesting to you? Explain your reasoning.

....

....

....

....

Deciphering Cuneiform

Below is a photo of a tablet from ancient Uruk, created around 3100 BC. The tablet is itself the record of the sale of livestock or produce in the city. With the guide to Sumerian cuneiform below, try and decipher the cune-iform tablet and the kinds of goods that were bought or sold. The answer key is available in the bottom right photo on the following page.

‖ A TABLET FROM URUK
(3,100 BC; Mieroop 31; Metropolitan Museum of Art)

‖ PROTO-CUNIFORM CHARACTERS
(3,100 and 2,700 BC)

Look above at the tablet left and using the symbols on the right, try to decode the cuneiform symbols written on it.

Hint: The circles indicate the size and the number of the goods being sold. Answer is in the bottom right photo on the opposite page.

....

....

....

‖ PROTO-CUNEIFORM

‖ EARLY CUNEIFORM

‖ DISTRIBUTION OF BEER

ANSWER KEY / URUK TABLET 3,100 BC

Metropolitan museum of Art

A Closer Look at Cuneiform

Sumerian Record Keeping Devices	Description	Photograph	Description of Photograph
Tablets	The Tigris and Euphrates river valley naturally possesses an endless supply of mud, which can be baked to make bricks or a smooth writing surface known as a tablet.		A tablet bearing a poem entitled *Inanna and Ebib*.
Cylinder Seals	Cylinder seals had ornate carvings upon them that could be used to leave an impression of a clay tablet and thereby show that tablet's authenticity.		A cylinder seal and the impression it leaves; available in the Louvre. Circa 3,100 BC
Bullae	These were small hollow balls upon which cuneiform was written; inside the ball, small objects (called "tokens") of different shapes and sizes were inserted. These tokens may have symbolized some agricultural commodity that had been bought or sold.		A bullae, on display at the Louvre.
Lexical Lists	These are lists of words in the same category, and they were copied and recopied by scribes trying to learn the cuneiform script. Those categories included: occupation, types of animals, types of crops, and other related groupings of things (Mieroop 33).		This tablet was a kind of *encyclopedia* of a number of different lexical lists that listed boats, wheeled vehicles, the names of constellations, and other important groupings of things.

Why did the Sumerians develop a written language? What did the process look like?

Of the Sumerian record-keeping devices–cylinder seals, bullae, lexical lists, and mud tablets–which one was your favorite and why?

Shouldn't writing be used for something more than just recording transactions? Why or why not? Explain your reasoning.

Writing Prompt

Writing is thinking, so we will spend considerable time this year writing and thinking about history. In the space provided, write a short essay answering the question: *Is it fair to credit ancient Sumer with being the founders of civilization? Do they or do they not deserve such a title? Cite at least three examples of why they should or not be credited with this title.*

Direct Instruction Review

The hardest part about history is memorizing all those facts, dates, and events. To make this process easier, we have included this short section called *Direct Instruction Review*. Direct Instruction (or DI) is a powerful pedagogical tool whereby teachers ask students a series of *call-and-response* questions, and students respond back with the aim of learning this material to *mastery*. Teacher's lines are in **bold**; student's lines in *italics*.

Where did the world's civilization rise? *Ancient Sumer.*

What did the Sumerians call themselves? *The Black-Haired Ones.*

And what did they call their land? *The land of the noble-kings.*

Where was ancient Sumer located? *On the banks of the Tigris and the Euphrates rivers.*

And where are the Tigris and the Euphrates rivers? *In what is today modern Iraq, Syria, and Iran.*

What did the Greeks call this region? *Mesopotamia!*

And what does Mesopotamia mean? *Mesopotamia means "the land between rivers."*

What was the first Sumerian city? *The first Sumerian city was called Eridu.*

And the biggest Sumerian city? *The biggest Sumerian city was Uruk, located in southern Iraq.*

What allowed Uruk to get so big? *Uruk was surrounded by productive farmland and could ship goods up and down the Euphrates River and across the Persian Gulf.*

And what did the Sumerians invent? *The Sumerians invented the calendar, the wheel, baskets, bronze-making, and sailboats!*

But what was their most important invention? *The Sumerians invented a kind of writing called cuneiform.*

And what is cuneiform? *Cuneiform means wedge-shaped writing, and it was written on clay tablets.*

What did the Sumerians use cuneiform for? *The Sumerians used cuneiform for keeping records–first of commercial transactions and later historical records and even poetry!*

And why might cuneiform be the most important invention the Sumerians passed down to history? *Because without writing and written records, we really don't have history!*

Map Practice: Ancient Sumer

Instructions: Carefully look over the maps below, which are identical to maps provided in the rest of this chapter aside from one crucial difference—they have blanks in the place of the name of a sea, region, or site. Fill in the appropriate blank with the term list provided above each map. *Note: The course of the Tigris and Euphrates rivers has shifted over time, so the exact placement of a Sumerian city may appear to have shifted, too.*

Ancient Sumer: Rivers such as the Tigris and the Euphrates; mountains such as the Zagros and the Taurus; bodies of water such as the Mediterranean Sea, the Persian Gulf, and the Caspian Sea; regions such as Sumer and Elam; and the city-states of Ur, Uruk, Umma, Lagash, Kish, Susa, Nippur, and Eridu.

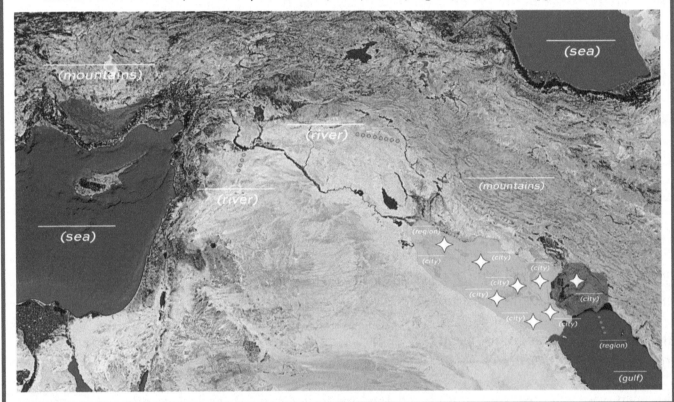

Want to study this map online? Type in the link below or scan the QR code to access an interactive diagram:
https://bit.ly/3okSogF

Timeline Practice / Ancient Sumer

The hardest part about history is memorizing all those facts, dates, and events. To make this process easier, check out the timeline below—well, technically, there are *two* timelines. Some entries are missing dates, and others are missing the event that occurred on that date. With the information available from both timelines, fill in the missing blanks to get a better sense of the timeline for this chapter.

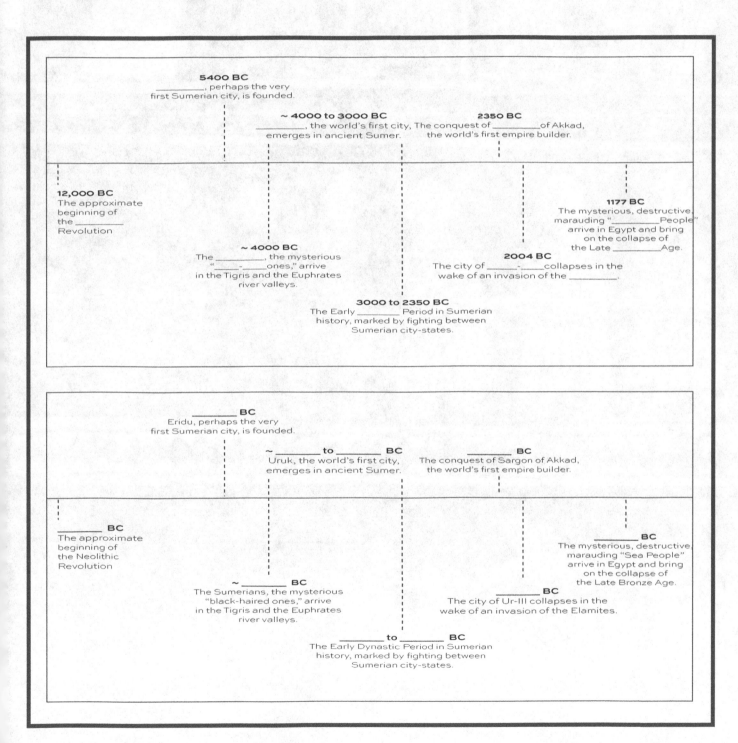

5400 BC
_____, perhaps the very first Sumerian city, is founded.

~ 4000 to 3000 BC
_____, the world's first city, emerges in ancient Sumer.

2350 BC
The conquest of _____ of Akkad, the world's first empire builder.

12,000 BC
The approximate beginning of the _____ Revolution

1177 BC
The mysterious, destructive, marauding "_____ People" arrive in Egypt and bring on the collapse of the Late _____ Age.

~ 4000 BC
The _____, the mysterious "_____-_____ ones," arrive in the Tigris and the Euphrates river valleys.

2004 BC
The city of _____-_____ collapses in the wake of an invasion of the _____.

3000 to 2350 BC
The Early _____ Period in Sumerian history, marked by fighting between Sumerian city-states.

_____ BC
Eridu, perhaps the very first Sumerian city, is founded.

~ _____ to _____ BC
Uruk, the world's first city, emerges in ancient Sumer.

_____ BC
The conquest of Sargon of Akkad, the world's first empire builder.

_____ BC
The approximate beginning of the Neolithic Revolution

_____ BC
The mysterious, destructive, marauding "Sea People" arrive in Egypt and bring on the collapse of the Late Bronze Age.

~ _____ BC
The Sumerians, the mysterious "black-haired ones," arrive in the Tigris and the Euphrates river valleys.

_____ BC
The city of Ur-III collapses in the wake of an invasion of the Elamites.

_____ to _____ BC
The Early Dynastic Period in Sumerian history, marked by fighting between Sumerian city-states.

THE STANDARD OF UR / WAR SIDE

Created around 2,600 BC, the Standard of Ur *was discovered in the royal tomb in the Sumerian city of Ur.*

The Rise & Fall of Sumer

ROADMAP

+ Learn about the ancient Sumerians and how they built their civilization.

+ Learn about the relationship between various city-states.

+ Study the fall of Sumerian civilization and the reasons why the Sumerians (largely) disappeared from history.

+ Practice our knowledge of maps and chronology, as well as our writing skills through reading comprehension questions and an essay.

THALES
OUTCOME
№ 8

*Someone who is **Astute Problem Solver** plans the best possible solutions to challenges to achieve optimal success..*

In this chapter, we look at the history of ancient Sumer as they react to and solve a number of problems: how to raise enough food to feed an ever-growing population, how to defend their cities from barbarian attacks, and how to integrate their economies in a larger and more organized system. But, sadly, Sumer tries solving some of their problems (like lack of resources) by fighting, which sadly creates more problems for the Sumerians to handle.

Do people typically fight to have control of all resources, or just the resources they have the greatest likelihood of controlling? If you and a sibling were to fight over toys, what would you fight over?

Fall of the Black-Haired Kings / Early Dynastic Period

THE PEOPLE OF ANCIENT SUMER lived in a network of independent city-states. This period is called the Early Dynastic Period, and it lasted from 3,000 to 2,350 BC. The bigger Sumerian city-states included Nippur, Kish, and Ur, each of which made their unique contributions to Sumer as a whole. For example, Nippur was located in northern Sumer, and the city had a huge temple dedicated to Enlil. That temple made Nippur something of a religious center for the whole of Sumer. Kish, meanwhile, lay almost right between the Tigris and Euphrates rivers. That position allowed them to control passage up and down those rivers and thus made Kish wealthy and powerful. Later, Sumerian kings would claim the title "King of Kish" to signal their great might and power. And there was Ur, whose location near the Persian Gulf allowed it to grow wealthy and prosperous off of trade.

But, this period is marked mostly by fighting between city-states. Those city-states fought for the limited resources on the edge of the plain, known in Sumerian as the **guedena**. The guedena was the border region between city-states such as a field or a stream that lay just in the middle between two city-states. Access to that field may help one city-state survive in the hostile environment of ancient Sumer. One particularly bad battle over the guedena is depicted in the Vulture Stele on the following page. The stele describes the city of Lagash fighting with the city of Umma over resources, with Lagash triumphing over Umma (and feeding their bodies to the birds).

Then, in 2350 BC, **Sargon of Akkad**, a commoner, built the world's first empire. An **empire** is one city or group of people who come to rule over many cities and many groups of people. This achievment was indeed Sargon's major accomplishment, conquering and uniting the formerly-independent Sumerian city-states into a cohesive political unit similar to an empire, a political unit whereby one city rules over a large geographic area encompassing many different groups of people.

Sargon of Akkad

This development from fractured city-states to unified empire has occurred many times throughout history. We will see it again in Greece with a king named Philip II of Macedon, who conquered the smaller, scattered Greek city-states, and we will see it eras in European history with kingdoms like Prussia and Piedmont-Sardinia absorbing the other states to form modern Germany and modern Italy, respectively. City-states fight against each other and grow weaker, while one state (like Akkad or Macedon or Prussia) bides its time and makes a bid to rule them all.

According to legend, Sargon was the illegitimate son of one of the temple priestesses of Inanna, the Sumerian goddess of love and war. For reasons unknown, his mother placed him in a basket and set him adrift in the Euphrates. This legend is a fairly-common birth story in the ancient world: a prince abandoned in the woods or at sea only to be miraculously rescued by the gods. These stories show that whoever was abandoned enjoyed the gods' favor or else they would not have survived. For example, Sargon was rescued by a nearby gardener.

Later, Sargon became the cup-bearer to the king of Kish, an important city that controlled much of the trade between northern and southern Sumer. But the king grew jealous of Sargon and tried to have him murdered, sending Sargon to the city of Uruk with a clay tablet bearing the message, "Kill the man (Sargon) who bears this tablet." The king of Uruk instead recruited Sargon, and Sargon was given charge of enough soldiers to carry on a war of conquest across northern Sumer. Later, Sargon conquered Uruk, too, and eventually conquered all of the Tigris and Euphrates river valleys. Sargon's empire stretched along the Tigris and Euphrates and ended only at the Persian Gulf.

Sargon implemented many new practices that we would associate with the building of an empire. First, Sargon tried to standardize practices in his kingdom. He made standard weights and measures merchants used to weigh out goods in the marketplace, taking out much of the guesswork involved in trade between cities. He also implemented something like a postal

VULTURE STELE / CIRCA 2550 BC
Lagash soldiers marching in formation

system to make communication between city-states more efficient. To send a "letter," a cuneiform tablet would be encased in a clay "envelope," sealed by the sender, with a name and address written on the outside. When the recipient received his "letter," he would simply break the outer encasing and pull out the tablet to read his message. In addition to these developments, Sargon founded a new capital which he named Agade, a city we know today as Akkad thanks to its Hebrew spelling. Lastly, Sargon replaced the rulers of a Sumerian city with his own trusted attendants; that way, Sargon had officials he could trust.

Those proud Sumerian city-states hung onto their local identities, and merchants did not want to convert one city's measurements to their own measurements. He put down rebellions with his soldiers, but he also ordered the leading families of every city to send representatives to serve at his court. These individuals were effectively hostages and ensured good behavior from their families back home (Bauer 100-102). According to legend, Sargon also founded the city of **Babylon**, and he conquered other cities like **Assur** and Nineveh.

These cities would later build empires not unlike Sargon's and rule over much of the Tigris and Euphrates river valleys–indeed, much of the known world (Bauer 96-99). But those empires only rose after the fall of the ancient Sumer.

The End of Ancient Sumer

Sargon ruled for 56 years and the empire was passed on to his son, Rimush, and later his grandson, Naram-Sin. Like many empires that followed, Sargon's empire collapsed in the face of barbarian invasion from a people called the Gutians. You see, Naram-Sin, the arrogant grandson of Sargon, brought the anger of the Sumerian gods down on his empire by sacking a temple dedicated to Enlil, one of the three most powerful and important gods in ancient Sumer. Enlil sent the Gutians down the slopes of the Zagros Mountains to destroy the land of the black-haired ones (Stearns 26; Bauer 121-123).

The **Gutians** could destroy Sumerian cities, but they did not know how to rule them. In place of the Gutians arose the city of Ur, located in southern Sumer near the Persian Gulf. The city of Ur drove out the Gutians and then took over the administration of much, but not all, of ancient Sumer. Ur was very wealthy thanks to its quick access to the Persian Gulf, and its most famous king Ur-Nammu used that wealth to rebuild Sumer. Ur-Nammu was of the 3rd dynasty, so this period is called Ur-III. He renovated many public buildings and ziggurats, and he even drafted a law code, called the Code of Ur-Nammu. This legal code appeared 300 years before the more-famous Code of Hammurabi. At its height, Ur had a population of 65,000 people (Mieroop; Bauer).

Vocabulary

Guedena

The term *guedena* refers to the border region between Sumerian city-states, which contained resources those city-states fought over.

Empire

An empire is one city or group of people who come to rule over many cities and many groups of people.

Sargon of Akkad

The world's first empire builder and the conqueror of the whole of the Tigris and Euphrates river valleys.

Babylon and Assyria

The two dominant states in the Tigris and Euphrates river valleys, who trace their history back, in part, to Sargon of Akkad.

The Gutians

A barbarian tribe from the Zagros Mountains that conquered large parts of the Tigris and Euphrates river valleys and put an end to the remnants of Sargon's empire.

Elam

A state to the southeast of Mesopotamia near the foothills of the Zagros Mountains.

The Zagros Mountains

The mountains to the east of ancient Sumer, separating the Tigris and Euphrates rivers from the Iranian plateau.

But the good times were not to last. Ur-Nammu was a great king, but his descendants of Ur-III could not stand up to the challenges posed by a new state called Elam. Elam was a state to the southeast of Mesopotamia, near the foothills of the Zagros Mountains. The Elamites were distant ancestors of the Medes and the Persians, and in 2004 BC, these people invaded Sumer and sacked the city of Ur. Although ancient Sumer had been invaded before and had experienced considerable fighting between cities, it would not recover from the invasion of the Elamites. The Elamites tore down the walls and destroyed its magnificent temples and palaces, leaving behind a trail of destruction so devastating that poets described the plains as "cracked like a kiln," (Bauer 143).

New civilizations would arise in the Tigris and the Euphrates, but they were nothing like the Sumerians. The civilization that gave us the wheel and writing disappeared, replaced by new and mighty states that imitated the cultural successes of the black-haired kings. From the ashes of ancient Sumer would arise new and mighty empires like Babylon and Assyria, terrifying states that would come to rule the whole world.

One man who fled from Ur before its destruction has had the most influential impact on world history. He was of small importance during his lifetime, for he was not a king or an empire builder. In fact, when he left Ur, he was old and childless. But by the time he passed away, this man, named Abraham, and his wife, Sarah, would give birth to a son whose descendants would become the ancient Israelites. Abraham is known to history as the father of the people of Israel, a people though small in stature may be the most significant of all the people we study this year. And shortly before 2004 BC, Abraham left the city of Ur and migrated north and west to the land of Canaan–but that tale is a story for another chapter.

THE MASK OF SARGON / CIRCA 2300 BC
Scholars speculated this artifact was a kind of funerary mask worn by a deceased Sargon of Akkad, but now historians and archaeologists think that it was for Sargon's grandson, Naram-Sin.

VICTORY STELE OF NARAM-SIN / 2254 BC
Naram-Sin, grandson of Sargon of Akkad, seen here in triumph over his enemies, wearing a helmet associated with the gods.

Why did city-states typically fight with each other?

Who was Sargon of Akkad, and what did he do that made him the world's first empire builder?

Describe the city of Ur. What did Ur do for ancient Sumer?

Primary Source Analysis / **Standard of Ur**

Recall that primary sources are documents (or similar artifacts) created at or very near the time of the event under investigation. They are a record created around the time of the event the historian is studying, and they can include the chronicles of great kings, letters, poems, songs, diaries, historical artifacts, even paintings.

Title: The Standard of Ur

Date: Circa 2600 BC

Location: The city of Ur, the center of the last significant moment in Sumerian history.

Description: Perhaps the most famous artifact from Sumerian civilization was the Standard of Ur, constructed sometime around 2,600 BC and made from lapis lazuli, a blue stone found in places like Afghanistan. British archaeologist Sir Leonard Woolley discovered the standard in AD 1927-28. The name "standard" comes from the object's placement next to a man who may have carried this "standard" on a pole, but whether it was a "standard" carried into battle is a matter of conjecture. The truth is no one knows what this object is or for what purpose it was constructed—only that the "Standard of Ur" is a beautiful, superb work of craftsmanship.

‖ STANDARD OF UR / PEACE SIDE

‖ STANDARD OF UR / WAR SIDE

Who is at the center of each scene? The War Side? The Peace Side?

Who are the other figures in this scene?

What might this scene be depicting? What exactly is the purpose of this object?

Writing Prompt

Writing is thinking, so we will spend considerable time this year writing and thinking about history. In the space provided, write a short essay answering the question: *What can we learn from the collapse of the world's first civilization, that of ancient Sumer? Why did Sumer fall apart in the way that it did? Could that collapse have been avoided? Why or why not?*

Direct Instruction Review

The hardest part about history is memorizing all those facts, dates, and events. To make this process easier, we have included this short section called *Direct Instruction Review*. Direct Instruction (or DI) is a powerful pedagogical tool whereby teachers ask students a series of *call-and-response* questions, and students respond back with the aim of learning this material to *mastery*. Teacher's lines are in **bold**; student's lines in *italics*.

What is a city-state? *A city-state is a city and the farmland around that city, so that the city can take care of itself and remain independent of anyone else.*

Did Sumerian city-states fight with each other? *Yes, the city-states of ancient Sumer fought all the time over resources such as a field or a river, anything that could help them survive.*

Did the city-states of ancient Sumer remain independent for very long? *No, they were conquered by Sargon of Akkad.*

And who was Sargon of Akkad? *Sargon was born a commoner but was entrusted with an army; eventually, he conquered all of Sumer and built the world's first empire.*

What is an empire? *An empire is one city or one group of people ruling over many cities and many groups of people.*

What did Sargon do to build the world's first empire? *Sargon not only conquered the cities of ancient Sumer, he also brought them closer together by standardizing weights and measures for trading and starting a postal system for communication.*

And what happened to Sargon's empire? *When Sargon's grandson Naram-Sin brought down the wrath of the gods, the gods sent the Gutians to destroy the empire.*

And who drove out the Gutians? *The city of Ur.*

And who was the king of Ur? *Ur-Nammu of Ur's third dynasty!*

What did the king of Ur do? *Ur-Nammu rebuilt many temples and drafted the first legal code, called the Code of Ur-Nammu.*

And what happened to the city of Ur? *A group of people called the Elamites sacked the city of Ur in 2004 BC.*

What else did the Sumerians give us? *Sumerian civilization would eventually give rise to new empires like Babylon and Assyria, and Abraham, the father of the Jewish people, came from the city of the Ur.*

Map Practice: Ancient Sumer

Instructions: Carefully look over the maps below, which are identical to maps provided in the rest of this chapter aside from one crucial difference—they have blanks in the place of the name of a sea, region, or site. Fill in the appropriate blank with the term list provided above each map. *Note: The course of the Tigris and Euphrates rivers has shifted over time, so the exact placement of a Sumerian city may appear to have shifted, too.*

Ancient Sumer: Rivers such as the Tigris and the Euphrates; mountains such as the Zagros and the Taurus; bodies of water such as the Mediterranean Sea, the Persian Gulf, and the Caspian Sea; regions such as Sumer and Elam; and the city-states of Ur, Uruk, Umma, Lagash, Kish, Susa, Nippur, and Eridu.

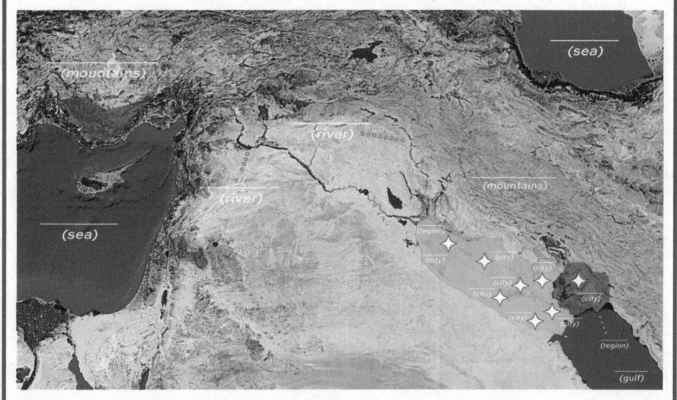

Want to study this map online? Type in the link below or scan the QR code to access an interactive diagram: https://bit.ly/3okSogF

Timeline Practice / Ancient Sumer

The hardest part about history is memorizing all those facts, dates, and events. To make this process easier, check out the timeline below—well, technically, there are *two* timelines. Some entries are missing dates, and others are missing the event that occurred on that date. With the information available from both timelines, fill in the missing blanks to get a better sense of the timeline for this chapter.

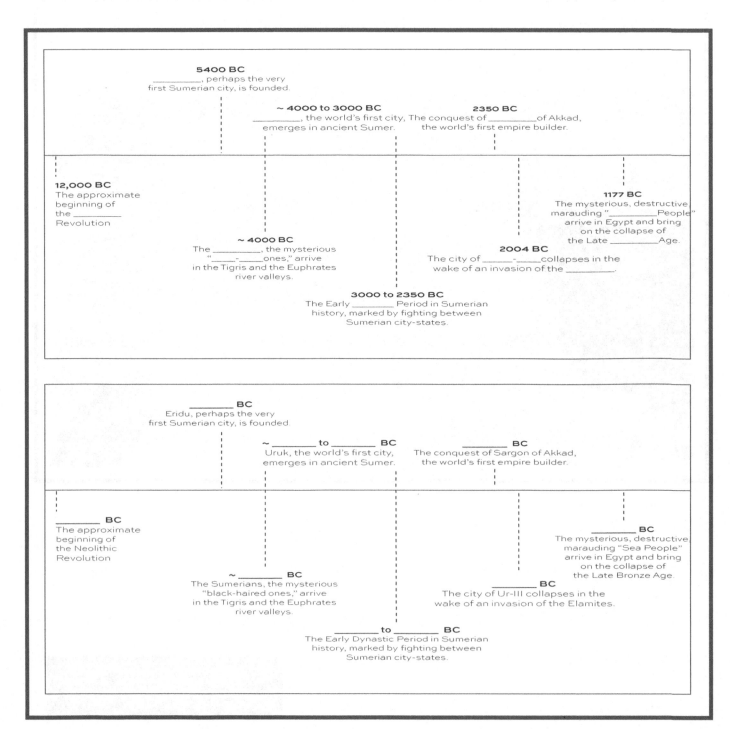

5400 BC
_____, perhaps the very
first Sumerian city, is founded.

~ 4000 to 3000 BC
_____, the world's first city,
emerges in ancient Sumer.

2350 BC
The conquest of _____ of Akkad,
the world's first empire builder.

12,000 BC
The approximate
beginning of
the _____
Revolution

1177 BC
The mysterious, destructive,
marauding "_____ People"
arrive in Egypt and bring
on the collapse of
the Late _____ Age.

~ 4000 BC
The _____, the mysterious
"_____-_____ ones," arrive
in the Tigris and the Euphrates
river valleys.

2004 BC
The city of _____-_____ collapses in the
wake of an invasion of the _____.

3000 to 2350 BC
The Early _____ Period in Sumerian
history, marked by fighting between
Sumerian city-states.

_____ BC
Eridu, perhaps the very
first Sumerian city, is founded.

~ _____ to _____ BC
Uruk, the world's first city,
emerges in ancient Sumer.

_____ BC
The conquest of Sargon of Akkad,
the world's first empire builder.

_____ BC
The approximate
beginning of
the Neolithic
Revolution

_____ BC
The mysterious, destructive,
marauding "Sea People"
arrive in Egypt and bring
on the collapse of
the Late Bronze Age.

~ _____ BC
The Sumerians, the mysterious
"black-haired ones," arrive
in the Tigris and the Euphrates
river valleys.

_____ BC
The city of Ur-III collapses in the
wake of an invasion of the Elamites.

_____ to _____ BC
The Early Dynastic Period in Sumerian
history, marked by fighting between
Sumerian city-states.

THE CODE OF HAMMURABI

Composed circa 1750 BC, the Code of Hammurabi is the world's first fully-developed legal code.

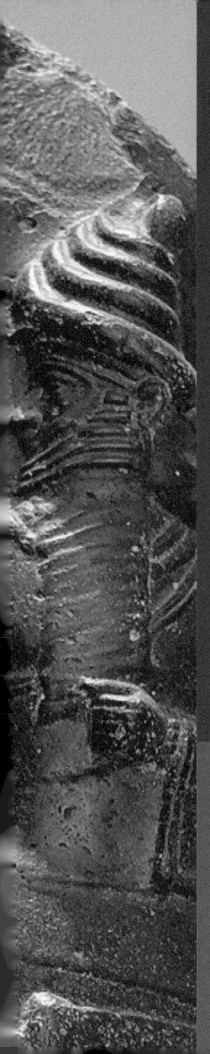

Babylon & Assyria

ROADMAP

✦ Examine the very beginnings of Assyria and Babylon, kingdoms that will become the world's first empires.

✦ Learn about the life, reign, and accomplishments of the Assyrian king Shamshi-Adad and the Babylonian king Hammurabi.

✦ Read the *Code of Hammurabi*, one of the world's earliest and most significant legal texts.

✦ Practice our knowledge of maps and chronology, as well as our writing skills through reading comprehension questions and an essay.

THALES
OUTCOME

№ 2

*A **Virtuous Leader** analyzes a variety of truth statements and/or observations through a dialectic examination of facts and assumptions.*

Kingdoms like Assyria and Babylon emerged largely due to the leadership of local rulers like Shamshi-Adad and Hammurabi the Great. While we should not certainly imitate many of the things these leaders did (they were warlords, after all), they help us to better understand the importance of virtuous leadership.

Enūma Eliš / Author Unknown, as early as 1900 BC...

IN THE BEGINNING, there was only the fresh water and the salt water, Apsu and Tiamat. Together, Apsu and Tiamat created the rest of the gods and brought them into being: Lahmu and Lahamu, Anshar and Kishar, Anu and Enki. But as they created more gods, conflict arose between Apsu and Tiamat and between all the gods they had created. Apsu, god of freshwater, hated the great noise made by these pesky, lower gods and plotted against them to kill them. In turn, the lower gods feared for their lives and plotted against Apsu. Then Enki, god of crafts and magic and knowledge, cast a spell on Apsu and killed him, and from the remains of Apsu, the god who both is and made the freshwaters, Enki made his dwelling place. From the remains of Apsu came forth Marduk, the greatest and most powerful of all the gods in heaven and earth.

Still, there was conflict, The lower gods disturbed Tiamat, and she plotted against them, too. Tiamat, the god of the salt waters, made monsters: dragons, sphinxes, vipers, and more terrible beasts to strike down the lower gods and avenge Apsu's death. Together with her consort Quingu, Tiamat waged terrible war upon the earth. These monsters were too much for Anu and Enki and the other gods, and they turned at once to Marduk, now the strongest of all the gods that had been made. Only Marduk, with four eyes and four arms, had the strength to defeat Tiamat and all her monsters, but Marduk's help came with a price: "Make me your king," he said, "and I will defeat Tiamat and slay all her host." The gods agreed.

And so Marduk took up arms against Tiamat. Tiamat cast spells, and Marduk unleashed the winds; Quingu attacked Marduk, and Marduk shot down Quingu with

MARDUK STANDING ON MUSHKHUSHSHU

8th c. BC Neo-Assyrian seal; Mushkhushshu was Marduk's pet dragon.

his arrows, and from Quingu's wounds came forth the Tigris and the Euphrates. Finally, Marduk shot down Tiamat with his fiery arrows and defeated the vengeful deity. Then Marduk defeated her minions, monsters like snakes and sphinxes and dragons, and at last, brought peace to the whole of the universe.

With Tiamat's remains, Marduk used one-half for the heavens and the other half for the earth. Then Marduk set about ordering the rest of creation, appointing the days of the year and the phases of the moon. At last, to give the gods rest from toil and hardship, Marduk made one last creation: man. From Quingu's remains, Marduk creates human beings, and to human beings, Marduk gives them the task of serving the gods and releasing them from all their toil.

Summarize the plot and, in your opinion, the moral of the *Enūma Eliš*.

Based on this brief reading, what seems to be man's purpose? For what was he created? Does this purpose seem noble and good, or something below man's talents and value?

Based on this story, the story that these people tell themselves about the creation of the world and man's purposes within it, what do you think life would be like in ancient Mesopotamia?

If Marduk is the most powerful god of the Babylonians, and Marduk is coming to rule over all the gods of Sumer, what might that say of Babylon, the city where Marduk makes his home?

Heirs to the Black-Haired Kings / Babylon & Assyria

SO READS THE CREATION MYTH from the city of Babylon, the *Enūma Eliš*. As Marduk rose in prominence to rule the gods of ancient Sumer, so Babylon will rise to rule over the cities and villages spread along the Tigris and the Euphrates river valleys. Babylon itself began as a small village on the banks of the Euphrates, but great kings such as Hammurabi would transform this small village into a great power that ruled all of southern Sumer.

Now that ancient Sumer is no more, we will refer to the whole region of the Tigris and the Euphrates river valleys by its Greek name: *Mesopotamia*. The word **Mesopotamia** is a combination of two Greek words, *mesos* meaning "the middle" or "in the midst of", and *potamos* meaning "river." (For comparison, think of a *hippopotamus*, which the Greeks considered a "river-horse," with the word *hippo* meaning "horse.") Thus, Mesopotamia is literally *the land between the rivers*, the rivers being the Tigris and the Euphrates. As we will see, one power comes to dominate northern Meso-

potamia–**Assyria**–and another power dominates the south–**Babylon**. So, we will at times use those names, Assyria and Babylon, to refer to the regions of **Upper** and **Lower Mesopotamia**, respectively. Like ancient Egypt, a civilization we will learn about soon, the history of Assyria is organized into periods designated by the words *kingdom* or *empire*. Let us begin with **Old Kingdom Assyria**, a period of Assyrian history that lasted from around 1813 to 1741 BC.

Assyria & Shamshi-Adad

The Elamites, a people from the Zagros mountains, invaded Sumer in and around 2004 BC. The Elamites sacked much of ancient Sumer, destroying its defensives and farmland that had taken the Sumerians generations to build up. Still, the region had a lot of potential with its cities, ziggurats, well-educated literate classes, and a leadership vacuum that other cities in the region attempted to fill. The city of Assur in northern Mesopotamia would fill that vacuum.

When one state or civilization "collapses," new states arise and continue on its legacy. They make use of the traditions and practices that had long been in use in that region, they use many of the same forms of writing and record-keeping, and they look back to the heights of that civilization for guidance. This use of past customs was the case with ancient Sumer and its successor states in Mesopotamia, Assyria and Babylon, as well as with the later Roman Empire and their successor states across Western Europe.

Vocabulary

Write down this vocabulary in your notebook. These terms will help you better learn and understand the material in this chapter.

Mesopotamia
A Greek word meaning "the land between the rivers" of the Tigris and the Euphrates.

Babylon and Assyria
The two dominant states in the Tigris and Euphrates river valleys, with Babylon controlling Lower Mesopotamia and Assyria Upper Mesopotamia.

Upper Mesopotamia
The upper, northern region of the "land between the rivers". This region was largely ruled by the city of Assyria.

Lower Mesopotamia
The lower, southern region of the "land between the rivers". This region was largely ruled by the city of Babylon.

Old Kingdom Assyria
The period of Assyrian history that begins with Shamshi-Adad's conquest of Assur but ends with his son's death in 1741, when Assyria would be superceded by the rising power of Old Kingdom Babylon, lasting from 1813-1741 BC.

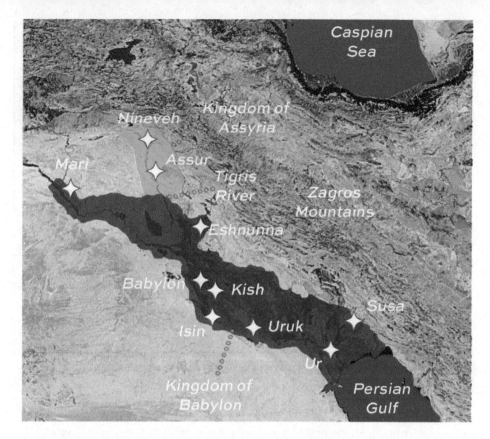

‖ **MAP OF ASSYRIA & BABYLON**

Assyrian history begins with the mysterious figure known only as **Shamshi-Adad**. We do not know much about him. We think he was an **Amorite**, a tribe of nomads from Canaan who had migrated into the Tigris and Euphrates river valleys. We think his name means *My god is the storm god Adad*. From his accomplishments, we can assume he was not only a great military leader but also a capable administrator. He not only conquered cities, but he knew how to organize them and make them work together. In time, Shamshi-Adad's conquests would bring together the whole of Upper Mesopotamia into a political unit similar to that of a state like North Carolina or Virginia: one dominant capital city supported by a vast network of smaller cities, administrative hubs, infrastructure like roads and bridges, and farmland. We might call this unit a **territorial state**, a small region comprised of one dominant city (like Babylon or Assyria), several smaller towns, and the adjoining farmland integrated into one economic and political unit. Shamshi-Adad began his conquests from his home city of Ekallatum, near the larger city of Assur. Hence, the name of the territorial state that Shamshi-Adad built: Assyria.

The three major cities in northern Mesopotamia fought with each other. Shamshi-Adad took advantage of the instability by attacking and capturing

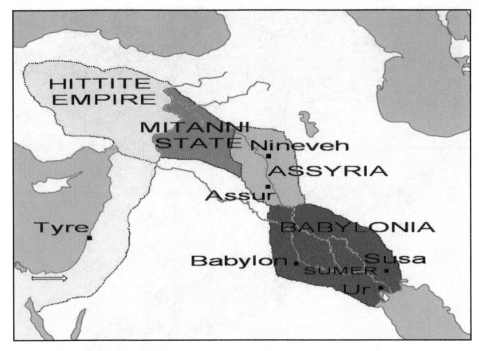

‖ **MAP OF MESOPOTAMIA / ASSYRIA & SURROUNDING STATES**

the much larger city of Assur for himself. With the cities of Ekallatum and Assur under his control, Shamshi-Adad attacked other cities in the region, installing his sons as the rulers of some of these cities. Shamshi-Adad allowed some of them to retain their rulers, provided they became his vassals and recognized he was in charge. A **vassal** is a local leader who has sworn an oath of loyalty to another, more powerful leader. Having conquered Upper Mesopotamia, Shamshi-Adad then set about integrating the economies of these cities into one cohesive unit, with Assur at its center (Mieroop 115).

After all, Upper Mesopotamia and Assur had immense potential. Assur sits on the northern reaches of the Tigris River near the Zagros Mountains. The fields around Assur were very productive and fertile. In contrast, the fields of southern Sumer had grown increasingly salty and less fertile thanks to centuries of intensive agriculture, but this decrease in land fertility was not true of northern Sumer. The region enjoyed some rainfall to water its crops, and that rainfall reduced the need for large-scale irrigation projects, as was the case in southern Sumer.

Assur's position in northeastern Mesopotamia gave them other benefits. The Assyrians had access to lots of valuable trade goods. These goods included sheep from Syria, a region just west of Mesopotamia. They also had access to the Zagros Mountains and the Iranian plateau, a region that provided wool, milk, and meat. Then, there was tin, a metal crucial for making bronze that came from Afghanistan. And, Assyria had access to commercial products from Lower Mesopotamia such as woolen textiles, ceramic jars and pots, and other products of fine craftsmanship. Lastly, Assur sent Assyrian residents abroad to

Shamshi-Adad
An Amorite warlord who conquered the city of Assur and founded Old Kingdom Assyria. He ruled from 1808-1776 BC.

Amorite
The Amorites were a tribe from Mesopotamia, Syria, and Canaan of Semitic origin, who settled in Sumer in and around the 3rd millenium BC. Figures like Shamshi-Adad of Assyria and Hammurabi of Babylon may have had Amorite roots.

Territorial State
A small region comprising one dominant city (like Babylon or Assyria), several smaller towns, and the adjoining farmland integrated into one economic and political unit.

Vassal
The word *vassal* refers to someone who has taken an oath of obedience to a more powerful ruler.

operate as merchants in foreign cities or in the lands that Assur had gained through conquest.

As with other Sumerian cities, the great city of Assur served one god whom they venerated above all the others. The city of Assur was (appropriately) dedicated to Assur, the god of war in ancient Sumerian mythology. When the Assyrians went to war every spring, they brought gifts and spoils back to Assur's temple as part of their worship of their war god Assur. In this way, Assyrian conquest and Assyrian religious identity were largely intertwined with each other to produce one of the most effective and brutal military machines in history. The Assyrians would eventually build roads, canals, and all kinds of infrastructure to move troops across the ancient Near East.

But then Shamshi-Adad died in 1776 BC. Much of the state he had built fell apart. Shamshi-Adad's son Ishme-Dagan managed to hold onto Assur and Ekallatum and keep cultural continuity from this Old Assyrian Kingdom into Assyria's Middle and New Kingdom periods. But Ishme-Dagan never managed to live up to his father's example—or his expectations, for that matter. When he was alive, Shamshi-Adad wrote letters to his son making fun of him, saying "Can't you behave like a man? Your brother has made a great name for himself; you should do the same in your own land" (Bauer 170). So while Shamshi-Adad was a good, capable warlord and king, he was not necessarily the best father who helped his children shoulder the heavy burdens placed upon them. In addition, a new power was growing in the south, one with a talented and capable ruler at the helm: Babylon, with its new king, Hammurabi.

Babylon & Hammurabi

The city of Babylon began as a small village on the banks of the Euphrates River. However, the city was made into a great power by a nomadic tribe-turned-settled-peoples known as the Amorites, whose chief, a man

❙ **DRAGON / ISHTAR GATE RECONSTRUCTION**

named Sumu-Abum, established Babylon's first dynasty and built its first defenses (Bauer 158; Stearns 26). The king most responsible for Babylon's future greatness was the grandson of Sumu-Abum, **Hammurabi** (sometimes spelled Hammurapi). Hammurabi ruled Babylon from 1792-1750 BC, and his accomplishments include conquering much of Upper and Lower Mesopotamia and drafting the famous Code of Hammurabi.

As king, Hammurabi boasted that he "made the four quarters of the earth obedient". Those four corners included the powerful state of Assur to the north, now run by Shamshi-Adad's son, Ishme-Dagan; Mari, a city on the Euphrates to the northwest, ruled by a king named Zimri-Lin; and Larsa, led by a king named Rim-Sin, Babylon's rival in Lower Mesopotamia. Each king hoped to become the next Sargon the Great, an empire-builder who could unite the "four corners" of Mesopotamia into one grand, powerful state. Hammurabi was the one who succeeded.

The way it happened went like this. Sometime around 1764 BC, two of those kings, Ishme-Dagan of Assur and Zimri-Lin of Mari, invaded Babylon. They had help from the Elamites, the same people who had invaded Sumer a generation or so earlier. Still, this attack was

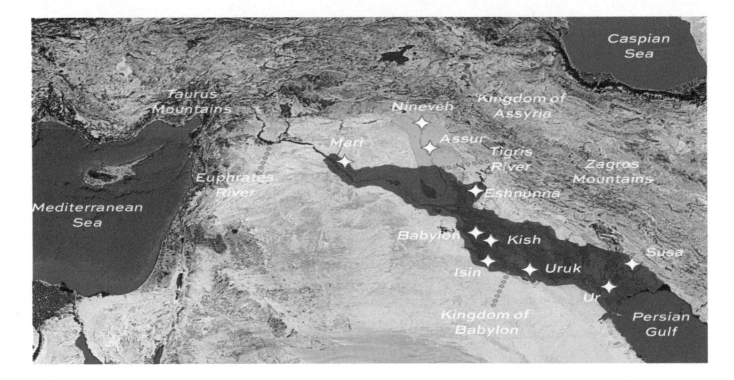

MAP OF HAMMURABI'S BABYLON

a bad idea. Hammurabi not only defeated the coalition of great powers assembled against him, but he invaded the land of Assur, defeated the armies defending it, and made Assyria part of *his* territory.

Hammurabi did not stop there. He invaded Elam next and sacked the city of Susa, looting its temples and bringing back statues of its gods to Babylon. Once the dust had settled, Hammurabi then attacked Larsa and Mari. He sacked both cities and removed their royal families from positions of power. Then, he made those cities an integral part of Babylon's economy.

That integration came about through relentless military campaigning, the drafting of a law code, and Hammurabi's close watch of Mesopotamia's entire economy. Hammurabi controlled the major entry points into and out of Mesopotamia, and he set up checkpoints at important cities throughout the region of Mesopotamia. That way, he could collect taxes from merchants buying and selling cedar from Syria, lapis lazuli from the mountains of modern-day Afghanistan and Pakistan, precious metals like gold and silver, and the bronze-making metals copper and tin (Bauer 175).

Hammurabi's tight control of the economy proved to be very effective. These efforts ensured that his newly-conquered subjects could not gain the metals they needed to make weapons, or the gold and silver required to buy them without him knowing about it. To an extent, Hammurabi's most famous contribution to world history—the **Code of Hammurabi**—was born out of Hammurabi's desire to govern the far-flung parts of his empire.

To watch over an area so large required a large number of scribes and bureaucrats. A scribe is essentially a bureaucrat or a record-keeper, an official who recorded the sale of a field or how much wheat was produced in a year. These record-keepers learned to read and write cuneiform in both Sumerian and Akkadian, and they went to schools connected to both the local ziggurat and local palaces. Wealthy members of the Babylonian elite could afford private instruction for their children. To learn how to read, they copied grammar charts and even whole poems, ones as long as Gilgamesh, an epic poem about a heroic but flawed Sumerian king (Mieroop 124-25).

Vocabulary

Hammurabi

A Babylonian king who turned Babylon into Lower Mesopotamia's most powerful state. He conquered much of the region, and he also drafted the famous Code of Hammurabi. He ruled Babylon from around 1792 to 1750 BC.

The Code of Hammurabi

A law code drafted by King Hammurabi of Babylon to help him govern his empire.

The Kassites

A tribe that conquered Babylon in the 1500s BC, but continued, preserved, and even furthered Babylon's seminal literary and diplomatic culture.

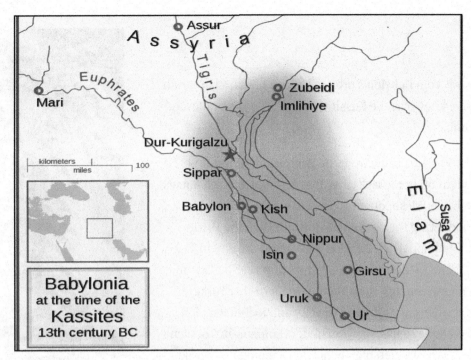

MAP OF MESOPOTAMIA / BABYLON UNDER THE KASSITES

Once they learned how to read and write, these scribes operated in many of the cities of Hammurabi's empire. As a result, Babylonian culture and writing were transmitted far across the Near East. These scribes and record keepers brought with them not only their knowledge of the cuneiform script, which could be adapted to other languages, but also examples of Akkadian and Babylonian literature such as hymns, myths, and other types of compositions. These scribes were also famous for their skill in mathematics, and they developed early forms of algebra to help in measuring fields and predicting harvests. They could also help with large building projects by estimating the number of bricks that had to be produced or volumes of earth moved in some grand building project (Mieroop 125-26).

Capable, transformational rulers like Hammurabi come around once in a generation. While they establish great states, those states rarely last for any length of time following their death. Babylon is an exception to this general principle since so many states would still look to Babylon for leadership. The Babylonian language, too, would be used for generations by the record keepers of other cities and kingdoms in a manner similar to the spread of Latin in the early Middle Ages.

Hammurabi died in or around 1750 BC, the causes being presumably sickness and old age. After his death, the city of Babylon declined in power and prestige. Virtue is not a condition one inherits, and Hammurabi's son Samsu-iluna was not the gifted administrator or the ruthless military conqueror his father was. Some faraway parts of Hammurabi's empire rebelled and broke away from Babylon's orbit. Closer to home, a barbarian tribe known as the **Kassites** moved into Lower Mesopotamia.

The Kassites came from the Zagros Mountains and fought on horseback (they may have introduced horses to Lower Mesopotamia). They were unsuccessful in conquering the city of Babylon, but then the Hittite Kingdom invaded Babylon and sacked the city in 1595 BC. The Hittites were the dominant power in Anatolia, a region roughly equivalent to modern-day Turkey, and when they attacked the city and looted Babylon's incredible riches, Babylon under Hammurabi's descendants was vulnerable. In Babylon's moment of weakness, the Kassites conquered Babylon and installed their own warrior-chieftains in various positions of power around the city. Hammurabi's Babylon was now over.

The Kassites were now Babylon's unquestioned rulers. Yet, they continued many of Hammurabi's policies and changed very little of what made Babylon so powerful and unique. Hammurabi's Babylon may have come to an end, but the Kassites gave Babylon and the surrounding region one of the era's longest dynasties, a period that lasted from approximately 1595 to 1200 BC and enjoyed extraordinary stability.

Conclusion

After the collapse of the Sumerian civilization, new powers would take their place and rule over the Tigris and Euphrates River valleys—namely, Babylon and Assyria. But Babylon and Assyria would not be city-states like those of ancient Sumer. Instead, they would be territorial states: political entities consisting of one large, principal city supported by a network of villages, farms, pasture lands, and complicated trade networks. Such states hoped to rule the entirety of the Tigris and the Euphrates river valleys, but the two powers that succeeded were Assyria in Upper Mesopotamia and Babylon in Lower Mesopotamia.

MARDUK SLAYING TIAMAT
8th c. BC Neo-Assyrian seal

These states succeeded in part because their founders—Shamshi-Adad in Assyria and Hammurabi in Babylon—were not only ruthless military conquerors but also gifted administrators, individuals who knew how to govern the peoples they defeated. From their example, we might recognize the value of taking care of the big things, such as defeating a hostile neighbor like Isin or Larsa, but also the little things that come along with conquest, such as record-keeping and other simple but necessary tasks.

But we would also do well to recognize that these early empire builders did not have the kind of character that we ourselves would want to cultivate. Shamshi-Adad seemed to be hard on the people closest to him, and while Hammurabi demonstrated strengths in some areas, we can analyze his most famous contribution to world history—the Code of Hammurabi—and see what kind of insights we can gain from his character and the kind of society he hoped to create. In both cases, these rulers seemed to be more concerned with ruling and exercising power for themselves and not necessarily for the people over whom they ruled. So, as a result, we would do well not to imitate their example.

Who was Shamshi-Adad, and what were his major accomplishments?

What advantages did Upper Mesopotamia have?

Who was Hammurabi, and what were his major accomplishments?

What can we learn from figures like Shamshi-Adad and Hammurabi?

Primary Source Analysis / Code of Hammurabi

Recall that primary sources are documents (or similar artifacts) created at or very near the time of the event under investigation. They are a record created around the time of the event the historian is studying, and they can include the chronicles of great kings, letters, poems, songs, diaries, historical artifacts, even paintings.

Title: Code of Hammurabi

Date: Circa 1755-1750 BC.

Location: Babylon, located in Lower Mesopotamia, although the stele photographed to the right was actually stolen by the Elamites and taken to Susa.

Description: The most famous example of Hammurabi's efforts to control the ever-growing city of Babylon is his law code, appropriately titled the *Code of Hammurabi*. With the code, Hammurabi seems to want to portray himself as a kind of ideal king, one who was instructed directly by the gods of ancient Sumer and Akkad (Mieroop 121). He inscribed his code of Hammurabi onto a massive stele made of jet-black basalt and diorite, with an image of Hammurabi receiving the law code from no less a source than the sun-god Shamash, the god of wisdom and justice in ancient Sumerian mythology. The code is most famous for containing the principle of **lex talionis** or "the law of retribution." The principle of *lex talionis* means that the punishment for a particular crime should, in part, resemble in kind or degree or be limited by the nature of the crime. That is, the punishment for a particular crime or offense could not go beyond the nature of the crime itself.

Preamble

When **Anu** the Sublime, King of the Anunaki, and Bel, the lord of Heaven and earth, who decreed the fate of the land, assigned to Marduk, the over-ruling son of Ea, God of righteousness, dominion over earthly man, and

CODE OF HAMMURABI / 1755-1750 BC

The Code was inscribed on a stele (which is a kind of monument or billboard to proclaim the accomplishment of a particular ruler) on diorite and basalt over 7 feet tall.

Vocabulary

Lex Talionis

The principle of *lex talionis*, or the "law of retribution" or "retaliation" means that the punishment for a crime should resemble or be limited by the nature of the crime itself.

Anu

Anu was the king of the Sumerian gods, while the Anunaki include Sumer's powerful sky gods.

...black-headed people

Hammurabi refers to the Sumerians, whose name meant "black-haired ones."

Shamash

Shamash was the god of the sun and was associated with wisdom.

Marduk

Marduk was the king of the gods in Sumerian mythology. His "home" was in the city of Babylon.

...two shekels of silver

A shekel is a both a measure of weight and a unit of currency that is one-sixtieth in value to a mina; a silver shekel was relatively-insignificant in value at about $1 to $2.

...his eye shall be put out

This passage demonstrates the principle of *lex talionis*, or *an eye for an eye*.

Mina

A mina is a unit of currency roughly equivalent to 60 shekels.

HAMMURABI & SHAMASH

Hammurabi received his legal code from no less wise and respected a source than Shamash, the god of the sun and wisdom. Shamash wears a helmet associated with the gods.

made him great among the Igigi, they called Babylon by his illustrious name, made it great on earth, and founded an everlasting kingdom in it, whose foundations are laid so solidly as those of heaven and earth; then Anu and Bel called by name me, Hammurabi, the exalted prince, who feared God, to bring about the rule of righteousness in the land, to destroy the wicked and the evil-doers; so that the strong should not harm the weak; so that I should rule over the **black-headed people** like **Shamash**, and enlighten the land, to further the well-being of mankind... When **Marduk** sent me to rule over men, to give the protection of right to the land, I did right and righteousness..., and brought about the well-being of the oppressed.

The Code of Laws

01 If any one ensnare another, putting a ban upon him, but he can not prove it, then he that ensnared him shall be put to death.

02 If any one bring an accusation against a man, and the accused go to the river and leap into the river, if he sink in the river his accuser shall take possession of his house. But if the river prove that the accused is not guilty, and he escape unhurt, then he who had brought the accusation shall be put to death, while he who leaped into the river shall take possession of the house that had belonged to his accuser.

03 If any one bring an accusation of any crime before the elders, and does not prove what he has charged, he shall, if it be a capital offense charged, be put to death.

06 If any one steal the property of a temple or of the court, he shall be put to death, and also the one who receives the stolen thing from him shall be put to death.

08 If any one steal cattle or sheep, or a donkey, or a pig or a goat, if it belong to a god or to the court, the thief shall pay thirtyfold therefor; if they belonged to a freed man of the king he shall pay tenfold; if the thief has nothing with which to pay he shall be put to death.

15 If any one take a male or female slave of the court, or a male or female slave of a freed man, outside the city gates, he shall be put to death.

16 If any one receive into his house a runaway male or female slave of the court, or of a freedman, and does not bring it out at the public proclamation of the major domus, the master of the house shall be put to death.

17 If any one find runaway male or female slaves in the open country and bring them to their masters, the master of the slaves shall pay him **two shekels of silver**.

21 If any one break into a house, he shall be put to death before that home and be buried.

22 If any one is committing a robbery and is caught, then he shall be put to death.

195 If a son strike his father, his hands shall be hewn off.

196 If a man put out the eye of another man, **his eye shall be put out**.

196 If he break another man's bone, his bone shall be broken.

198 If he put out the eye of a freed man, or break the bone of a freed man, he shall pay one gold **mina**

199 If he put out the eye of a man's slave, or break the bone of a man's slave, he shall pay one-half of its value.

200 If a man knock out the teeth of his equal, his teeth shall be knocked out. [*editor's note: this passage also demonstrates, the principle of lex talionis, or a tooth for an tooth*]

201 If he knock out the teeth of a freed man, he shall pay one-third of a gold mina.

202 If any one strike the body of a man higher in rank than he, he shall receive sixty blows with an ox-whip in public.

203 If a free-born man strike the body of another free-born man or equal rank, he shall pay one gold mina.

204 If a freed man strike the body of another freed man, he shall pay ten shekels in money.

205 If the slave of a freed man strike the body of a freed man, his ear shall be cut off.

222 If he were a freed man he shall pay three shekels.

245 If any one hire oxen, and kill them by bad treatment or blows, he shall compensate the owner, oxen for oxen.

246 If a man hire an ox, and he break its leg or cut the ligament of its neck, he shall compensate the owner with ox for ox.

251 If an ox be a goring ox, and it shown that he is a gorer, and he do not bind his horns, or fasten the ox up, and the ox gore a free-born man and kill him, the owner shall pay one-half a mina in money.

252 If he kill a man's slave, he shall pay one-third of a mina.

281 If a slave say to his master: "You are not my master," if they convict him his master shall cut off his ear...

Of the following laws, which one struck out to you the most? Which one seemed to be the most out of place, the most outdated, the most outlandish?

On what kinds of crimes does the Code of Hammurabi focus? Cite as many laws as you can, and consider what you can learn about life in Hammurabi's Babylon?

Why were there so many laws about slavery, and what to do with real, human beings in a series of different scenarios? What does these laws tell you about life in Hammurabi's Babylon?

Why are there different punishments given, depending on the person who was hurt or injured? What does these laws tell you about life in Hammurabi's Babylon?

Writing Prompt

Writing is thinking, so we will spend considerable time this year writing and thinking about history. In the space provided, write a short essay answering the question: *Why does the Code of Hammurabi have different consequences for different groups of people? Why does it not have one set of punishments that are applied equally to everyone?*

Primary Source Analysis / Code of Hammurabi

LET'S TAKE A MOMENT to break down and better understand the Code of Hammurabi. The Code of Hammurabi is significant as one of the world's first promulgated—that is, published—law codes in world history. It may not technically be the first law code. The Code of Ur-Nammu is earlier, written during the 3rd Dynasty of Ur circa 2,000 BC. The Code of Hammurabi is also technically not the most significant law code, an honor that goes to the Mosaic Law and the Ten Commandments, a law code found in the Hebrew and Christian Bible and which influenced preceding law codes right up to the present day. The biblical prophet and Israelite Moses, the author of the book of Exodus that contains the Ten Commandments, most likely knew about the Code of Hammurabi, since Moses grew up in an Egyptian palace and presumably received an excellent education. But the influence of the Code of Hammurabi on the Ten Commandments may be overstated.

Still, the Code of Hammurabi is significant for several reasons. First, the Code of Hammurabi helped establish the *principle of lex talionis*, Latin for "the law of retaliation." Lex talionis refers to the idea that the nature of the crime also limits the punishment for that crime. The phrase *an eye for an eye and a tooth for a tooth* summarizes the principle of lex talionis, in that the punishment should in some way, shape, or form, fit the crime. For example, laws #196 and 200 read that if a free man "destroyed the eye of a member of the aristocracy, they shall destroy his eye," and if he "has broken a(nother) freeman's bone, they shall break his bone" (Pritchard 174). This principle is crucial because it limits the actions the state can take in punishing crimes; one person

CODE OF HAMMURABI / 1755-1750 BC

cannot lose ten teeth because he wounded a popular and influential member of the aristocracy.

But, as you may have guessed, the laws in the Code of Hammurabi did not apply to all members of society equally. If a high-ranking aristocrat harmed a member of a lower class, they might pay a fine but suffer no other penalties ("if he has destroyed the eye of a commoner or broken the bone of a commoner, he shall pay one mina of silver," Law 198 in Pritchard 174). We can gain a reasonably accurate picture of the socioeconomic structures of ancient Babylon. That is, if we could read the original cuneiform and could identify more precise definitions of words like free men and slaves, which corresponded to the class structure of ancient Babylon. Three parts comprised Babylon's social hierarchy: free men, dependents, and slaves, along with small-scale artisans who did contract work for the temple. In Babylon, free men were known as *Awilum*, the dependents were *Mushkenum*, and the slaves were known as *Wardum*. The structure is somewhat fluid and relative, so that "a high court official was still a 'slave' to the king," and dependents beneath the free men "slaves" to the individuals who presumably owned enough land to merit this "free" designation (Mieroop 121).

Lastly, the Code of Hammurabi may signal something about the aims and goals of Hammurabi and the way Hammurabi wanted to be perceived. Hammurabi wanted to govern his new territory effectively, aims that required he control commerce, standardize weights and measurements (notice the reference to shekels, minas, and gerahs), and punish individuals who steal goods or defraud their customers. Hence, the Code of Hammurabi lays out clear punishments for common offenses like stealing, an occurrence we can imagine happened often in various markets across Hammurabi's Babylon. Certainly, stealing must have happened often if so many of the laws in the Code of Hammurabi focus on stealing. Other laws focus on slavery and the treatment of real, human beings who were treated as property, laboring either as farm workers or domestic servants. Given the likelihood that a slave would want to escape and other similar scenarios, Hammurabi also dictates what people are to do, which is, sadly, to respect the institution and the owners of those human beings.

And how did Hammurabi want to be perceived by his subjects? Hammurabi wanted to be perceived as the ideal king, a ruler who could give his people just laws and ensure fair treatment amongst his people. If new, conquered territories followed Hammurabi's laws, things would go well for them. Hammurabi received these laws from no less a source than Shamash himself, the Sumerian god of the sun and wisdom, and Hammurabi then relayed these divinely-given laws to his people for their benefit. Monarchs from Hammurabi to Napoleon have established legal codes, not unlike the Code of Hammurabi. A good king (or queen, for that matter) should both define and dispense justice and thereby create the conditions for his or her people to flourish. But, at the same time, these legal codes are often based upon the force that ruler provides to enforce his or her edicts, as was the case with Hammurabi's Babylon.

When Hammurabi died in 1750, his state largely disintegrated. His heirs were not up to the task of governing so vast a territory as Hammurabi himself conquered, and Babylon was left with territory in Lower Mesopotamia. The Elamites invaded Babylon and took the massive basalt stele of the Code of Hammurabi as a trophy back to the Elamite capital Susa, effectively declaring that Hammurabi's influence was over. While Hammurabi's Babylon decreased in size and controlled just the territory in Lower Mesopotamia, Babylon still enjoyed considerable advantages that would help this state reemerge as a great power in the generations. Indeed, both Assyria and Babylon, states founded by warlords like Shamshi-Adad and Hammurabi, would one day become empires that would rule the entirety of the known world.

Direct Instruction Review

The hardest part about history is memorizing all those facts, dates, and events. To make this process easier, we have included this short section called *Direct Instruction Review*. Direct Instruction (or DI) is a powerful pedagogical tool whereby teachers ask students a series of *call-and-response* questions, and students respond back with the aim of learning this material to *mastery*. Teacher's lines are in **bold**; student's lines in *italics*.

What happened after the fall of the city of Ur? *New powers arose in the Tigris and Euphrates Rivers to take their place.*

What does the name "Mesopotamia" mean? *Mesopotamia is Greek for the* land between rivers, *with those rivers being the Tigris and the Euphrates.*

How was Mesopotamia divided up? *Mesopotamia was divided up into Upper Mesopotamia and Lower Mesopotamia.*

What was the dominant power in Upper Mesopotamia? *The city of Assyria was the dominant power in Upper Mesopotamia and was located on the Tigris River.*

What was the dominant power in Lower Mesopotamia? *The city of Babylon was the dominant power in Lower Mesopotamia and was located on the Euphrates River.*

Who founded Assyria? *Assyria began as a small village devoted to the war god Assur, but Shamshi-Adad conquered Assur and turned this village into a much larger and more powerful state.*

Who founded Babylon? *The Amorites turned the small village of Babylon into a larger city, and Hammurabi turned Babylon into a much larger, more powerful state.*

What were the accomplishments of King Hammurabi of Babylon? *Hammurabi conquered almost all of Mesopotamia, promoted trade and commerce, spread cuneiform and Babylonian culture, and promulgated a legal code, the Code of Hammurabi.*

What made the Code of Hammurabi so unique and significant? *The Code of Hammurabi promoted the idea of* lex talionis, *the idea that* the punishment should fit the crime.

What happened to Assyria and Babylon following the deaths of Shamshi-Adad and Hammurabi? *The states of Assyria and Babylon decreased radically in size but still enjoyed advantages that would help them become great, powerful states in the generations to come.*

Map Practice: Babylon & Assyria

Instructions: Carefully look over the maps below, which are identical to maps provided in the rest of this chapter aside from one crucial difference—they have blanks in the place of the name of a sea, region, or site. Fill in the appropriate blank with the term list provided above each map. *Note: The course of the Tigris and Euphrates rivers has shifted over time, so the exact placement of a Sumerian city may appear to have shifted, too.*

Babylon & Assyria: Bodies of water such as the Tigris and the Euphrates Rivers, the Mediterranean and the Caspian Sea, the Persian Gulf; mountains such as the Zagros and the Taurus; kingdoms of Hammurabi and Shamshi-Adad; and the city-states of Ur, Uruk, Isin, Mari, Babylon, Susa, Nineveh, Assur, Eshnunna, and Kish.

 Want to study this map online? Type in the link below or scan the QR code to access an interactive diagram: **https://bit.ly/3okSogF**

Timeline Practice / Babylon & Assyria

The hardest part about history is memorizing all those facts, dates, and events. To make this process easier, check out the timeline below—well, technically, there are *two* timelines. Some entries are missing dates, and others are missing the event that occurred on that date. With the information available from both timelines, fill in the missing blanks to get a better sense of the timeline for this chapter.

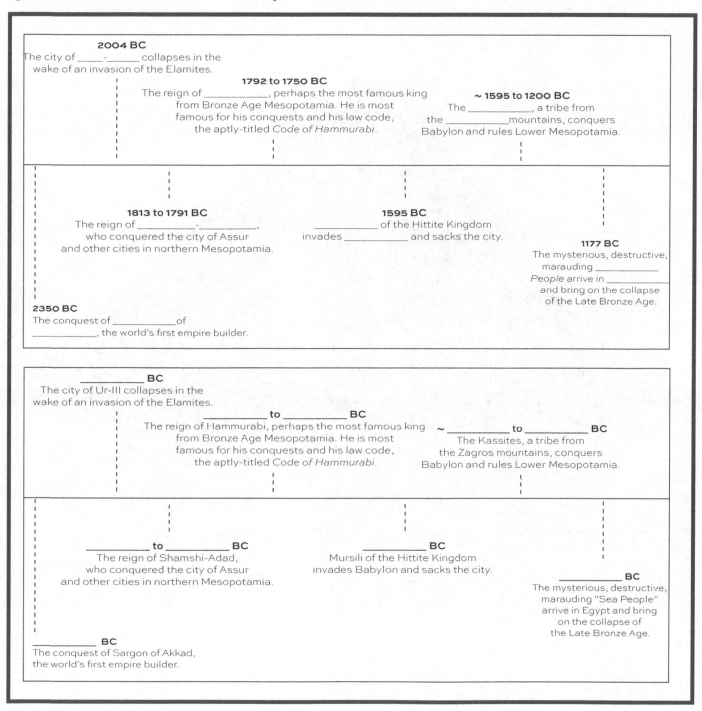

2004 BC
The city of ____-____ collapses in the wake of an invasion of the Elamites.

1792 to 1750 BC
The reign of _____, perhaps the most famous king from Bronze Age Mesopotamia. He is most famous for his conquests and his law code, the aptly-titled *Code of Hammurabi*.

~ 1595 to 1200 BC
The _____, a tribe from the _____mountains, conquers Babylon and rules Lower Mesopotamia.

1813 to 1791 BC
The reign of _____-_____, who conquered the city of Assur and other cities in northern Mesopotamia.

1595 BC
_____ of the Hittite Kingdom invades _____ and sacks the city.

1177 BC
The mysterious, destructive, marauding _____ *People* arrive in _____ and bring on the collapse of the Late Bronze Age.

2350 BC
The conquest of _____of _____, the world's first empire builder.

_____ BC
The city of Ur-III collapses in the wake of an invasion of the Elamites.

_____ to _____ BC
The reign of Hammurabi, perhaps the most famous king from Bronze Age Mesopotamia. He is most famous for his conquests and his law code, the aptly-titled *Code of Hammurabi*.

~ _____ to _____ BC
The Kassites, a tribe from the Zagros mountains, conquers Babylon and rules Lower Mesopotamia.

_____ to _____ BC
The reign of Shamshi-Adad, who conquered the city of Assur and other cities in northern Mesopotamia.

_____ BC
Mursili of the Hittite Kingdom invades Babylon and sacks the city.

_____ BC
The mysterious, destructive, marauding "Sea People" arrive in Egypt and bring on the collapse of the Late Bronze Age.

_____ BC
The conquest of Sargon of Akkad, the world's first empire builder.

THE GREAT PYRAMIDS AT GIZA / 2,600 BC

Photo by Leonardo Ramos

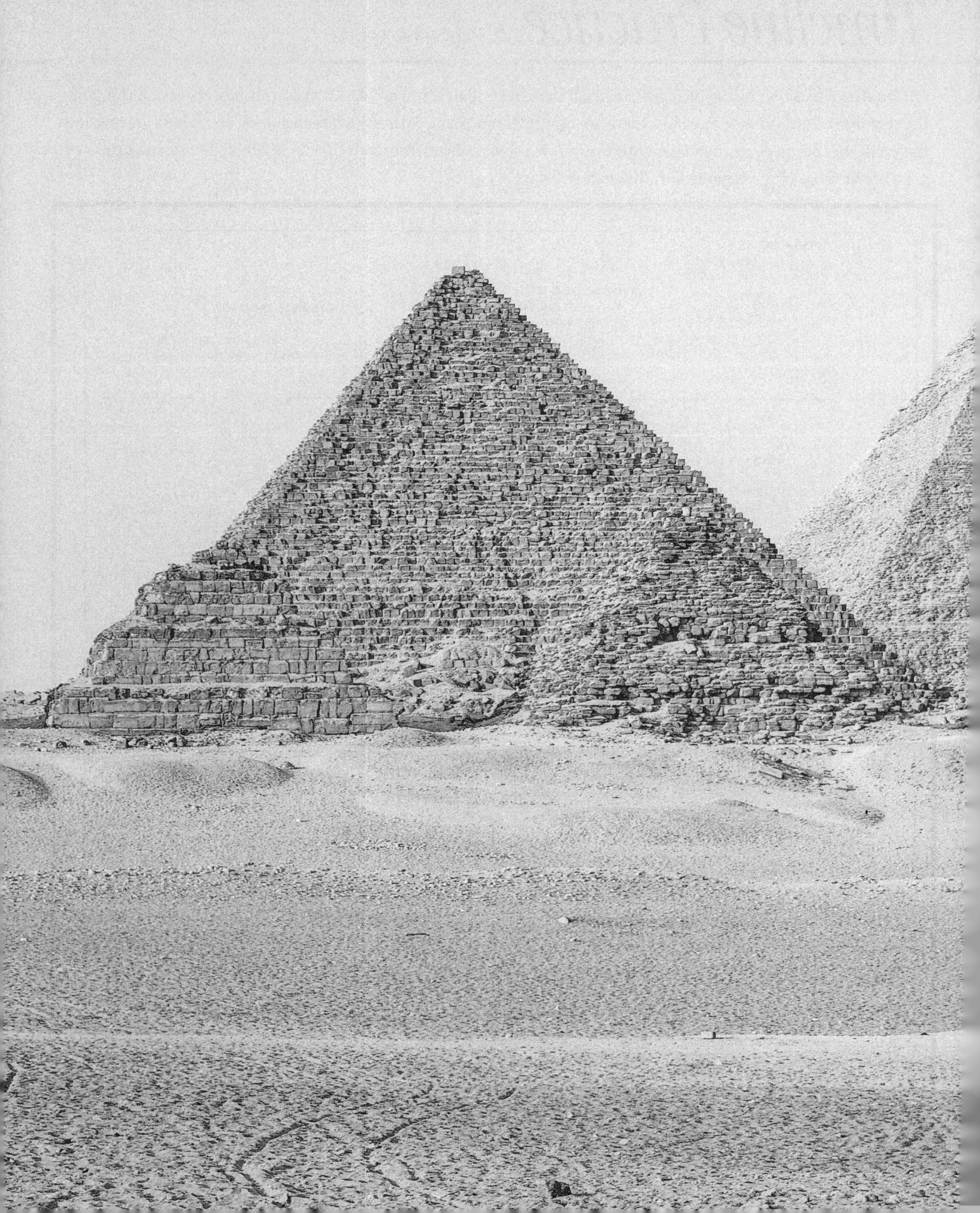

CHAPTER

Old Kingdom Egypt

ROADMAP

✦ Learn about ancient Egyptian geography and chronology, why Egypt was called the "Gift of the Nile", and how these factors influenced Egyptian history.

✦ Take a closer look at the most significant contributions of the Egyptians, including mummies, pyramids, pharaohs, and hieroglyphics.

✦ Read an Egyptian myth about Isis and Osiris, as well as study the Narmer Palette, which chronicles the unification of ancient Egypt and is one of the earliest written "documents" in ancient history.

✦ Practice our knowledge of maps and chronology, as well as our writing skills through reading comprehension questions and an essay.

THALES OUTCOME

N° 3

Self-Reliance *evaluates his/her interdependence, independence, and dependence on local, national, and global communities in relation to oneself.*

Herodotus called Egyptian civilization the "Gift of the Nile" for good reason: the regular, predictable flooding of the Nile River helped produce untold prosperity and material flourishing in ancient Egypt. Over time, the ancient Egyptians thought of themselves as superior to other peoples and largely self-sufficient, not needing other city-states or territorial states as much as they needed help from the Egyptian pharaoh.

Myth of Isis & Osiris /

Author Unknown...

AFTER THE BEGINNING, Osiris, the king of the gods of Egypt, held a feast. Osiris had inherited the throne from Ra, the god of the sun and the creator of everything good in the lands within and without Egypt, and Osiris was a good and noble king. Osiris upheld ma'at, gave good laws, and blessed the people of Egypt with good harvests from the lands beside the Nile. But Osiris was too trusting, and he invited his worthless brother Seth to a feast, Seth who had planned a trick to steal from Osiris the throne.

Seth, in secret, while the good king Osiris slept, measured Osiris' body. Then, Seth fitted a casket for him and outlaid the casket in gold and beautiful images. Then, at the banquet Osiris hosted for all the gods of Egypt, after the gods played games and sang songs and feasted to their hearts' content, Seth brought the casket and invited everyone to see who could fit inside of it. When they could not, Seth turned to his brother the king, and asked, his smile hiding the evil in his heart. "Can you fit into this chest, decorated with gold?"

"I shall try," Osiris answered and lowered himself into the chest. Osiris falling for the trick, Seth slammed the lid of the casket and nailed it shut. Then the wicked Seth threw the chest into the Nile, whose roaring waters carried it far away from the palace.

Isis, the wife of Osiris, mourned for her husband, and Isis searched everywhere for him. When she found him, she hid his body in the reeds. When Seth found Osiris' body, he chopped it into pieces and scattered them across the land of Egypt. When Isis discovered Seth's evil deed, she transformed herself into a bird to search for every piece of Osiris her husband. When she found them, she cast a spell to bring him back to life. And

SETH, THE KING, & HORUS
The Temple of Ramses II at Abu Simbel

when she brought him back to life, Osiris her husband, the king, spoke these words to her,

"Do not worry Isis, for you shall bear a son. His name shall be Horus, and he shall avenge me and defeat his uncle Seth, bringer of storms, sower of chaos. Then Horus will become a king over Egypt, and I will return to the land of the dead, where I will rule and judge those who wish to pass from the land of Egypt to the blessed field of reeds."

So Isis bore a son, whom she named Horus. And Horus defeated Seth and banished him to the red lands, the deserts beyond the Nile. And Horus henceforth ruled the lands of Egypt in and through the person of the Pharaoh, Egypt's wise kings, who upheld ma'at, gave good laws, and blessed the people of Egypt with good harvests from the lands beside the Nile. When Pharaoh died, he passed into the underworld, where he became Osiris, the king of the dead, who judges the souls of those who wish to pass from the land of Egypt to the field of reeds, weighing their hearts against a feather, judging them for how well they, too, upheld ma'at...

Summarize the plot and, in your opinion, the moral of the myth of Isis and Osiris.

This myth is not focused on mankind in general, but on the beginnings of an institution. What institution might this myth be trying to explain?

What might be the importance of this institution to the people of Egypt?

The Gift of the Nile / The Ancient Egyptians

EGYPT HAS LONG BEEN ONE of the most powerful and most interesting kingdoms to study of the ancient world. The Greeks saw Egypt as a land famed for its wealth, luxuries, and power, and the ancient Romans toured the ruins of ancient Egypt the way Americans visit Rome today. Egypt produced an incredible array of material culture from which to study that includes massive pyramids, towering obelisks, huge statues, and tons of letters, documents, and inscriptions. The sheer abundance of sources makes studying Egyptian history a difficult but rewarding task.

Other factors make it difficult to study Egyptian history. The land of Egypt has been incorporated into multiple empires over the past thousands of years, so that its place names have Greek or modern Arabic names that make locating Egyptian sites more difficult. In fact, the name *Egypt* is actually Greek, given to it by Greek conquerors in the 3rd century BC. The Macedonian prince Alexander the Great had conquered Egypt, a land already thousands of years old. The word the Egyptians used for their own country was Kemet, which means *Black Land* in reference to Egypt's fertile soil. Then, in the mid-7th century AD, Egypt was conquered by Muslim armies from the Arabian peninsula, so many of Egypt's towns and cities have Arabic names. Still, one geographical feature hasn't changed its name: the Nile River.

The Geography of Ancient Egypt

Herodotus famously remarked that Egyptian civilization was the "gift of the Nile," a river that is one of the longest rivers in the world at over 4,000 miles long. The harsh desert landscape surrounds Egypt, so the Egyptians depended on the Nile to help them grow wheat, barley, and other crops. The desert, though, did protect Egypt from invasion by all but the most determined armies or barbarian tribes.

The most important thing to remember is that the Nile River flooded regularly. Each year, when a star known as Sirius, or the "Dog Star" (think of Sirius Black from Harry Potter), appeared in the sky, Egypt's well-educated priests knew that the flooding of the Nile would begin soon. The Nile's flooding would deposit a layer of nutrient-rich topsoil across Egypt like clockwork–well, like a calendar, as the Egyptians marked their calendars by the flooding of the Nile. Egypt is a desert and receives little to no rainfall each year, making the flooding of the Nile that much more important (Stearns 28).

BIG IDEA

Herodotus called Egypt the "Gift of the Nile" because the Nile River made the difficult task of farming so much easier for the Egyptians. The Nile floods at a regular, predictable time each year, and this allows the Egyptians to prepare their canals and irrigation systems to bring as much farmland under cultivation as possible. As a result, Egypt would become one of the wealthiest and most powerful kingdoms in the ancient world.

Vocabulary

Write down this vocabulary in your notebook. These terms will help you better learn and understand the material in this chapter.

Egypt

One of the world's oldest civilizations, this word is the Greek term for the land of the Nile River and the civilization that arose on its banks.

Kemet

The word the Egyptians used called for their own country; the word means "Black Land" in ancient Egyptian and refers to the fertile soil of Egypt.

The Nile River

One of the longest rivers in the world, the Nile flows from sub-Saharan Africa northwards into the Mediterranean Sea; its regular, predictable annual flooding deposited nutrient-rich topsoil onto Egyptian farmland and enabled ancient Egyptian civilization to flourish.

Upper Egypt

The southern region of Egypt down to the first cataract, whose ruler wore a white crown called the "Hedjet," adorned with a vulture.

Lower Egypt

The northern region of Egypt that included the Nile Delta, whose ruler wore a red crown called the "Deshret," featuring an upreared cobra.

‖ **UPPER AND LOWER EGYPT**

The 365-day-long calendar is yet another gift of the Nile. The priests developed a calendar to help them prepare for the annual flooding of the Nile; they recognized that Sirius, a constellation that looks like a dog, would appear in the sky a short time before the waters of the Nile rose and flooded their banks. That short, intervening period gave the Egyptians time to make whatever preparations were needed to take advantage of the rising floodwaters. The priests counted the days between the arrival of Sirius in the sky and recorded it as a period of 365 days, which they further divided into 12 months of 30 days each: "the calendar was so accurate that it fell short of the true solar year by only six hours," (Beck, et. al 40-41). The Egyptians made other advancements as well. These included an early form of algebra and geometry as a means of predicting how large a harvest a particular plot of land should produce.

The Nile River flows south to north, which makes Egyptian geography a bit confusing. Because the Nile originates in southern Africa in Ethiopia and flows north to the Mediterranean Sea, the region of southern Egypt is actually called **Upper Egypt**. Upper Egypt stands at a higher elevation than **Lower Egypt**, so Upper Egypt contains the upper waters of the Nile River. Lower Egypt is in the north of Egypt, the region known as the Nile River Delta where the Nile meets **the Mediterranean Sea.**

The Nile River runs into a series of **cataracts**, areas where the river becomes too shallow and rocky to permit travel. Cataracts prohibited travel any fur-

‖ **FIRST CATARACT / SOUTH OF MODERN-DAY ASWAN**

ther south without disembarking and unloading one's boat and its cargo, so the cataracts became convenient borders for the extent of the Egyptian kingdom. Most of the time, Egypt stretched at least as far down as the first cataract, but a powerful, ambitious, energetic pharaoh might conquer land down into the third and fourth cataracts. Those cataracts were then part of the **Kingdom of Nubia**, today's Sudan.

Egypt has other geographical features that helped them to flourish. Egypt is almost entirely desert, a region that receives very little rainfall; the desert provides natural defenses against invaders who, generally, do not want to cross a desert with an army. Only the most determined barbarian tribes or empires would risk crossing these deserts to attack Egypt. (One army actually disappeared in those deserts, but we will save that story for a later chapter.) Egypt is also surrounded by the Mediterranean Sea to the north and the Red Sea to the east, so that the Egyptians could trade with a wide variety of people from all across the ancient world. That trade would make Egypt even more wealthy and prosperous in later centuries.

The regular flooding of the Nile led the Egyptians to very different conclusions about their gods. If you remember, the Tigris and the Euphrates rivers flooded, but there was little to no way to predict when these floods would occur. That made the ancient Sumerians believe that the forces of nature, and the gods who controlled those forces, actually hated them. In contrast, the Egyptians believed that the gods were fairly benevolent, and that their king, the **pharaoh,** actually was a god. In Egyptian mythology, the pharaoh, a title that comes from an ancient Egyptian word for "big house," was the embodiment of the sun god Horus in his lifetime but then became Osiris, the king of the underworld, once he died. (The *Myth of Osiris and Isis* explains this nuance in greater detail.)

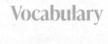

Vocabulary

The Mediterranean Sea
From the Latin for "in the middle of the land," the Mediterranean Sea has long been the center of Western civilization and is surrounded by the coastlines of southern Europe, northern Africa, and western Asia.

Cataracts
The falls of the Nile River, which mark the southernmost penetration of Egyptian power into Nubia.

The Kingdom of Nubia
The deserts to the south of Egypt that corresponded to modern-day Sudan; at times, Egyptian pharaohs would invade Nubia to obtain soldiers for its armies or to gain access to Nubia's considerable gold mines.

Pharaoh
Pharaoh comes from the Egyptian word for "great house," the title that refers to the king of Egypt.

Ma'at
Ma'at was the ideal of truth, harmony, and balance in ancient Egyptian religion and culture. The pharaoh was responsible for upholding *ma'at*.

Deshret
The Egyptian word for "Red Land," which is the desert region of Egypt.

In life, the pharaoh lived to promote Egypt's prosperity and uphold an ideal called **ma'at**, the idea of truth, harmony, and balance. There was also a goddess named Ma'at associated with these qualities, and for the Egyptians, the ideal was characterized by the balance between opposing forces. This idea was evident in Egyptian geography, in the balance between the Kemet, the rich lands of the valley and the Deshret, the barren, desert west of the Nile from which death comes, as well as between Upper and Lower Egypt.

In summary, the sheer abundance of sources, and the vast expanse of time Egypt has existed, makes studying ancient Egypt a difficult task. But certain themes carry over for all of the history of ancient Egypt, from its earliest days as a series of small, scattered villages to its peak as an empire that stretched from the Euphrates River to the western desert. Those themes included:

The Gift of the Nile:
Egyptian civilization depended heavily on the Nile River, which flooded at a regular, predictable time each year. That regular flooding allowed the Egyptians to prepare their fields and their network of canals in time for these floods and the nutrient-rich topsoil the Nile deposited along its banks.

The Benefits of Geography:
Natural barriers like deserts protected Egypt from possible invaders, while the Mediterranean Sea and the Red Sea facilitated seafaring trade and communication with the other kingdoms of the ancient world. This prosperity gave

PHARAOH KHAFRE / CIRCA 2570 BC

Horus sits behind Khafre, showing Horus' link to the living pharaoh.

Egyptians immense wealth that they would use on building projects like pyramids and other examples of monumental architecture (i.e., really big buildings).

The Role of the Pharaoh:
The Egyptians called their king *pharaoh*, from an Egyptian word for *big house*. In Egyptian mythology, the pharaoh was the embodiment of the sungod Horus while the pharaoh was alive and became Osiris, the king of the underworld, when he died. The immense prosperity of Egypt and the regular, predictable flooding of the Nile added to the idea that the pharaoh really was a god, a god fit to be worshiped. As a result, much of Egyptian society revolved around pharaoh—following his orders in life, building his final home in death, and supporting an elaborate series of rituals for his mortuary cult—but more on these items in our next section.

Why is Egyptian history so hard to study?

....

....

....

....

What geographical advantages did Egypt have, features that helped Egypt to grow and prosper as a country? What was "the gift of the Nile"?

....

....

....

....

What is a cataract, and why was a cataract a convenient border for Egypt?

....

....

....

....

Why is Egyptian geography confusing? Where is Upper Egypt, as opposed to Lower Egypt?

Who (or what) was the *Pharaoh*? What does the name mean, and what was his function over the land of Egypt?

What is *Ma'at*, and how is it reflected in the geography of Egypt?

What is chronology, and how do we come to understand how chronology works? How are historical events organized, and what makes the topic of chronology so difficult?

An Old, Old Kingdom / Old Kingdom Egypt

THE HISTORY OF EGYPT is divided into three periods: an **Old Kingdom**, a Middle Kingdom, and a New Kingdom. A 3ʳᵈ-century BC priest named **Manetho** devised this system and centered it on the strength of the pharaoh, the king of Egypt, and his ability to hold all of Egypt together. These kingdom periods are divided by an "Interregnum Period," periods when Egypt did not have a strong pharaoh. Instead, the few dozen districts or "nomes" making up Egypt became independent and took care of themselves–or fought against each other. The Kingdom periods were times of peace and prosperity, whereas the Interregnum periods were considered violent and chaotic. In an Interregnum period, the nomes fought with each other or were overrun by foreign enemies.

The land of Egypt boasts one of the oldest continually-inhabited civilizations in the world, dating back to the early 10ᵗʰ millennium BC. Hunter-gatherers and cattle drivers went back and forth between the Nile and the oases dotting the western desert. Somewhere around 6,000 BC, agriculture took root in the Nile River valley, and people grew wheat and barley (Stearns 14). These early farming villages became city-states, and the Nile made it easier for these city-states to trade with each other.

But of course, the Nile River also made it easier for an ambitious ruler to come and conquer the cities along the banks. The first ruler who may have attempted to conquer Egypt is known only as the "Scorpion King," The name comes from the glyphs (Egyptian writing) found on the Scorpion King. In 1897-1898, two British archeologists found a macehead at the Temple of Horus at Hierakonpolis, and on each side is presumably the same king. On one side he wears the White Crown of Upper Egypt; on the other, he wears the Red Crown of Lower Egypt; and next to his person is a scorpion. Thus, we know him simply as the "Scorpion King," a Pre-Dynastic Pharaoh who may have ruled sometime around 3,200 BC. Sadly, we do not know much about the Scorpion King.

In contrast, we know much more about a later Egyptian king generally credited with unifying Egypt: **Narmer**. Narmer, whose name means fierce catfish or raging catfish, was the king of Upper Egypt who successfully conquered Lower Egypt around 3150 BC. Narmer may

The Scorpion King & Egyptian Crowns

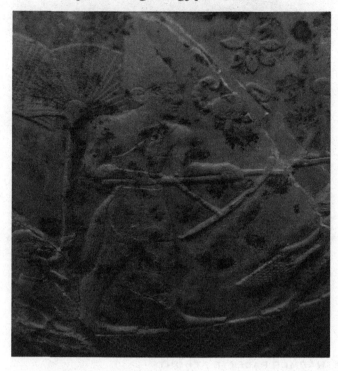

SCORPION KING MACEHEAD

Notice the hedjet (white) crown and a scorpion next to the central figure.

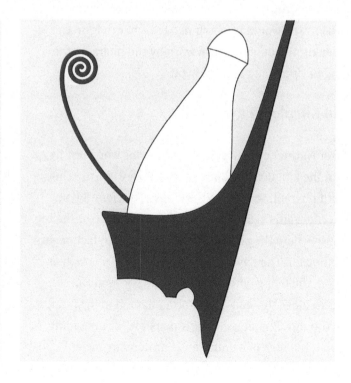

‖ **HEDJET CROWN / UPPER EGYPT**

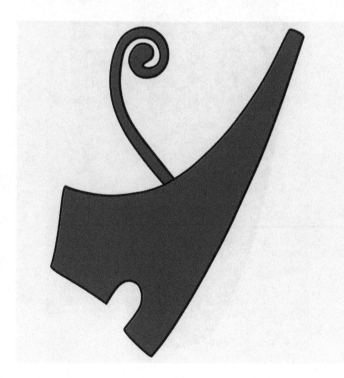

‖ **DESHRET CROWN / LOWER EGYPT**

‖ **PSCHENT / DOUBLE CROWN OF UNIFIED EGYPT**

be the same person as Menes, the first pharaoh that Manetho records in his chronology (Stearns 29). It was Menes who built a new capital at Memphis, located at the southernmost post of the Nile Delta to help control the delta to the north and the long, flowing river to the south. Narmer's conquest brought together Upper and Lower Egypt, an event documented in the Narmer Palette presented in this section. Narmer reigned for 64 years until he died hunting hippopotami in the Nile River, with Egypt's first real pharaoh being buried at the necropolis in the city of Abydos.

The Narmer Palette (seen to the right) is thought to commemorate the conquest of Upper Egypt (the delta) by Lower Egypt (the desert regions to the south). Narmer wears two different crowns in the Narmer Palette. On one side, Narmer is wearing the Hedjet, the white crown of Upper Egypt. On the other side, Narmer is wearing the deshret, the red crown of Lower Egypt. The two crowns, at least, imply that Narmer unified Upper and Lower Egypt (plus, Narmer is clearly hitting someone from the Nile Delta on the head). Later, these two crowns would be combined together to form the Pschent, the double crown worn by the pharaoh, the king of Upper and Lower Egypt.

Old Kingdom Egypt

After Narmer came a series of pharaohs who built Egypt into the kingdom we know so well today. We use the word pharaoh to refer to the kings of ancient Egypt, but the word originally referred to the palace or the big house where the pharaoh lived (pharaoh, in fact, means big house). The Egyptians worshiped that pharaoh as a god, the living embodiment of the sun-god Horus. Ra, an older sun deity, became a pharaoh in Egyptian mythology. Pharaohs were responsible for upholding ma'at, the idea of balance and harmony in ancient Egypt, and making sure Egypt would have large harvests each year. Because of these things, almost all of Egyp-

▌ NARMER PALETTE / FRONT

▌ NARMER PALETTE / BACK

Vocabulary

Old Kingdom Egypt
Lasting from 2686-2181, this period includes the earliest pharaohs in Egyptian history, the unification of Upper and Lower Egypt, and the building of the Great Pyramid and the Sphinx, both located in Giza.

Manetho
An Egyptian priest who devised the chronological system by which we organize ancient Egyptian history.

Hedjet & Deshret
The white crown of Upper Egypt and the red crown of Lower Egypt, respectively.

Pschent
The double crown worn by the pharaohs, the king of Upper and Lower Egypt.

Narmer
Narmer is credited with unifying ancient Egypt and is the first pharaoh of the First Dynasty, reigning circa 3150 BC.

Imhotep
Imhoteph was a government official, a priest of the sun god Ra, and an architect credited with building the first pyramid-like structures in ancient Egypt.

Pyramids
A pyramid is an example of monumental architecture that served as the final resting place for an Egyptian pharaoh.

THE GREAT PYRAMID OF GIZA / COMPLETED, CIRCA 2600, BC
In front are mastaba *tombs, earlier examples of Egyptian monumental architecture.*

tian society served the needs of the pharaohs and helped to build their final resting places, the pyramids.

Old Kingdom pharaohs included kings like Djoser, pharaoh of the 3rd dynasty. Djoser, along with his advisor **Imhotep**, built the first pyramids. Then there was Khufu, builder of the Great Pyramid at Giza, and Khufu's son Khafre, who built the Sphinx. During the Old Kingdom, Egypt became wealthy and prosperous, and they used that wealth to build magnificent pyramids at Giza. Egypt's rulers and their well-educated class of priestly bureaucrats also invented a form of writing called hieroglyphics and developed the famous Egyptian practice of mummifying the bodies of pharaohs, wealthy Egyptians, important servants, and even pets.

First, let's talk about **pyramids.** The purpose of the pyramids is to serve as a final resting place for the pharaohs, with the massive, sloping sides of pyramids channeling the soul of that pharaoh into the afterlife. At the center of a typical pyramid was a burial chamber adorned with beautiful illustrations of what the Egyptians believed happened in the afterlife. A coffin in the center of the burial chamber was also covered in such illustrations, and the burial chamber was filled with not only treasure like gold and precious jewels but also ordinary household items the Egyptians believed the pharaoh would need in the afterlife. The pharaoh **Djoser** began the process of building these massive pyramids. Djoser wanted a huge final resting place for himself, and he

STEP PYRAMID OF DJOSER / COMPLETED, CIRCA 2575 BC

This first example of pyramid architecture is essentially six mastaba tombs, stacked on top of each other

told a priest named Imhotep to build him one. One can trace a kind of progression from the mastaba tombs that earlier Egyptian rulers were buried in. The word **mastaba** comes from the Arabic word for *bench*, which is exactly what a mastaba tomb looks like (see photo above). Imhotep's insight was to stack one mastaba on top of another so that tombs would be taller and thus look bigger and grander. The Egyptians learned along the way how to make the sides of these pyramids look smoother and more uniform, making gradual improvements with each new pyramid.

The largest and most famous pyramid is the Great Pyramid at Giza, built by the pharaoh **Khufu** (2589-2566 BC). The Great Pyramid is one of the Seven Wonders of the World and for centuries, the Great Pyramid was the world's tallest building. To build the Great Pyramid, the Egyptians assembled over 2 million bricks, giving the pyramid a total weight of 16 tons and a height of 455 feet. Khufu's son and successor Khafre tried to outdo his father in pyramid construction, but eventually, he settled for building the Sphinx, a monstrous half-man and half-lion from Egyptian mythology. Khafre may have built the Sphinx as a kind of watchful guardian to protect the pyramids at Giza and the pharaohs resting there. Giza and other burial sites are called a **necropolis**, meaning a "city of the dead." Pyramid construction took years, so pharaohs would begin building their pyramids almost as soon as they became pharaohs. At first, scholars assumed that the Great Pyramid was built with slaves and other forms of forced labor.

Vocabulary

Djoser
A 3rd dynasty pharaoh whose desire to have the largest and most exquisite resting place resulted in one of the first pyramid-like structures ever built.

Mastaba
A flat-roofed temple used as the burial site of many prominent Egyptians in its "Old Kingdom" period before the construction of the pyramids.

Necropolis
Literally a "city of the dead"; these were the massive burial sites for Egypt's pharaohs built near the capitals from which Egypt's pharaohs ruled.

Khufu
A 4th dynasty pharaoh who built the largest pyramid in all of Egyptian history, the Great Pyramid at Giza. His reign lasted from 2589–2566 BC. Herodotus referred to him by his Greek name *Cheops*.

Hieroglyphics
From the Greek for *temple writing*, hieroglyphics were the writing system used by ancient Egypt's well-educated priests. Like cuneiform, hieroglyphics were pictographic in nature, with each symbol derived from an image of the object or idea being represented.

With further research, it seems that Egypt's massive peasant class worked on the pyramids for food during the times they were not planting or harvesting.

To build a pyramid, Egyptian laborers cut out huge blocks of limestone and floated them down the Nile River to the construction site. They would drag the limestone blocks into place, rolling them on logs. Then, with the help of oxen, laborers would push the limestone blocks up wooden scaffolding built along the sides of the pyramids. Once all the blocks were in place, the Egyptians would cover the pyramids in limestone to give the sides a smooth, uniform finish. The sides came together at a triangular point covered in gold.

Mummies & Mummification

And what about inside the pyramids? Egyptian architects would build a central burial chamber deep inside the pyramid. Then they would fill the burial chambers with all sorts of gold, jewels, furniture, plates, cups, and even food, anything that the pharaoh might need in the afterlife. Often, the pyramid (or a similar tomb) was part of a massive "mortuary complex," as the construction of new pyramids, the maintenance of old pyramids, and the rituals needed to take care of the pharaoh in the afterlife required the work of Egypt's well-educated priests.

The body of the pharaoh, meanwhile, was **mummified** to preserve as much of his appearance as possible. At first, mummification was reserved for pharaohs. But, as Egypt grew wealthier, Egyptian noblemen could pay to be mummified. Poorer Egyptians could pay for some sort of ceremonies or purchase some sort of spell book that might assist them in their journey through the afterlife. And that soul would need all the help it could get.

KHAFRE'S PYRAMID / EXTERIOR
The Egyptians believed that the soul existed after

INTERIOR OF THE GREAT PYRAMID
See Photo Credits *for citation and author information.*

WEIGHING OF THE HEART / EGYPTIAN BOOK OF THE DEAD

Egyptians believed that to enter the Blessed Field of Reeds, *their hearts must be lighter than a feather, a feather that symbolized* ma'at.

death. But, the soul would face a series of trials that determined whether or not that Egyptian soul was pure and innocent enough to enter *A'Aru*, the *blessed field of reeds*, a heavenly realm in ancient Egyptian mythology not unlike that of the Elysium Fields in Greek mythology. At death, the soul undertook a perilous journey that culminated in a moment called the *weighing of the heart*. At that moment, the heart of the deceased would be weighed against a feather, symbolizing that Egyptian ideal of balance and harmony called *ma'at*. If that soul had led a good life and pursued ma'at, their heart would be lighter than a feather and they would enter *A'Aru*, the *blessed field of reeds*. If not, their soul would be eaten by Ammit, a monster that had the head of a crocodile and the body of a lion and a hippopotamus. Once eaten, that soul ceased to be, a fate the Egyptians considered to be the absolute worst thing that could happen to a pharaoh. Thus, Egypt's priests and their people did everything they could to ensure the pharaoh would be well-taken care of in the afterlife. Later, in Egyptian history, this process would open up to Egyptians of other social classes.

BIG IDEA

Thanks to the Nile, ancient Egypt grew wealthy and prosperous. That wealth gave the Pharaoh, the king of Egypt, the wealth, the resources, and the leisure time needed to support the building of massive pyramids and the education of Egypt's priests.

Who was Narmer, and what do historians and archaeologists think he did for the two lands of Egypt?

Why did the Egyptians build pyramids?

What were the accomplishments of pharaohs like Khufu and Khafre?

A Closer Look at Mummies & Mummification

LET'S TAKE A CLOSER LOOK at mummies and mummification, perhaps the most fascinating and well-known practice among the ancient Egyptians. The ancient Egyptians believed that the soul, the personality of the deceased person called their *ka*, existed after death and that the soul may have a better experience in the afterlife if the priests completed a series of rituals meant to help sustain the life force of that individual after death. They even buried the pharaoh with food and furniture, anything that the *ka* of the pharaoh might need in the afterlife. Chief amongst these rituals was mummification, which Egyptians practiced to preserve the body of the pharaoh and thus sustain their *ka* in the afterlife.

Initially, only the pharaoh was mummified. The process was very expensive, and only the well-educated priestly class of Egypt could do it. Later in Egyptian history, wealthier Egyptians could pay for these elaborate rituals. Egyptians may have come upon this practice by chance, by necessity, or some mix of the two. Egypt is a desert everywhere outside of the Nile River valley so if a body is left in the desert, its features do not decompose and rot away. Instead, those features just dry out, similar to the more elaborate process of mummification. So how does a person get mummified?

First, Egyptian priests removed the organs of the deceased pharaoh. The priests stored the organs in special containers called *canopic jars*, sealed with the head of an Egyptian god like Hapi (the hippo-headed god of the Nile) or Duamutef (a son of Horus with the head of a jackal). Since the Egyptians believed that the heart was really the personality and soul of a person, the heart remained in the body. The priests covered the heart with a *heart scarab,* an amulet decorated with spells to assist the Pharaoh's *ka* in the afterlife. The priests then dried out the body using natron salt over a period of forty days. Then, they wrapped the body in linen and placed it in a wooden coffin called a *sarcophagus*, a Greek word for *eater of flesh*. That sarcophagus would be covered in gold and spells, its grandeur dependent on the wealth and status of the person being mummified.

‖ CANOPIC JARS

The mummification process allowed doctors to examine and learn about the human body at an unprecedented level. For that reason, medical knowledge and practices in Egypt far exceeded what was available in other regions of the ancient Near East at this time in history. Doctors learned important skills such as sewing up cuts, setting broken bones, and using herbs and drugs to treat illnesses.

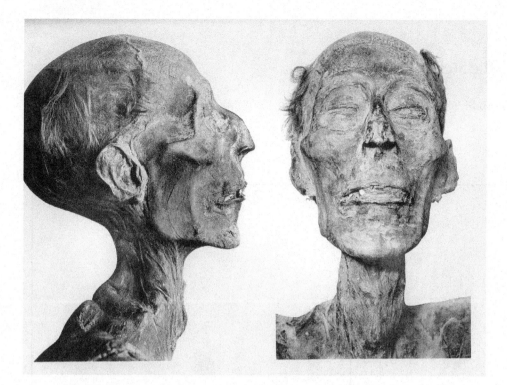

RAMESSES II / 1279 - 1213 BC

Mummified head of Ramesses II

Herodotus described the process like this:

> *First, with a crooked iron tool they draw out the brain through the nostrils, extracting it with the tool and partly by pouring in medicines and herbs. After this, with a sharp stone procured from the land of Ethiopia, they make a cut along the side of the belly and take out the whole contents of the stomach. Once they have cleared out the abdomen, they clean it with palm-wine and again with spices, pounded and mixed together.*
>
> *They then fill the belly with pure myrrh, pounded up and mixed with cassia and many other spices except, notably, frankincense. They then sew the abdomen together again. Having so done, they cover the body in natron salt for seventy days, but for a longer time than this it is not permitted to embalm it. When the seventy days have passed, they wash the body and roll its whole body up in fine linen, the linen having been cut into bands and smearing the body beneath with gum, a rubbery substance the Egyptians use generally instead of glue.*
>
> *Then the family of the deceased receive the body from them and have a wooden figure, a coffin, made in the shape of a man. Then, they shut the body inside the coffin and store it in a tomb, setting the cask standing upright against the wall,* (Book II, 86).

On the following page, we have provided some quotations from the passage above. Read each quotation and draw a picture to illustrate the step described in the mummification process. Refer to the passage as necessary.

Close Reading & Drawing : The Steps of Mummification

Read each quote and draw a picture to illustrate the step described in the mummification process. Refer to the passage on the previous page as necessary.

‖ *...with a crooked iron tool...*

‖ *...draw out the brain...*

‖ *...by pouring in medicines and herbs...*

‖ *...the whole contents of the stomach...*

Close Reading & Drawing : The Steps of Mummification

Continue the exercise begun on the previous page.

‖ *...cover the body with natron salt...*

‖ *...wash the body...*

‖ *...roll its whole body up in fine linen...*

‖ *...shut the body inside the coffin...*

The Steps of Mummification

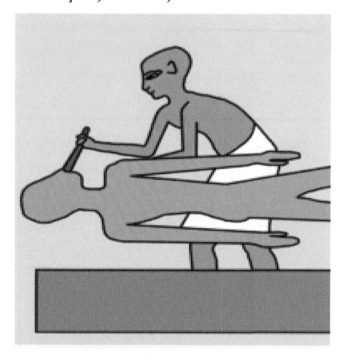

‖ STEP 1 / REMOVE BRAIN

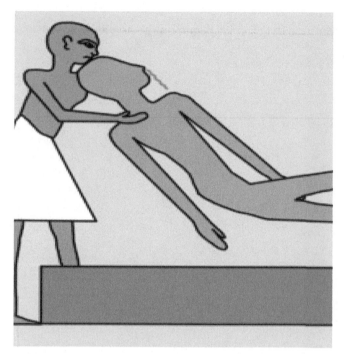

‖ STEP 2 / BRAIN DRAINS OUT VIA NOSE

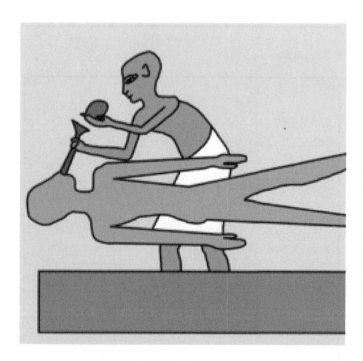

‖ STEP 3 / FILL SKULL WITH MEDICINES

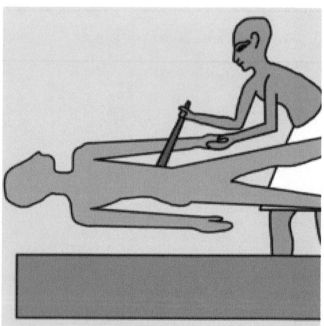

‖ STEP 4 / REMOVE ORGANS

‖ *The organs were placed in* canopic jars *once removed from the body.*

The Steps of Mummification

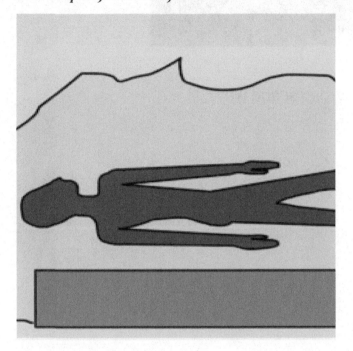

STEP 5 / SOAK BODY IN NATRON SALT
The body was left in this state for 35 to 70 days.

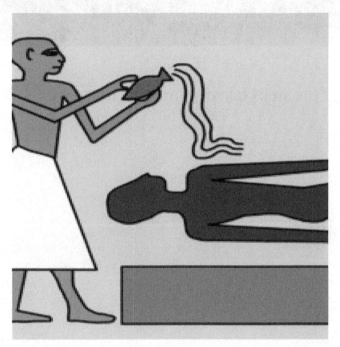

STEP 6 / WASH BODY
The body was washed and anointed with oils and resin

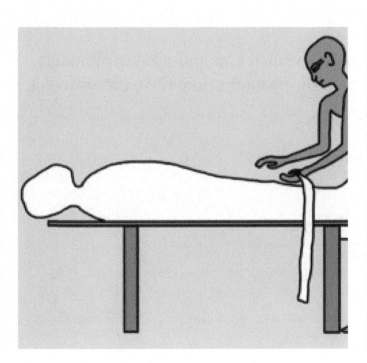

STEP 7 / WRAP BODY IN LINEN FABRIC

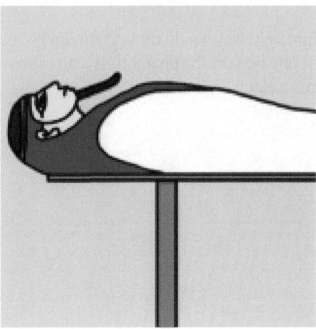

STEP 8 / PLACE IN COFFIN
The body may have been anointed with death masks or shrouds, depending on the wealth and status of the person being mummified.

Of the steps taken above, which one seems the grossest and why?

Ultimately, why would the ancient Egyptians spend so much time and effort to mummify just one person, the pharaoh? Is it an expression of the pharaoh's power? An expression of man's search for immortality?

A Closer Look at Hieroglyphics

LIKE THE SUMERIANS, THE EGYPTIANS developed their own writing system. Similar to cuneiform, Egyptian hieroglyphics were also "pictographic." The symbols began as pictures of the real objects those symbols represented, with the language becoming more and more difficult to learn as the number of symbols increased. Like cuneiform, the study of hieroglyphics was reserved for the priestly class of ancient Egypt, the only individuals who received any kind of education.

The word *hieroglyphic* is itself composed of two Greek words: *hieros* meaning "sacred" and *glypho* meaning "carve" or "engrave." Each Egyptian symbol originally represented whole words or parts of words, but the priests devised signs that rendered common phonetic sounds or a combination of vowel sounds. Hieroglyphics was written on the walls of pyramids (hence the *hiero* in *hieroglyphyics*), but later it would be written on coffins and, most famously, on papyrus scrolls. Papyrus was a kind of paper that the Egyptians made from reeds that grew in the Nile River.

The knowledge of hieroglyphics was lost for centuries. We may never have deciphered this ancient, pictographic script if it had not been for the discovery of the *Rosetta Stone* in 1799. Napoleon Bonaparte had invaded Egypt, and one of his soldiers happened upon a mysterious, massive black stele upon which was inscribed a message in three different languages: hieroglyphics, the Demotic script, and finally Greek, as the stele was written during the Ptolemaic period of Egyptian history.

Whereas hieroglyphics was virtually indecipherable, historians, archaeologists, and Egyptologists (historians dedicated to the study of ancient Egypt) could use their knowledge of ancient Greek to decipher the meaning of the hieroglyphics. This translation of hieroglyphics happened only in 1822 when a French scholar and a prodigious student of ancient languages, one well-versed enough in Egyptian Demotic to give a paper on the topic at the age of 16, named Jean François Champollion successfully translated the hieroglyphic script (Beck, et al., 40).

As in Sumer, the purpose of hieroglyphics was to maintain records of commercial transactions. The evolution of a written language would go from hieroglyphics to a hieratic script not unlike cursive writing. The hieratic script was written right to left (not unlike the Hebrew or Arabic languages today), was used for commercial purposes as well as religious ones, and has been found on both shards of pottery and papyrus, a kind of paper made from a papyrus reed that grows in the Nile River. The hieratic script was used by priests from 3,000 BC to 1,000 BC, when it was replaced by a script known as the Demotic. Demotic means "popular" and came in use circa the 7th century BC; the Egyptians called it "sekh shat," or "writing for documents"; unlike hieratic, demotic script has no noticeable links to hieroglyphics. After Alexander the Great conquered Egypt, the Egyptians devised a new written language called Coptic, which used the Greek alphabet to render Egyptian words.

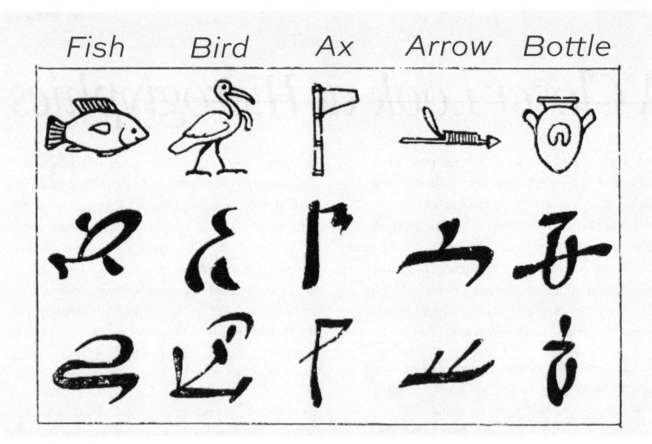

| Fish | Bird | Ax | Arrow | Bottle |

HIEROGLYPHICS

As with cuneiform, hieroglyphics began as a series of pictures that, with use, became more simplified over time.

Look at the hieroglyphic script above. What symbols seem the most interesting to you? Explain your reasoning.

....

....

....

....

....

....

Primary Source Analysis / Narmer Palette

Recall that primary sources are documents (or similar artifacts) created at or very near the time of the event under investigation. They are a record created around the time of the event the historian is studying, and they can include the chronicles of great kings, letters, poems, songs, diaries, historical artifacts, even paintings.

Title: The Narmer Palette

Date: Circa 3200 BC

Location: The archaeological site at the city of Nekhen, a capital of predynastic Egypt (i.e., Egypt *before* Egypt unified).

Description: A palette is typically used for grinding grain, but the Narmer Palette tells a story. Today, most historians believe that the Narmer Palette depicts the story of the unification of Egypt. The central figure is presumably Narmer, the *fighting catfish* credited with unifying Egypt–defeating enemies who presumably come from the Nile Delta. The Narmer Palette is an example of a relief carving, a work of art created by re-moving material from a flat surface. The Narmer Palette is made from siltstone. As a primary source, the Narmer Palette is telling a story, but what kind of story? Who are its characters and its central message?

‖ **NARMER PALETTE / FRONT**

‖ **NARMER PALETTE / BACK**

Primary Source Analysis / Narmer Palette

Instructions: Examine the Narmer Palette below and the highlighted areas on the document. Each highlighted area is paired with a question, which you can answer below or in the corresponding pages if you would like more room.

The Front

The Serekh
The symbol below is a special type of hieroglyphic called a *serekh*, a symbol that helps identify the document as official. What does this symbol look like to you?

The Crown
What about this crown seems familiar to you? Might it be the crown of Upper Egypt, or of Lower Egypt?

The Falcon
Would this falcon be associated with any of the gods of ancient Egypt? And, if so, why would it be included in this document?

The Reeds
Are these reeds the same kind that grow in the Nile Delta? And, if so, what might they symbolize?

The Figures
Who are these individuals? Are they vanquished foes? And if so, where did they come from?

Primary Source Analysis / Narmer Palette

Instructions: *Continued from the previous page.*

The Back

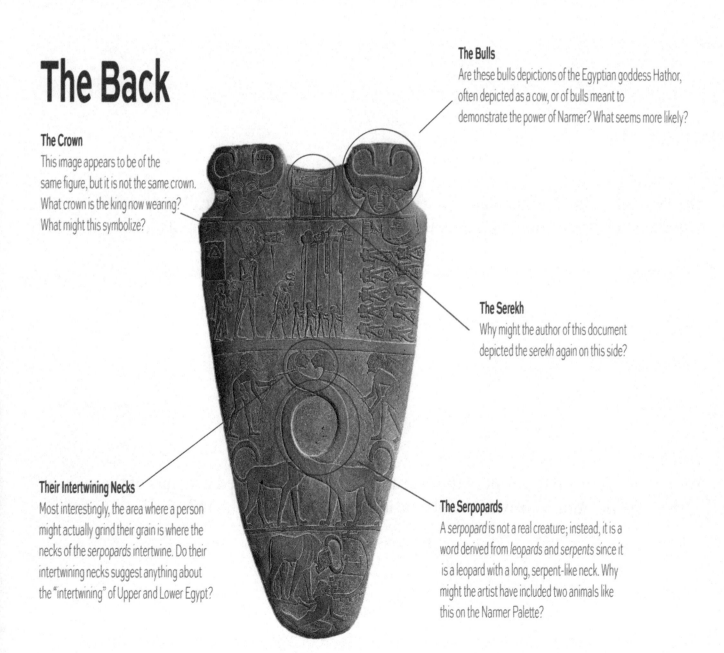

The Crown
This image appears to be of the same figure, but it is not the same crown. What crown is the king now wearing? What might this symbolize?

The Bulls
Are these bulls depictions of the Egyptian goddess Hathor, often depicted as a cow, or of bulls meant to demonstrate the power of Narmer? What seems more likely?

The Serekh
Why might the author of this document depicted the serekh again on this side?

Their Intertwining Necks
Most interestingly, the area where a person might actually grind their grain is where the necks of the serpopards intertwine. Do their intertwining necks suggest anything about the "intertwining" of Upper and Lower Egypt?

The Serpopards
A serpopard is not a real creature; instead, it is a word derived from *leopards* and *serpents* since it is a leopard with a long, serpent-like neck. Why might the artist have included two animals like this on the Narmer Palette?

What about this crown seems familiar to you? Might it be the crown of Upper Egypt, or of Lower Egypt?

The symbol on the Narmer Palette is a special type of hieroglyphic called a *serekh*, a symbol that helps identify a document as official. What does this symbol look like to you?

Would the falcon on the front of the Narmer Palette be associated with any of the gods of ancient Egypt? And, if so, why would it be included in this document?

May these reeds be of the same kind of reeds that grow in the Nile Delta? And, if so, what might they symbolize?

Look at the images on the front and back of the Narmer Palette. Are they meant to be depictions of the Egyptian goddess Hathor, often depicted as a cow, or of bulls meant to demonstrate the power of Narmer? What seems more likely?

Who are the individuals, whether on the front or on the back of the palette? Are they vanquished foes? And if so, where did they come from?

Why might the author of this document depict the *serekh* two more times on this side?

....

....

....

....

This image appears to be of the same figure, but it is not the same crown. What crown is the king now wearing? What might this symbolize?

....

....

....

....

A *serpopard* is not a real creature; instead, it is a word derived from the words *leopards* and *serpents* and thus is a leopard with a long, serpent-like neck. Why might the artist have included two animals like these on the Narmer Palette?

....

....

....

....

Most interestingly, the area where a person might actually grind their grain is where the necks of the *serpopards* intertwine. Do their intertwining necks suggest anything about the "intertwining" of Upper and Lower Egypt?

The conventional narrative is that the Narmer Palette tells the story of the unification of Egypt. What details on the front and back of the Narmer Palette support this interpretation?

What if the conventional narrative concerning the Narmer Palette is wrong? What clues can you find on the Narmer Palette that suggests it may be depicting an entirely different scene?

Writing Prompt

Writing is thinking, so we will spend considerable time this year writing and thinking about history. In the space provided, write a short essay answering the question: *Compare and contrast the history of ancient Egypt with that of ancient Sumer. How are these two civilizations so similar, and how are they also so different?*

Direct Instruction Review

The hardest part about history is memorizing all those facts, dates, and events. To make this process easier, we have included this short section called *Direct Instruction Review*. Direct Instruction (or DI) is a powerful pedagogical tool whereby teachers ask students a series of *call-and-response* questions, and students respond back with the aim of learning this material to *mastery*. Teacher's lines are in **bold**; student's lines in *italics*.

Where is Egypt located? *Egypt is located in North Africa, along the Nile river.*

How is Egyptian history organized? *The history of ancient Egypt is organized into three parts: an Old Kingdom, a Middle Kingdom, and a New Kingdom.*

Was the Nile River important? *Yes, the land of Egypt is surrounded by deserts, so their farmers depended on the regular flooding of the Nile River.*

And how regular was the flooding of the Nile River? *The Nile's flooding was so regular they could (and did) set their calendars in and around the event.*

What happened when the Nile flooded? *The Nile dropped nutrient-rich topsoil along its banks which helped the Egyptians have abundant crop harvests each year.*

What are the two parts of Egypt? *There is Upper Egypt, which is southern Egypt, and there is Lower Egypt, located in northern Egypt in the Nile River Delta.*

Did the Egyptians have a form of writing? *Yes, the Egyptians used a form of writing called hieroglyphics, in which words were represented by pictures.*

And who were the rulers of Egypt? *The land of Egypt was ruled by a king called* Pharaoh, *so named for the "Big House" in which the pharaoh lived.*

What did the Egyptians believe about pharaoh? *They believed that the pharaoh was actually a god— Horus when the pharaoh was alive, and Osiris when the pharaoh died.*

Where was the Pharaoh buried? *The pharaohs were buried in a massive tomb known as a pyramid.*

Who built the first pyramids? *A pharaoh named Djoser built the first pyramid, based on a design by Imhotep.*

Who built the biggest pyramid? *The pharaoh Khufu built the Great Pyramid at Giza.*

And how big is the Great Pyramid at Giza? *The Great Pyramid stands at a height of 455 feet and had, in total, over 2 million bricks!*

Map Practice: Ancient Egypt

Instructions: Carefully look over the maps below, which are identical to maps provided in the rest of this chapter aside from one crucial difference—they have blanks in the place of the name of a sea, region, or site. Fill in the appropriate blank with the term list provided above each map.

Ancient Egypt: Bodies of water such as the Nile River and the Red Sea; regions such as the Nile Delta, Upper Egypt, Lower Egypt, Kush, and the Nubian Desert; and the cataracts that helped separate Egypt from Kush, Nubia, and other civilizations further south.

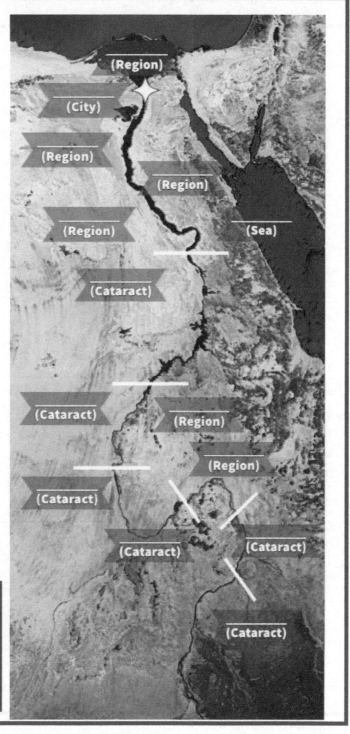

Want to study this map online? Type in the link below or scan the QR code to access an interactive diagram: https://bit.ly/3okSogF

Timeline Practice / Ancient Egypt

The hardest part about history is memorizing all those facts, dates, and events. To make this process easier, check out the timeline below—well, technically, there are *two* timelines. Some entries are missing dates, and others are missing the event that occurred on that date. With the information available from both timelines, fill in the missing blanks to get a better sense of the timeline for this chapter.

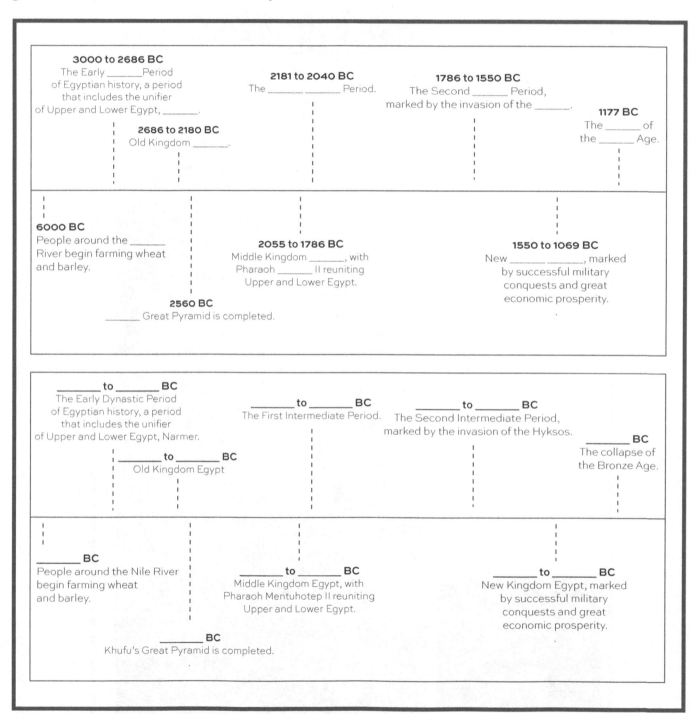

3000 to 2686 BC
The Early _____ Period of Egyptian history, a period that includes the unifier of Upper and Lower Egypt, _____.

2686 to 2180 BC
Old Kingdom _____.

2181 to 2040 BC
The _____ _____ Period.

1786 to 1550 BC
The Second _____ Period, marked by the invasion of the _____.

1177 BC
The _____ of the _____ Age.

6000 BC
People around the _____ River begin farming wheat and barley.

2055 to 1786 BC
Middle Kingdom _____, with Pharaoh _____ II reuniting Upper and Lower Egypt.

1550 to 1069 BC
New _____ _____, marked by successful military conquests and great economic prosperity.

2560 BC
_____ Great Pyramid is completed.

_____ to _____ BC
The Early Dynastic Period of Egyptian history, a period that includes the unifier of Upper and Lower Egypt, Narmer.

_____ to _____ BC
Old Kingdom Egypt

_____ to _____ BC
The First Intermediate Period.

_____ to _____ BC
The Second Intermediate Period, marked by the invasion of the Hyksos.

_____ BC
The collapse of the Bronze Age.

_____ BC
People around the Nile River begin farming wheat and barley.

_____ to _____ BC
Middle Kingdom Egypt, with Pharaoh Mentuhotep II reuniting Upper and Lower Egypt.

_____ to _____ BC
New Kingdom Egypt, marked by successful military conquests and great economic prosperity.

_____ BC
Khufu's Great Pyramid is completed.

7

CHAPTER

The Middle & New Kingdom

ROADMAP

✦ Study Egyptian primary sources like the Egyptian Book of the Dead and the Battle of Qadesh.

✦ Learn about Middle and New Kingdom Egypt and the accomplishments the Egyptians made during this time.

✦ Learn more about the pharaohs of Middle and New Kingdom Egypt, as well as the Intermediate Periods between each Kingdom period.

✦ Practice our knowledge of maps and chronology, as well as our writing skills through reading comprehension questions and an essay.

THALES
OUTCOME

№ 3

Someone with a **Healthy Mind, Body, and Spirit** *implements a plan to maintain a healthy mind, spirit, and body to allow for optimal personal and educational outcomes..*

Herodotus called Egyptian civilization the "gift of the Nile" for good reason: the regular, predictable flooding of the Nile river helped produce untold prosperity and material flourishing in ancient Egypt. Over time, the ancient Egyptians thought of themselves as superior to other peoples and largely self-sufficient, not needing other city-states or territorial states as much as they needed help from the Egyptian pharaoh.

Primary Source Analysis / Egyptian Book of the Dead

Recall that primary sources are documents (or similar artifacts) created at or very near the time of the event under investigation. They are a record created around the time of the event the historian is studying, and they can include the chronicles of great kings, letters, poems, songs, diaries, historical artifacts, and even paintings. So, what does the document below from the *Egyptian Book of the Dead*, tell us?

WEIGHING OF THE HEART / EGYPTIAN BOOK OF THE DEAD

Egyptians believed that to enter the Blessed Field of Reeds, their hearts must be lighter than a feather, a feather that symbolized ma'at.

Look at the picture above and the close-ups on the preceding page, each of which focus on a different scene from the Egyptian Book of the Dead. Who are the principal characters? What is going on in this climatic scene in the Egyptian afterlife?

....

....

....

....

....

Primary Source Analysis / **Egyptian Book of the Dead**

Title: *The Egyptian Book of the Dead*: The Papyrus of Hunefer

Date: Circa 1300 BC

Location: Found in the tomb of a scribe named Hunefer, the Papyrus of Hunefer is now in the British Museum.

Primary Source Analysis / Egyptian Book of the Dead

THE EGYPTIAN BOOK OF THE DEAD was at heart, a spell book. In fact, it contained hundreds of spells to help guide the recently deceased through the perils of the Egyptian afterlife. At first, these spells and similar incantations were painted on the walls of the pyramids, the massive tombs for the pharaohs. As the centuries wore on and Egypt grew wealthier, these spell books became more widely available. They were painted on pyramids and later on, scrolls included in the coffins of more relatively-affluent Egyptians. This copy of the Book of the Dead comes from the *Scroll of Hunefer*, an Egyptian scribe who lived during Egypt's New Kingdom circa 1275 BC. It is his *ba* below whose heart is about to be weighed against a feather.

Those photos come from the climax of the Egyptian Book of the Dead, a scene called "The Weighing of the Heart." Herein, the heart of the dead soul would be weighed against a feather. Anubis, the god of the dead, escorts the *ba* of the deceased scribe Hunefer. Thoth, the god of wisdom, records the proceeding, and Osiris, the king of the underworld, presides over the entire ceremony. If the heart of the dead soul was lighter than a feather, he would go into the *Blessed Field of Reeds*, Egypt's vision of a good and happy afterlife. If the heart was *not* lighter than a feather, the soul was immediately eaten by Amut, the half-crocodile, half-lion, half-hippopotamus monster sitting at Anubis's feet. For the average Egyptian, this end was the worst fate imaginable, for the *ba*, the spiritual entity of a person, would simply cease to exist. The priests of Egypt composed the Book of the Dead so that Egyptians from the mightiest pharaoh to the average peasant might have some chance of making it through the realm of the dead and into the Blessed Field of Reeds.

✦ Primary Source Questions

What was the purpose of the Egyptian Book of the Dead?

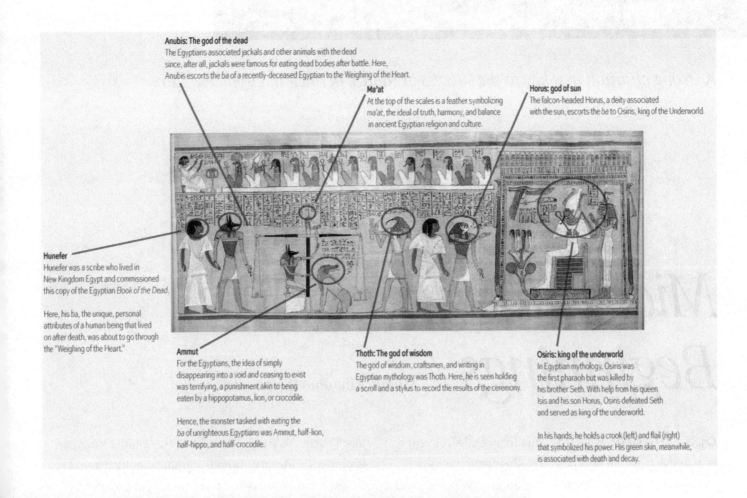

Anubis: The god of the dead
The Egyptians associated jackals and other animals with the dead since, after all, jackals were famous for eating dead bodies after battle. Here, Anubis escorts the *ba* of a recently-deceased Egyptian to the Weighing of the Heart.

Ma'at
At the top of the scales is a feather symbolizing *ma'at*, the ideal of truth, harmony, and balance in ancient Egyptian religion and culture.

Horus: god of sun
The falcon-headed Horus, a deity associated with the sun, escorts the *ba* to Osiris, king of the Underworld.

Hunefer
Hunefer was a scribe who lived in New Kingdom Egypt and commissioned this copy of the Egyptian *Book of the Dead*.

Here, his *ba*, the unique, personal attributes of a human being that lived on after death, was about to go through the "Weighing of the Heart."

Ammut
For the Egyptians, the idea of simply disappearing into a void and ceasing to exist was terrifying, a punishment akin to being eaten by a hippopotamus, lion, or crocodile.

Hence, the monster tasked with eating the *ba* of unrighteous Egyptians was Ammut, half-lion, half-hippo, and half-crocodile.

Thoth: The god of wisdom
The god of wisdom, craftsmen, and writing in Egyptian mythology was Thoth. Here, he is seen holding a scroll and a stylus to record the results of the ceremony.

Osiris: king of the underworld
In Egyptian mythology, Osiris was the first pharaoh but was killed by his brother Seth. With help from his queen Isis and his son Horus, Osiris defeated Seth and served as king of the underworld.

In his hands, he holds a crook (left) and flail (right) that symbolized his power. His green skin, meanwhile, is associated with death and decay.

✦ Primary Source Questions

What seems sad, lamentable, and tragic about the *Egyptian Book of the Dead*?

A strong pharaoh was key to the success or failure of ancient Egypt. Explain.

....

....

....

Middle Kingdom, New Beginnings / Middle Kingdom Egypt

OLD KINGDOM EGYPT came to an end after years of massive pyramid building. Old Kingdom pharaohs following Khufe and Khafre lost their grip on power, and the districts of ancient Egypt—called nomes—became independent. Without a strong pharaoh holding them together, these nomes started fighting against each other in a period called the First Intermediate—that is, a kind of break between Old and Middle Kingdom Egypt. The fighting between nomes became violent and bloody. The Egyptian historian Manetho recorded that there were "70 kings in 70 days", with kings fighting against each other for more power. The chaos finally came to an end with the rise of the king of Thebes, Mentuhotep II. Mentuhotep conquered the other nomes and brought them all back under the control of one strong, powerful pharaoh.

So began the Middle Kingdom of Egyptian history. While the Old Kingdom is characterized by its pyramids, and the New Kingdom by great military leaders like Thutmosis III and Ramses II, the Middle Kingdom is more of a literary and philosophical golden age. At times, historians use the term *golden age* to refer to a period of great cultural flourishing. These are times when a culture becomes particularly wealthy, as Egypt became wealthy through both agriculture and trade with areas south of Egypt like Nubia and east of Egypt like the Arabian peninsula. Then, that wealth was used to support the writing and copying of books, and the Middle Kingdom produced a number of classics: *The Tale of Sinuhe*, the story of an Egyptian official who lived among the nomadic, Bedouin tribes of ancient Syria-Palestine (Bauer 150), and *The Tale of the Shipwrecked Sailor*, the story of a sailor who discovers the meaning of life while shipwrecked on a mysterious island (hint: the meaning of life is to accept the things one cannot control). And then there were the *Coffin Texts*, special groups of written spells and illustrations that covered the coffins of ordinary Egyptians.

Vocabulary

Write down this vocabulary in your notebook. These terms will help you better learn and understand the material in this chapter.

Nomes
In ancient Egypt, a *nome* was an administrative district in ancient Egypt.

First Intermediate
A period marked by infighting between the various nomes of Egypt for control and influence over the rest of Egypt without a single, powerful pharaoh to maintain stability and order for the people of Egypt.

Mentuhotep II
Mentuhotep II was the Egyptian pharaoh who reunited Upper and Lower Egypt and founded Egypt's Middle Kingdom.

Middle Kingdom Egypt
Egypt's Middle Kingdom was a *golden age* of Egyptian culture, one that lasted from 2040 to 1782 BC.

Second Intermediate
Lasting from 1786-1552, this period was characterized by the invasion and rule of the Hyksos, a race of chariot-driving, bow-shooting foreigners from Palestine and Syria.

MENTUHOTEP II / REIGN 2060–2009 BC

Illustration from the mortuary temple at Deir el-Bahari

Unfortunately, the good times of the Middle Kingdom did not last.

The Middle Kingdom came to an end with the arrival of the Hyksos, whose name meant "kings from foreign lands." The **Hyksos** were a Semitic people from Canaan and Syria, and they conquered Egypt with a combination of bows, horses, and chariots. The Hyksos then ruled Egypt as part of the Second Intermediate Period. The Egyptian historian Manetho described their conquest "as a blast of the gods [that] smote us" with invaders of obscure race march[ing] in confidence of victory against our land" and "burn[ing] our cities ruthlessly," (Bauer 179). The Hyksos set up a new capital city at Avaris, located in the Nile Delta. The Hyksos obviously intended to stay and rule Egypt. The Hyksos even worshiped Baal, the brother of Seth, the god who murdered Osiris. How could things get any worse?

New Kingdom Egypt

Thankfully for the Egyptians, the Second Intermediate Kingdom did not last long. The Hyksos ruled Egypt for a short period of time. While the Hyksos may have played a part in the story of the Israelites, another people of Semitic origin, they only ruled Egypt from 1786 to 1552 BC. That's a fairly short time in Egypt's 3,000-year history. So as quickly as they came in, the Hyksos were driven out circa 1570 BC.

In that year, King **Ahmose** of Thebes, a city in Upper Egypt, invaded the Nile Delta. He attacked the city of Avaris and forced the Hyksos to abandon their capital city and leave the delta altogether (Bauer 203-205). Then, Ahmose made himself the new pharaoh of Egypt. The Second Intermediate came to an end and New Kingdom Egypt rose in its place.

New Kingdom Egypt

New Kingdom Egypt would see Egypt reach its highest point of power and influence. The world outside of Egypt was filled with strong, powerful states like Assyria and Babylon in Mesopotamia, and the **Hittites** in the region of Anatolia. These states had grown very rich and powerful thanks to huge, international trade networks. Merchants from places like Phoenicia sailed along the coast of North Africa to lands as far as Italy and Greece trading for copper and tin, the metals needed to make bronze. Then, states like Assyria, the Hittites, and Babylon would trade for copper and tin, as well as for gold and precious metals. During the Late Bronze Age, all of these kingdoms became very wealthy and powerful, but Egypt was always richer and more prosperous than its neighbors. Thanks to its deserts, Egypt was isolated from most attacks, but it still had access to the Mediterranean and the Red Sea. The Nile kept flooding each year, and the Egyptians enjoyed huge harvests of grain and other food.

And beginning with Ahmose, the pharaohs of New Kingdom Egypt were ambitious and capable generals. At times, pharaohs would boast of bringing Egyptian power "below the fourth cataract," one of the southernmost falls of the Nile river that typically divided Egypt from Nubia, in what is today's Sudan. These conquests gave Egypt access to precious metals like gold. In fact, the Egyptians obtained so much gold from their mines in Nubia that foreigners said that "gold was like dust" in Egypt.

‖ HATSHEPSUT / 1479 – 1458 BC

‖ THUTMOSIS III / 1479 – 1429 BC

Vocabulary

THE VALLEY OF THE KINGS / COMPLETED, CIRCA 2600, BC

The final resting place for many of Egypt's most famous rulers, including Thutmosis III, Tutankhamun, and Ramses II.

One of the most successful of these pharaohs is **Thutmosis III** (reign, 1479 to 1425 BC). When Thutmosis III's father died and Thutmosis III was still too young to become pharaoh, Thutmosis III's aunt, **Hatshepsut**, took over as the ruler of Egypt. She had been ruling Egypt for years because Thutmosis II was sickly and weak, and she seized the opportunity to rule Egypt in her own right. She even called herself a pharaoh, a male pharaoh, not as some queen serving as a placeholder between pharaohs. She undertook a huge mortuary temple in the **Valley of the Kings**, where many of Egypt's most famous pharaohs are buried. Hapshutset shut Thutmosis III out of power and influence in Egypt, who may have gravitated to the life of a soldier to get around Hatshepsut's influence.

When he became pharaoh, Thutmosis III conquered many kingdoms to the east and south of Egypt. He expanded Egyptian power into today's Syria and far to the south of Egypt to the kingdoms of Nubia, today's modern-day Sudan. He also tried to erase Hapshutset's name and image from public monuments, as if he personally resented all the years during which she kept him from the throne.

Not all of New Kingdom Egypt's pharaohs were great military conquerors. The pharaoh **Akhenaten** (reign, circa 1351 to 1334 BC) is famous not for military conquests but for trying (and failing) to force all of Egypt to worship only one god, the image of the sun disk called the Aten. Egypt, you see, may have been

AKHENATEN & NEFERTITI WORSHIPPING ATEN

Circa 1350 BC

QUEEN NEFERTITI / 1370 - 1330 BC

German archaeologists hid this bust of Nefertiti in a pile of garbage

the most slow-moving kingdom in human history. Even their artwork barely changed as Egyptian painters and craftsmen used the same proportions when they drew human figures or Egyptian gods. So how could a pharaoh ask all of Egypt to abandon the religious traditions they had held since 3,000 BC?

Akhenaten and his queen, Nefertiti, succeeded in the short term. They commissioned works of art that departed from what the Egyptians were used to, works of art that are exceedingly beautiful in their own right. They also tried to start Egyptian history over by building a new capital at Amarna, from which they exchanged letters with kings from all over the ancient world. But, Akhenaten's plan did not work, and the capital was abandoned at his death. Thankfully, for historians, the treasure trove of documents and letters lay hidden for hundreds of years until they were found by an Egyptian peasant.

Amongst the famous part of Akhentan's reign were his children, who abandoned their father's devotion to Aten and restored Egypt's religious traditions. Akhenaten's son would change his name from Tutankhaten (the *living image of the Aten*) to a name more familiar to students, **Tutankhamun**, meaning the *living image of Amun*, the traditional sun god of ancient Egypt). Tutankhaum died young and under mysterious circumstances, circumstances explored in a special section entitled, *What happened to Tutankhamun?*

The last and perhaps the most significant of the New Kingdom pharaohs was **Ramses II** (reign, 1279 to 1213 BC). Ramses II's father Seti founded Egypt's 19th dynasty and, as a great military general reconquered many towns in Syria and Canaan. Ramses II's reign is one of the longest in Egyptian history, and during that time Ramses II supported huge building projects: huge mortuary temples, grand palaces, and colossal statues of

Vocabulary

ABU SIMBEL / EGYPT'S 19ᵀᴴ DYNASTY

Located on the western bank of Lake Nasser in Upper Egypt, Ramses II began the construction of these massive rock-cut relief statues during his reign.

himself. Ramses II's tomb complex at Ramesseum and Abu Simbel and other necropolises are among the most impressive ruins from the ancient world. Ramses also campaigned in Libya, a region to the west of Egypt, and north into Syria.

Ramses' expeditions into Syria brought him into conflict with another of the ancient world's most powerful kingdoms, the Hittites. The Hittites came from Anatolia, a region sometimes called Asia Minor and which today is called Turkey. The Hittites conquered Anatolia, and at times they grew powerful enough to attack cities in Mesopotamia or Syria. The Hittites were at their peak at the same time New Kingdom Egypt was at its peak. The Egyptians and the Hittites fought over the towns and villages at the borders of their respective empires until finally, war broke out between Egypt and the Hittites with what was the largest battle of the ancient world: the Battle of Kadesh (or Qadesh) in 1274. So what happened?

The battle began when the Egyptian army stumbled upon the front lines of the Hittite army, commanded by Muwatalli II of the Hittites. The Egyptians and the Hittites quickly brought all of their soldiers and upwards of 5,000 chariots into the battle, the largest such chariot battle in the ancient world. Kadesh essentially ended in a draw, with the Egyptians withdrawing further south and leaving the battlefield to the Hittites. The Egyptians and Hittites signed a peace treaty with each other–the first of its kind in the ancient

‖ THE BATTLE OF QADESH / 1274 BC

The illustration above is a reproduction of the paintings found on the mortuary temple of Ramses II, called the Ramesseum.

world—and Ramses II went home, but commissioned monuments that gave a very strong impression that he won the battle. Ramses could do that since, after all, he ruled Egypt until 1213 BC, dying of natural causes at the age of 90. Egypt's New Kingdom would not last much longer than the reign of its most famous and longest-ruling pharaoh. For dark storm clouds were gathering on the horizon, and Ramses II's successors would have to defend their homeland from barbarians hailing from the lands beyond the sea. The arrival of these mysterious invaders, known to us only as the Sea People, would bring an end to New Kingdom Egypt and all the other civilizations of the Bronze Age.

The defining feature of New Kingdom Egypt was that of military expansion, beginning under Thutmosis III and including the conquest of parts of Syria, Canaan, and the kingdom of Nubia (modern-day Sudan). These conquests gave Egypt access to gold mines that they used to increase their power and become the envy of the Late Bronze Age.

How was the Middle Kingdom of Egypt different from other periods of Egyptian history?

....

....

....

....

Who was Hapshetsut, and why was she so unique amongst figures from the ancient world?

....

....

....

....

Who was Akhenaten, and why was he considered a "heretic" pharaoh?

....

....

....

....

What were the accomplishments of Ramses II's reign?

....

....

....

....

Closer Look: What Happened to Tutankhamun?

THE DISCOVERY OF KING Tutankhamun's tomb was one of the most famous archaeological discoveries of the past two hundred years. The British archaeologist Howard Carter hypothesized that a tomb of no small significance lay undiscovered somewhere in the Valley of the Kings. Carter, bottom right, discovered the tomb in 1922 AD. Most pharaohs were buried in large and elaborate tombs that were easy targets for tomb robbers, and most tombs had been discovered and excavated by archaeologists by the early 19th century. Tutankhamun's tomb lay undiscovered because this young pharaoh was not buried in a grand pyramid, one that tempted grave robbers. Instead, Tutankhamun was buried in an easily-overlooked tomb whose entrance was even covered up by other building projects. Tutankhamun died too young to have finished his grand mortuary temple, but his tomb was still filled with all the treasure a pharaoh might need in the afterlife.

Most intriguing, however, is that no one is sure how Tutankhamun died. His death could have been caused by an infection from an arrow wound (Bauer 243), or it may have arisen naturally from a degenerative bone disease, malaria, or even a broken bone (Cline). Yet, court intrigue in and around at the time of Tutankhamun's death has raised the question, was Tutantkhaum's death an accident? What if Tutankhamun was assassinated, part of an elaborate plot to steal the throne from Akhenaten's children?

‖ DEATH MASK OF TUTANKHAMUN

‖ HOWARD CARTER /
TUTANKHAMUN'S MUMMY

Evidence #1 / Tutankhamun's DNA

Recall the process of mummification by which the bodies of deceased pharaohs are carefully preserved. Those bodies are so well-preserved that archaeologists and doctors can actually perform tests on the mummified bodies of pharaohs and gain new insights. For instance, Dr. Zahi Hawass, the head of Egypt's Supreme Council of Antiquities, led a series of DNA tests on the mummy of Tutankhamun and other family members found in the Valley of the Kings. The DNA tests showed that Tutankhamun may have died from malaria, traces of which appeared on the test. However, the same malaria traces were found in tests on other family members, which suggests that this malaria trace may have been a trait Tutankhamun inherited and not a disease from which he died. These tests and similar tests suggest Tutankhamun may have suffered from degenerative bone diseases that also may have contributed to his early death (Tutankhamun Exhibit).

Evidence #2 / Tutankhamun's Mummy

Tutankhamun's body was x-rayed in 1968. The X-rays found fragments of bone in Tutankhamun's skull, giving rise to the idea that Tutankhamun had died of a skull fracture. That is, Tutankhamun *could* have been killed by some of sort of blow on the back of the head. Further evidence, however, suggests the damage may have been done in the mummification process or by Carter and his team of archaeologists. The resins used in the embalming process acted as a kind of glue that glued Tutankhamun's body to his coffin, and the archaeologists damaged his body when they removed it from the coffin. As a result, the injury to the skull found by the X-ray may have been accidental, not murder. Lastly, CT scans on Tutankhamun's mummy suggest he died from an infection following a broken leg (Lovgren).

Evidence #3 / The Zannanza Affair

Tutankhamun's sister and wife Ankhesenamun may have suspected foul play. For in the months after his death, the young queen Ankhesenamun wrote to the king of the Hittites, Suppiluliuma I, and proposed a marriage alliance under the following terms: *My husband died, and I have no son. But you have many. If you would give me one of your sons, I would make him my husband. I cannot pick out one of my servants and make him my husband...and I am afraid,"* (Bauer 244). On principle, Egyptian princesses did not marry foreigners, so for Ankhesenamun to propose a marriage alliance on her suggests that her life was very much in danger—or, at least, she thought it was.

At first, the Hittite king Suppiluliuma did not believe the proposal. But once Suppiluliuma verified the proposal was legit, he sent one of his lesser sons, a prince named Zannanza, to Egypt to marry Ankhesenamun. Then, even more mysterious, the Hittite prince died while traveling through the Nile Delta. An Egyptian general named Horemheb met Zannanza at the border, and while details were murky, it was apparent that the prince was dead (Bauer 244). With the young prince dead, war between the Hittites and the Egyptians seemed imminent (Mieroop 167-168). War most likely would have come, had not a plague struck the kingdom of the Hittites. That Ankhesenamun later married a much-older adviser and court official named Ay, who had served both Akhenaten and Tutankhamun, only adds to the mystery: what *really* happened to Tutankhamun? Answer the questions on the following page and work through the evidence available to us.

What evidence is there that Tutankhamun died of natural causes? What are the strengths and the weakness of that evidence?

What evidence is there that Tutankhamun was murdered? What are the strengths and the weakness of that evidence?

Primary Source Analysis / Battle of Qadesh

RECALL THAT PRIMARY SOURCES are documents (or similar artifacts) created at or very near the time of the event under investigation. They are a record created around the time of the event the historian is studying, and they can include the chronicles of great kings, letters, poems, songs, diaries, historical artifacts, even paintings.

Title: The Battle of Qadesh

Date: Circa 1274 BC.

Location: The respective capitals of the Egyptian New Kingdom and the Hittite New Kingdom, following the Battle of Qadesh.

Description: The largest battle in the ancient world, Qadesh fought between New Kingdom Egypt under Ramses II and the Hittite Empire under Muwatalli II at the city of Qadesh, located in Syria. The treaty is often cited as the first document of its kind in recorded history: two great powers treating each other as equals and promising cooperation (Mieroop 146). The text of the Egyptian-Hittite Peace Treat comes from J.B. Pritchard's *Ancient Near Eastern Texts Related to the Old Testament*, pages 199-201.

Preamble

The regulations which the Great Prince of Hatti [*the name the Hittites gave their kingdom*], Hattusilis, the powerful, the son of Mursilis, the Great Prince of Hatti, the powerful, the son of the son of Suppiluliumas, the Great Prince of Hatti, the powerful, made upon a tablet of silver for User-maat-Re [*hereafter, Ramses II*], the great ruler of Egypt, the powerful, the son of Men-maat-Re, the great ruler of Egypt, the powerful, the son of Men-pe-

‖ EGYPTIAN DEFEATING A HITTITE / ABU SIMBEL

‖ EGYPTIAN-HITTITE TREATY / CUNEIFORM TABLET

hti-Re [*Seti I, father of Ramses II*], the great ruler of Egypt, the powerful; the good regulations of peace and of brotherhood, giving peace . . . forever.

A Defensive Alliance for Egypt

If another enemy come against the lands of Ramses II, the great ruler of Egypt, and he send[s] to the Great Prince of Hatti, saying: "Come with me as reinforcement against him," the Great Prince of Hatti shall come to him and the Great Prince of Hatti shall slay his enemy. However, if it is not the desire of the Great Prince of Hatti to go (himself), he shall send his infantry and his chariotry, and he shall slay his enemy. Or, if Ramses II, the great ruler of Egypt, is enraged against servants belonging to him, and they commit offenses against him, and he go to slay them, the Great Prince of Hatti shall act with him to slay everyone against whom they shall be enraged.

A Defensive Alliance for Hatti

But if another enemy come against the Great Prince of Hatti, Ramses II, the great ruler of Egypt, shall] come to him as reinforcement to slay his enemy. If it is (not)the desire of Ramses II, the great ruler of Egypt, to come, he shall send his infantry and his chariotry.

Extradition of Refugees to Egypt

If a great man flee from the land of Egypt and come to the Great Prince of Hatti, or a town belonging to the lands of Ramses II, the great ruler of Egypt, and they come to the Great Prince of Hatti, the Great Prince of Hatti shall not receive them. The Great Prince of Hatti shall cause them to be brought to Ramses II, the great ruler of Egypt, their lord, because of it. Or if a man or two men flee, and they come to the land of Hatti to be servants of someone else, they shall not be left in the land of Hatti. They shall be brought back to Ramses II, the great ruler of Egypt.

Extradition of Refugees to Hatti

Or if a great man flee from the land of Hatti and come to Ramses II, the great ruler of Egypt, or a town or a district or a . . . belonging to the land of Hatti, and they come to Ramses II, the great ruler of Egypt, (then) Ramses II shall not receive them. Ramses II shall cause them to be brought to the Prince of Hatti. They shall not be left. Similarly, if a man or two men flee, and they come to the land of Egypt to be servants of other people, Ramses II, the great ruler of Egypt, shall not leave them. He shall cause them to be brought to the Great Prince of Hatti.

The Divine Witness to the Treaty

As for these words of the regulation which the Great Prince of Hatti made with Ramses II, the great ruler of Egypt, in writing upon this tablet of silver, as for these words, a thousand gods of the male gods and of the female gods of them of the land of Hatti, together with a thousand gods of the male gods and of the female gods of them of the land of Egypt, and the mountains; and the rivers of the land of Egypt; the sky; the earth; the great sea; the winds; and the clouds, are all with me as witnesses hearing these words.

Blessings and Curses for this Treaty

As for these words which are on this tablet of silver of the land of Hatti and of the land of Egypt—as for him who shall not keep them, a thousand gods of the land of Hatti, together with a thousand gods of the land of Egypt, shall destroy his house, his land, and his servants. But, as for him who shall keep these words which are this tablet of silver, whether they are Hatti or whether they are Egyptians, and they are not neglectful of them, a thousand gods of the land of Hatti and of the land of Egypt, shall cause that he be well... shall cause that he live, together with his houses and his (land) and his servants.

What was the format of this document? What was unique about it? As far as its subject matter and what the treaty outlined, why do you think the Egyptians and the Hittites focused on these items and not others?

....

....

....

....

....

....

Technically, the Battle of Qadesh was a draw, with neither the Egyptians nor the Hittites gaining any significant advantage over the other. Yet, Egyptian king Ramses II depicted himself as having defeated his enemies at Qadesh. What evidence in the treaty suggests that this battle was a draw after all?

....

....

....

....

....

Writing Prompt

Writing is thinking, so we will spend considerable time this year writing and thinking about history. In the space provided, write a short essay answering the question: *What enabled Middle Kingdom and New Kingdom Egypt to become such powerful, wealthy states? Was it the natural advantages that Egypt possessed, or was it the decisions made by its more successful rulers? Explain your reasoning.*

Direct Instruction Review

The hardest part about history is memorizing all those facts, dates, and events. To make this process easier, we have included this short section called *Direct Instruction Review*. Direct Instruction (or DI) is a powerful pedagogical tool whereby teachers ask students a series of *call-and-response* questions, and students respond back with the aim of learning this material to *mastery*. Teacher's lines are in **bold**; student's lines in *italics*.

How is Egyptian history organized? *The history of ancient Egypt is organized into three parts: an old, a middle, and a new kingdom.*

When was Old Kingdom Egypt? *Old Kingdom Egypt lasted from 2686 to 2160 and included the building of the Great Pyramid at Giza and the Sphinx.*

When was Middle Kingdom Egypt? *Middle Kingdom Egypt lasted from 2055 to 1786 and was a period when Egypt was rich and produced great works of literature.*

When was New Kingdom Egypt? *New Kingdom Egypt lasted from 1550 to 1069 and was a period of great military expansion.*

Who were the most famous pharaohs of New Kingdom Egypt? *Hatshepsut, Thutmosis III, Akhenaten, and Ramses II.*

Who were Thutmosis III and Hatshepsut? *Queen Hatshepsut tried to rule Egypt as pharaoh and shut out her nephew Thutmosis III from power; when he became pharaoh, he expanded the borders of Egypt east to Syria and south to Nubia.*

For what deed was Akhenaten famous? *Akhenaten tried to impose a new religion devoted to the worship of the sun disk, Aten, but this new religion failed.*

And Ramses II? *Ramses II was one of the longest-ruling pharaohs of Egypt; he built massive monuments to himself and new cities in the Nile River delta, and he fought in the Battle of Qadesh.*

What was the Battle of Qadesh? *Fought in 1274 BC, Qadesh was the largest battle of the ancient world.*

And who won the Battle of Qadesh? *The battle was technically a draw and neither side won much advantage, but Ramses II still issued monuments to himself depicting him defeating the Hittites.*

Timeline Practice / Ancient Egypt

The hardest part about history is memorizing all those facts, dates, and events. To make this process easier, check out the timeline below—well, technically, there are *two* timelines. Some entries are missing dates, and others are missing the event that occurred on that date. With the information available from both timelines, fill in the missing blanks to get a better sense of the timeline for this chapter.

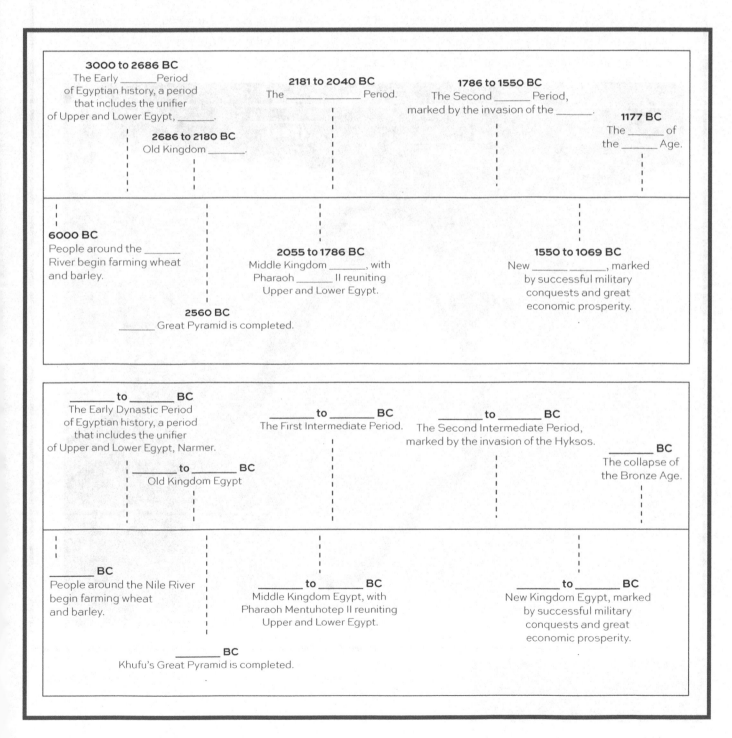

3000 to 2686 BC
The Early _____Period of Egyptian history, a period that includes the unifier of Upper and Lower Egypt, _____.

2686 to 2180 BC
Old Kingdom _____.

2181 to 2040 BC
The _____ _____ Period.

1786 to 1550 BC
The Second _____ Period, marked by the invasion of the _____.

1177 BC
The _____ of the _____ Age.

6000 BC
People around the _____ River begin farming wheat and barley.

2055 to 1786 BC
Middle Kingdom _____, with Pharaoh _____ II reuniting Upper and Lower Egypt.

2560 BC
_____ Great Pyramid is completed.

1550 to 1069 BC
New _____ _____, marked by successful military conquests and great economic prosperity.

_____ to _____ BC
The Early Dynastic Period of Egyptian history, a period that includes the unifier of Upper and Lower Egypt, Narmer.

_____ to _____ BC
Old Kingdom Egypt

_____ to _____ BC
The First Intermediate Period.

_____ to _____ BC
The Second Intermediate Period, marked by the invasion of the Hyksos.

_____ BC
The collapse of the Bronze Age.

_____ BC
People around the Nile River begin farming wheat and barley.

_____ to _____ BC
Middle Kingdom Egypt, with Pharaoh Mentuhotep II reuniting Upper and Lower Egypt.

_____ to _____ BC
New Kingdom Egypt, marked by successful military conquests and great economic prosperity.

_____ BC
Khufu's Great Pyramid is completed.

Map Practice: Ancient Egypt

Instructions: Carefully look over the maps below, which are identical to maps provided in the rest of this chapter aside from one crucial difference—they have blanks in the place of the name of a sea, region, or site. Fill in the appropriate blank with the term list provided above each map.

Ancient Egypt: Bodies of water such as the Nile River, the Mediterranean Sea, and Red Sea; regions such as the Nile Delta, Upper Egypt, Lower Egypt, and the Sinai Peninsula; and the cities of Avaris, Amarna, Karnak, Luxor, Giza, Saqqara, and Memphis.

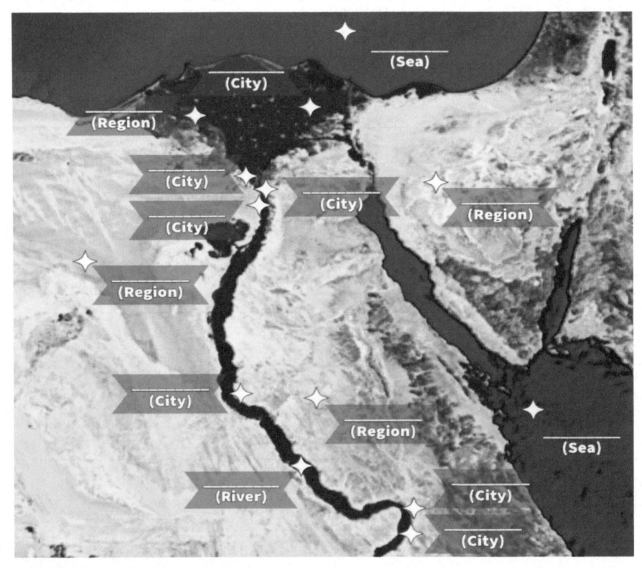

Want to study this map online? Type in the link below or scan the QR code to access an interactive diagram:
https://bit.ly/3okSogF

Section III
Bronze Age Civilizations

CHAPTER

The Hittites

ROADMAP

- ✦ Study the history of the Hittite Kingdom, the dominant power in the region of Anatolia.

- ✦ Compare and contrast the Old, Middle, and New Kingdom Hittites with that of ancient Egypt, Babylon, and Assyria.

- ✦ Learn about the earliest examples of the *Indo-European people*, namely, the civilization of the Hittites and the impact they left on world history.

- ✦ Practice our knowledge of maps and chronology, as well as our writing skills through reading comprehension questions and an essay.

THALES OUTCOME

№ 08

*Someone who is an **Astute Problem-Solver** Plans the best possible solutions to challenges to achieve optimal success.*

The people of the Hittite Kingdom solve the complex problems of building, extending and preserving their large, complicated states, but we have to solve difficult problems of our own: studying cultures that are a part of our heritage, but are so far from us geographically and chronologically that it is hard to recognize them.

Can an entire kingdom be lost and found again? Explain how such a thing might happen.

...Lost & Found / **The Hittites**

FOR A CIVILIZATION to flourish, location is one of the most important factors. A **civilization** is a society that enjoys a high degree of technical, political, and social organization. Often, that society stretches across a time period of hundreds, if not thousands, of years. The location of such a civilization should have access to natural resources like fertile farmland and rivers that make the process of farming easier. That way, the land can support the large numbers of people needed to enjoy a **division of labor**, and individuals can engage in activities outside of farming but contribute to a high and meaningful standard of living.

That location should have natural defensive barriers. Those barriers include rivers, mountains, and deserts that shield that civilization from attackers and raiders.

But that civilization should not be so isolated that they cannot trade with other nearby kingdoms and cities. After all, it's **trade**—the intellectual and commercial interactions between people to obtain new goods and services and share ideas—that helps civilizations to flourish.

The region of **Anatolia** enjoys many of these advantages and more. Over the past 6,000 years, Anatolia has been the home of many different civilizations and kingdoms, all of which have contributed meaningfully to world history. Anatolia is sometimes called Asia Minor (*minor* is Latin for *smaller* or *lesser*) because it is effectively a **peninsula** jutting out from the much larger continent of Asia. Anatolia is surrounded by seas: the Black Sea to the North, the Mediterranean to the South,

BIG IDEA

The Hittites built one of the most impressive civilizations of the Bronze Age. Yet, for all their historical significance, the Hittite civilization was lost to the point that historians and archaeologists did not even believe this kingdom ever existed, raising the question: what cool, historical treasures are still out there, just waiting for us to discover?

Vocabulary

Write down this vocabulary in your notebook. These terms will help you better learn and understand the material in this chapter.

Civilization

A society that enjoys a high degree of technical knowledge and political organization; often, we speak of a civilization as having existed for a period in the hundreds, if not thousands, of years.

Division of Labor

As communities grow in population, fewer people need to be directly engaged in farming and agriculture.

Trade

The commercial and intellectual interactions between people as individuals seek to obtain goods and services abundant in one area but lacking in their own.

Anatolia

A peninsula surrounded by the Aegean, the Black Sea, and the Mediterranean; the region is also referred to as Asia Minor. Today it corresponds to the Republic of Turkey.

Peninsula

A peninsula is literally *almost an island*, surrounded on three sides by water.

The Hittites

The dominant kingdom in the region of Anatolia and a significant player on the international scene during the Late Bronze Age.

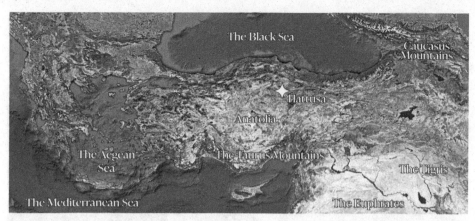

ANATOLIA AND HATTUSA / OLD KINGDOM HITTITES
Map from Google Earth

and the Aegean Sea to its west which connects Anatolia to the Greek world. In fact, many of the cities on the west coast of Anatolia were founded by Greeks, and Anatolia would later form the heartland of the Eastern Roman Empire, the half of the Roman world that lived on even after the city of Rome fell to barbarian invasions in AD 410 and 476. Today, the region of Anatolia roughly corresponds to the Republic of Turkey, named for the Turkish peoples who engaged in a centuries-long conquest of the region that finally ended in 1453.

The first kingdom to rule the fabled region of Anatolia arose during the Bronze Age: the **Hittites**. For as long as they existed, the Hittites were one of the most powerful and sophisticated of civilizations in the world of the Bronze Age. The Hittites ruled Anatolia like the Egyptians ruled Egypt and the Babylonians Babylon, even fighting New Kingdom Egypt to a draw at Qadesh and sacking Babylon on one occasion. But when the Hittites collapsed near the end of the Bronze Age, they disappeared, and they disappeared so thoroughly that historians actually thought they never existed, to begin with. But then, the ruins of the Hittite Old Kingdom were discovered in the 19th century and Hittite records written in cuneiform later in the 20th. This mix of archaeological remains and written sources allows student historians like us to study the people that once ruled over the whole of Anatolia.

So who exactly were the Hittites, and what can we learn from them?

The Hittite Old Kingdom

The Hittites were originally an **Indo-European** people—meaning that they spoke a language not unlike Latin or Greek or the English we speak today. They referred to their land as the "land of **Hatti**" and to themselves as the people of "Nesa" and of Hatti (Mieroop 127). The founder of the Hittite Old Kingdom was a mysterious figure named **Hattusili I**. Sometime around 1650, Hattusili I conquered the once-independent cities in central Anatolia (Mieroop 129). Like Shamshi-Adad in Assyria and Hammurabi in Babylon, Hattusili integrated these once-free and independent cities into a territorial state with himself at the top of its society.

‖ LION'S GATE / HATTUSA

The most significant of these conquests was the city of **Hattusa**. Hattusa sat on a hilltop that gave it a commanding position over the Anatolian heartland. The city was also surrounded by numerous springs that gave the city a steady supply of fresh water, as well as villages that the new Hittite kingdom could conquer and economically integrate into this new Hittite kingdom (Bauer 197-198; Mieroop 129-131). Hattusili built up his new capital into a formidable fortress.

Once completed, Hattusa possessed walls eight meters thick that stretched more than four miles around the city. A network of towers thirteen meters high rose above the walls while a network of tunnels ran below the fortifications. His capital established, the Hittite founder Hattusili got to work conquering neighboring cities and integrating them into his new state, the Kingdom of Hatti.

Hattusili's reign was marked by campaigns in southwest Anatolia and Syria. He conquered many of the smaller, more scattered, less politically sophisticated cities in southwest Anatolia. These small cities, villages, and kingdoms near the west coast of Asia would become more significant later for the Hittites because of their connections to Mycenaean Greece, ancient Troy, and the legendary story of the Trojan War (Mieroop 130). The Hittites were drawn into the orbit of the ancient Near East thanks to Assyrian merchants operating in Anatolia, who exposed to the Hittites the record-keeping practices of ancient Mesopotamia. Hattusili also moved south of the Taurus Mountains into Syria for further conquests.

But the Hittite kingdom faced two threats, one external, the other internal. The external threats came from barbarian tribes along the Black Sea coast. Not much is known about these Black Sea tribes aside from their name—the Kaska.

As the Gutians did to the Sumerians in Sumer, the Kaska would periodically attack the Hittites and keep them from expanding too far northwards (Mieroop 129-130).

But it was the disputes among Hattusili's successors that would destroy the Hittite kingdom. When Hattusili was on his deathbed, he denounced his sons and many other family members for being greedy and rebellious (they had rebelled against him, after all). Hattusili disinherited all of them, and then he appointed his grandson as his heir, a teenage boy named **Mursili** (Mieroop 130). The rule of a young king and the lack of a clear succession plan for the Hittites' king would ultimately destroy the Hittite royal house.

This boy king Mursili was initially supported by the Hittite warrior nobility and his relatives. As king, Mursili had some significant accomplishments: he sacked the Syrian city of Aleppo in 1600, and in 1595, he sacked the city of Babylon. But when Mursili returned home from his campaign in Babylon, his brother-in-law Hantili murdered him and took the throne for himself. This coup set off a violent chain reaction as other would-be kings murdered each other, one after another, in a fierce scramble for power (Bauer 199-200; Mieroop 130).

The Hittite Old Kingdom lasted from 1650 to 1500. The Old Kingdom began with Hattusili I and lasted until the reign of Telepinu, a Hittite prince who came from outside the Hittite royal family. The young prince **Telepinu** was also almost assassinated by his evil brother-in-law, who was next in line to the throne and had already assassinated other potential threats (Bauer 215). Instead, Telepinu defeated the cruel, would-be tyrant and set himself up as king instead.

To help avert future threats, Telepinu issued a new law code—the **Edict of Telepinu**—which was both a law code and a succession plan for new Hittite kings.

HITTITE DEITIES / HATTUSA

That way, the Hittite kingdom could be spared from the violent power struggles that followed the close of one reign and the start of another. Unfortunately for the Hittites, while the Edict of Telepinu may have been a farsighted document on par with Hammurabi's Code, its effects did not last very long. The Hittites had gotten used to solving succession disputes through violence and bloodshed, and once a kingdom or any ruling body of people turns to violence to solve their problems, it is almost impossible to turn back. Without the legitimacy of a good king like Telepinu, the cuneiform document was not worth the hardened mud tablet upon which the words were inscribed.

At Telepinu's death, the Hittite kingdom was plunged into more deadly assassination plots, plots that would bring an end to the Old Kingdom. The Hittite Middle Kingdom, moreover, was little more than a century of these succession battles (Bauer 216). Unlike the Egyptian Old Kingdom which lasted for half a millennium, the Hittite Old Kingdom lasted only from its founder Hattusili to Telepinu, and the Hittites would not emerge again as a great power in the region until the reign of Suppiluliuma I.

What advantages did the land of Anatolia provide for the kingdom of the Hittites?

Who founded the kingdom of the Hittites? What was this individual like?

How were the Hittites "like" the other kingdoms of the Near East?

Could the problems that plagued the Hittites have been avoided? Why or why not?

New Starts, Same Ends / The Hittites

The Hittite Middle Kingdom was little more than a century of assassination plots. The Hittites lost much of their territory in Syria to a new upstart power called **Mitanni**, who were also of Indo-European ancestry (Mieroop 167). The fortunes of the Hittites changed with the accession of **Suppiluliuma I** (reign, 1344-1322, although dates vary, Mieroop 167). Suppiluliuma united the troublesome Hittites together and established the **Hittite New Kingdom**. He accomplished this unity by directing their energies outwards. Instead of fighting each other, he brought them to fight enemies outwards of Hattusa. Most importantly for Suppiluliuma, these enemies were wealthy, and these conquests gave him land and treasure with which to reward nobles who might have fought against him. So who were these enemies?

First was the great state of Mitanni to the south. Once Suppiluliuma had firm control over Anatolia, he pushed south of the Taurus Mountains into Mitanni, conquering the city of Washukanni and making the Mitannians his vassals. Suppiluliuma moved through Syria, conquering some territories and accepting the **vassalage**, or pledges of military service and treasure of others. These states included the ancient Syrian city of Damascus, the city of Ugarit, one of the wealthiest and most prosperous port cities in Phoenicia, and the smaller kingdom of Amurru, also in Syria. These conquests gave the Hittites the resources needed to take on the region's most powerful player: New Kingdom Egypt.

As we learned earlier, Egypt was at its highest point during the Late Bronze Age. Yet, despite being so powerful, Egypt treated the Hittites almost as equals. For example, the Treaty of Qadesh includes clauses of mutual assistance between the Egyptians and the Hittites. And the Egyptian princess Ankhesenamun,

ANATOLIA / 14TH TO 12TH C. BC

who lived from approximately 1348 to 1322 BC, wrote to the king of the Hittites for help against scheming court advisers, not to the kings of Babylon or Assyria. Of course, the Hittite prince pledged to marry Ankhesenamun was killed under mysterious circumstances near the Egyptian border, and war might have come between the Hittites and the Egyptians.

That war would almost have certainly come, had it not been for a plague striking the Hittite kingdom. Suppiluliuma I died, perhaps from the plague. Suppiluliuma's state was held together by sheer force and, as typically happens at the death of a conquering king, his Syrian vassals rebelled against their Hittite overlords as soon as they could. Suppiluliuma's son and heir Mursili II, who reigned from 1321 to 1295, put down the rebellions.

Most significant among these conquests is a small state known as **Arzawa**. Arzawa is on the west coast of Anatolia, on the Aegean Sea. They served as a kind of middleman between the Hittites to the east and the kingdoms of **Mycenaean Greece** to the west. During the Late Bronze Age, in the 14th through the 12th centuries, the Greek city of Mycenae developed a sophisticated trading network. They traded with cities in Greece, as well as port cities of Phoenicia and even New Kingdom Egypt. The Mycenaeans grew fabulously wealthy from their trade with the Egyptians and the Phoenicians.

The connections between Mycenaean Greece and the Hittites may have been more valuable in the long run. The Greeks imitated practices mostly from Egypt (both Egyptian gods and mathematics) and the Phoenicians (their alphabet). Since the Hittites speak an Indo-European language more similar to that of Mycenaean Greek, Hittite influences still passed from Anatolia to Greece.

Such influences include iron weapons, for the Hittites may have even introduced iron metallurgy to Greece. Other advantages and inventions include lighter chariots and monumental architecture, as the gates of Hattusa bear more than a passing similarity to those built at Mycenae.

‖ LION'S GATE / HATTUSA

‖ LION'S GATE / MYCENAE

Later Greek authors like Hesiod borrowed elements of Hittite mythology. Hittite texts may even refer to events as seminal as the Trojan War and the mysterious *King of Ahhiyawa*, the Hittite word for the Mycenaeans. But we will turn to such developments at the close of this chapter.

At last, war came between the Egyptians under Ramses II and the Hittite king Muwatalli II (reigned 1295-1272). The battle came at the Syrian city of Qadesh (or Kadesh) in 1274. Qadesh was a city in Syria on the border between the great powers of Egypt and the Hittite kingdom, and both powers wanted to extend their influence deeper into the territory of their rivals, a rivalry the Hittites took personally on account of the mysterious and unavenged death of Zannanza. The battle broke out when the Egyptian army happened upon a Hittite army also operating in the area. What began as a skirmish between each army's vanguards quickly turned into the largest battle of the Bronze Age.

Often, powerful states fight over the regions on their borders as in the Egyptians and the Hittites over Syria, or, for example, the city-states of Renaissance Italy over towns and estates on their respective borders, and Germany and France over the Alsace-Lorraine in the twentieth century. These fights arise because states view the possession of these regions as a "zero-sum game": the resources gained from these regions could help one state survive and the other decline. In international diplomacy and warfare, states can behave very much like animals fighting over resources.

The treaty is often cited as the first document of its kind in recorded history: two great powers treating each other as equals and promising cooperation. The Egyptians and the Hittites promised to come to their aid in case the other was attacked, and they pledged to send back anyone who had escaped from one kingdom and sought refuge in another (Mieroop 146). This treaty, sadly, is the high water mark of Hittite power and influence, having stood up to the Bronze Age's most powerful state—Egypt — and perhaps its most ambitious and energetic ruler — Ramses II. Now all that awaits the fabled Hittite kingdom is its fall as part of a deafening and epoch-ending collapse that will see not only the end of the Hittites, but indeed, of all the civilizations of the ancient Bronze Age.

✦✦ Primary Source Analysis Questions

How did Suppululiuma manage to unite the warring Hittites?

How did Hittite culture influence later Greek culture?

Writing Prompt

Writing is thinking, so we will spend considerable time this year writing and thinking about history. In the space provided, write a short essay answering the question:
If the Hittites were effectively lost to historians for hundreds of years, are they even worth studying? Why or why not?

Direct Instruction Review

The hardest part about history is memorizing all those facts, dates, and events. To make this process easier, we have included this short section called *Direct Instruction Review*. Direct Instruction (or DI) is a powerful pedagogical tool whereby teachers ask students a series of *call-and-response* questions, and students respond back with the aim of learning this material to *mastery*. Teacher's lines are in **bold**; student's lines in *italics*.

How is the history of the Hittite Kingdom organized? *The history of the Hittites is organized into three parts: an Old Kingdom, a Middle Kingdom, and a New Kingdom.*

When was the Hittite Old Kingdom? *The Hittite Old Kingdom lasted from 1650 to 1500.*

And who founded the Hittite Old Kingdom? *Hattusili founded the Hittite Old Kingdom.*

What was the capital of the Hittite Kingdom? *Hattusa was the capital of the Hittite Old Kingdom.*

Where was the Hittite Old Kingdom located? *The Hittites ruled over the region of Anatolia.*

What is Anatolia? *Anatolia is a peninsula jutting out from the much larger continent of Asia.*

What happened after Hattusili, the founder of the Hittite kingdom, died? *Hattusili tried to make his grandson, Mursili, his heir.*

But what happened to Mursili? *Mursili was murdered by his brother-in-law, who took the throne. From that point forward, the Hittites were plagued by violent, constant in-fighting for the throne.*

How long did this violent fighting last? *The fighting lasted until the reign of Telepinu.*

Who was Telepinu? *Telepinu ruled from 1525 to 1500, and he issued the Edict of Telepinu that tried to set in place a clear succession plan.*

And did the Edict of Telepinu work? *Nope! The Hittites were plagued by violent fighting for the throne until the reign of Suppiluliuma I and the start of the Hittite New Kingdom.*

What did Suppiluliuma I do for the Hittites? *Suppiluliuma I united warring Hittite tribes, conquered Anatolia, invaded Syrian lands south of the Taurus Mountains, and fought New Kingdom Egypt at the battle of Qadesh.*

And who won the Battle of Qadesh? *The battle was technically a draw and neither side won much advantage, but Ramses II still issued monuments to himself depicting him defeating the Hittites.*

Timeline Practice / The Hittites

The hardest part about history is memorizing all those facts, dates, and events. To make this process easier, check out the timeline below—well, technically, there are *two* timelines. Some entries are missing dates, and others are missing the event that occurred on that date. With the information available from both timelines, fill in the missing blanks to get a better sense of the timeline for this chapter.

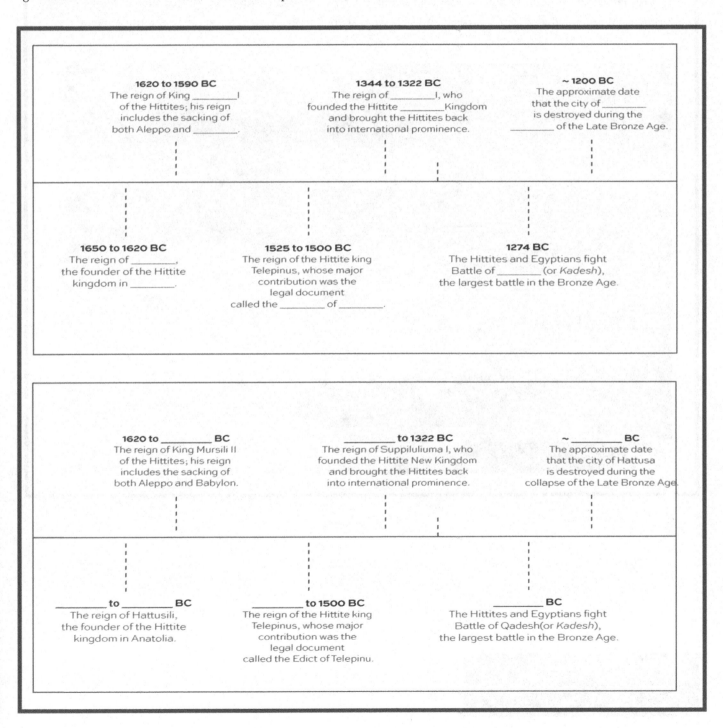

1620 to 1590 BC
The reign of King _____ I of the Hittites; his reign includes the sacking of both Aleppo and _____.

1344 to 1322 BC
The reign of _____ I, who founded the Hittite _____ Kingdom and brought the Hittites back into international prominence.

~ 1200 BC
The approximate date that the city of _____ is destroyed during the _____ of the Late Bronze Age.

1650 to 1620 BC
The reign of _____, the founder of the Hittite kingdom in _____.

1525 to 1500 BC
The reign of the Hittite king Telepinus, whose major contribution was the legal document called the _____ of _____.

1274 BC
The Hittites and Egyptians fight Battle of _____ (or *Kadesh*), the largest battle in the Bronze Age.

1620 to _____ BC
The reign of King Mursili II of the Hittites; his reign includes the sacking of both Aleppo and Babylon.

_____ to 1322 BC
The reign of Suppiluliuma I, who founded the Hittite New Kingdom and brought the Hittites back into international prominence.

~ _____ BC
The approximate date that the city of Hattusa is destroyed during the collapse of the Late Bronze Age.

_____ to _____ BC
The reign of Hattusili, the founder of the Hittite kingdom in Anatolia.

_____ to 1500 BC
The reign of the Hittite king Telepinus, whose major contribution was the legal document called the Edict of Telepinu.

_____ BC
The Hittites and Egyptians fight Battle of Qadesh (or *Kadesh*), the largest battle in the Bronze Age.

Map Practice: The Hittites

Instructions: Carefully look over the maps below, which are identical to maps provided in the rest of this chapter aside from one crucial difference—they have blanks in the place of the name of a sea, region, or site. Fill in the appropriate blank with the term list provided above each map.

The Hittites: Mountains such as the Taurus and the Caucasus; and important places such as Qadesh, Anatolia, Babylon, and Hattusa; and seas such as the Mediterranean, the Black, and the Aegean.

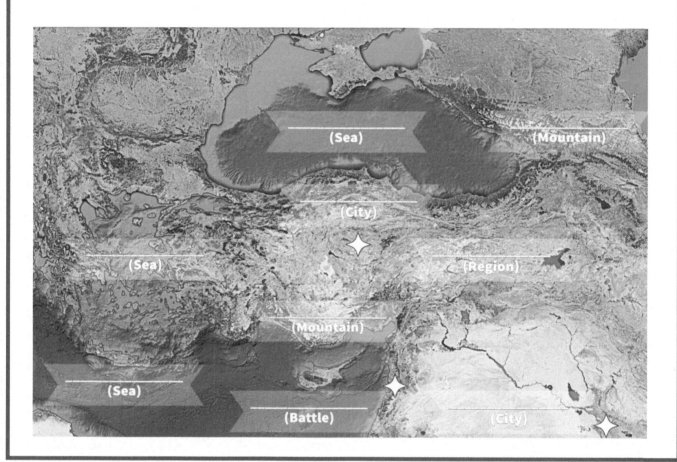

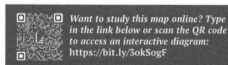
Want to study this map online? Type in the link below or scan the QR code to access an interactive diagram:
https://bit.ly/3okSogF

COASTLINE OF PHOE2NICIA / MODERN-DAY LEBANON
Photo by Kassem Mahfouz

CHAPTER

The Phoenicians

ROADMAP

✦ Study the history of ancient Phoenicia and learn about the trade routes the Phoenicians developed.

✦ Examine the value of trade and economics to world history.

✦ Learn about the innovations the Phoenicians contributed to world history—most importantly, their alphabet.

✦ Take a closer look at the Uluburun Shipwreck, a ship that sunk off the coast of Turkey filled with relics and treasures from the ancient world.

✦ Practice our knowledge of maps and geography, as well as our writing skills through reading comprehension questions and an essay.

THALES
OUTCOME

№ 12

Someone with **Traditional American Values and Entrepreneurialism** *recognizes the importance of traditional American entrepreneurialism, innovation, and values.*

The world in which we live today owes much to the Phoenicians, an ancient civilization that lived on the eastern coast of the Mediterranean Sea. These seafaring merchants devised the first phonetic alphabet, from which our own English alphabet derived, pioneered commerce and trades across the Mediterranean world, and imparted a bold, intrepid disposition to the civilization of the Greeks and Romans who, despite being rivals of the Phoenicians, imitated many of their best practices.

What is easier, to fight or to trade with your neighbors? Explain your reasoning.

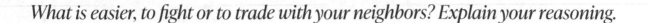

The First Seafarers / The Phoenicians

NOW, WE MOVE into a period known as the Late Bronze Age. Recall that we designate many time periods in the ancient world by the building materials with which they worked, and in the centuries from around 4,000 BC to around 1,200 BC, the peoples of the ancient world used **bronze**, a metal alloy made from copper and tin. If you can mix nine parts copper and one part tin, you can form a much stronger bronze than if you used copper or tin on their own. The problem? Copper and tin are rarely if ever, found in the same place.

Thus, vast trading networks formed across the ancient world to bring copper and tin together into one place. Tin came from areas as far-flung as Spain and Afghanistan and copper from isolated pockets in Cyprus, Anatolia, and Arabia. The kingdoms and territorial states that flourished during this time communicated and traded with each other to help bring the kinds of goods they needed but did not produce on their own. Those goods included not just precious metals like copper, tin, and gold, but also goods like grain, wine, and other kinds of foodstuffs for people to eat. These trading networks between states saw the free flow of goods and metals

needed to produce bronze, and these trade networks operated on a scale not seen yet in human history.

And at the center of it all? The coastal cities of Tyre and Sidon and the region situated on the eastern coastline of the Mediterranean Sea are known as **Phoenicia**. The **Phoenicians** are the first seafaring peoples we have come across in our history book—that is, they took to the high seas and all the adventures and dangers that the sea poses to get the goods they needed and make their fortunes. Later, we will come across other seafaring peoples that engaged in commerce and business, peoples like the ancient Athenians and the modern-day Venetians, Dutch, and the British. But for now, we start with Phoenicia and the commercial cities sitting on its coastline.

Ancient Phoenicia corresponds to the modern-day countries of Lebanon and Syria, countries just north of Israel and to the west of the Tigris and Euphrates River valleys. Sumer's great accomplishments included the wheel, urban centers, and cuneiform, but Phoenicia's great accomplishments were quite different. Phoenicia developed large, intricate trading networks across the

Vocabulary

Write down this vocabulary in your notebook. These terms will help you better learn and understand the material in this chapter.

Bronze

A metal alloy composed of nine parts of copper to every one part of tin. Because the components needed to make bronze were rarely, if ever, found in the same place, complicated trade networks developed across the ancient world to transport bronze.

Phoenicians

A seafaring, commercial people on the eastern coast of the Mediterranean; their commercial networks knit together the far-flung civilizations of the Late Bronze Age.

Ugarit

Along with Byblos, Ugarit was one of the principal cities of Bronze Age Phoenicia.

Byblos

Along with Ugarit, Byblos was one of the principal cities of Bronze Age Phoenicia.

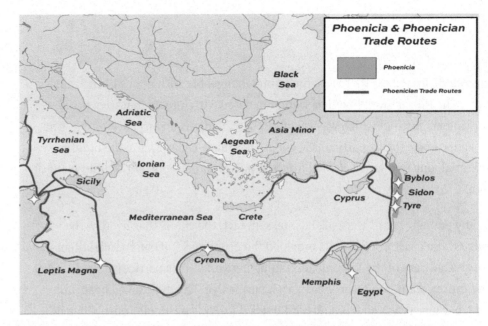

‖ **MAP OF PHOENICIAN TRADE ROUTES / EASTERN MEDITERRANEAN**

Mediterranean world. They also developed a phonetic alphabet, one that would make writing much easier, streamlining the record-keeping process. Phoenicia had several advantages that helped them develop these networks.

The Advantages of the Phoenicians

First, the coastline of Phoenicia had relatively deep harbors that could serve as ports. It was these ports that became the commercial centers of **Ugarit** and **Byblos** in the Bronze Age (which you might already know from the myth of Osiris and Isis), and later ports like Tyre and Sidon. One could compare these commercial centers to modern-day ports like New York City or London. Second, Phoenicia was located between three other large, interdependent regions. To the south of Phoenicia was Egypt, with its exotic goods like ivory and ebony and its huge gold reserves. Then, Babylon and Assyria lay to the east with their manufactured goods. Lastly, there was the Kingdom of the Hittites to the north ruling a region called Anatolia. The archaeological excavations at Ugarit, for instance, have found texts in Hurrian, Egyptian, Babylonian, and Hittite, among other languages. These texts imply that Ugarit was at the center of far-flung trade networks, and archaeological finds there at Ugarit include "dyed wool, linen garments, oil, lead, copper, and bronze objects" that testify to the vast trade networks the Phoenicians maintained (Cline 104). Cities that can serve as middlemen between larger, wealthier countries can often grow exceptionally rich through trade and commerce.

But Phoenicia had other advantages that made them so successful—namely, timber and snails. Timber and the dye produced from these snails are called

commodities, goods that are largely interchangeable with goods of the same type. The hills above Phoenicia were populated with forests that they could use for timber, much of which was valuable cedar. Cedar is an aromatic wood—that is, cedar wood smells particularly good. That made cedar a valuable building material, one that kings wanted for their palaces and important buildings (Beck et al., 75).

Oddly enough, snails were big business. In fact, the snails that lived in the waters off the coast of Phoenicia provided the economic and commercial lifeblood for the entirety of the Phoenician trading networks. This particular snail, called the **murex snail**, produced a deep, rich purple dye. The dye looked beautiful and, because it was so rare and hard to produce, this particular purple dye became a major status symbol in the ancient world. If anyone wanted to show off how wealthy they were, they wore garments dyed in purple. Each murex shell produced a tiny amount of purple dye, so little in fact that it took something on the order of 10,000 shells to produce *one gram of dye*—one gram was barely enough to dye even the edge of a garment.

‖ **MUREX SHELLS**

The city of Sidon, a Phoenician port city that came into prominence later in ancient history, had a mound of discarded shells over 130 feet high. You may know already, too, that Roman senators wore a purple stripe called the *toga praetexta* to identify themselves as wealthy, upper-class Romans. The merchants of Phoenicia had a near-monopoly on the production and sale of this Tyrian purple dye, which enabled them to trade across the Mediterranean world for other goods.

As a result, Phoenician merchants had two things in great abundance that they would need for trading and seafaring. The first was wood for their ships; the second was not one but two valuable commodities, cedar and purple dye. Thus,

Vocabulary

Commodity
Goods that are largely interchangeable with goods of the same kind.

Cedar
An aromatic, sweet-smelling wood valued as a building material by kings of the ancient world; this wood was readily available in Syria and Phoenicia.

Murex Snail
Found off the coast of Phoenicia, the murex snail produced a rare, valuable purple dye used for clothing and prized by the wealthy elites of the ancient world.

Carthage
Carthage was the most successful of the trading posts founded by the people of Phoenicia to aid in their overseas voyages.

Bireme
A Phoenician warship with *two* banks of oars and a ram at its prows used for hitting enemy ships.

Phonetic Alphabet
First developed by the Phoenicians, this alphabet was a writing system where symbols are attached to sounds, the symbols being what we know of as letters, and the sounds being combined together until they form words we can recognize.

they had timber both for ships and for trading, and the murex snail was a highly-valuable good for trading. Phoenician sailors could sail practically anywhere in the ancient Mediterranean world and find buyers eager to purchase that valuable purple dye.

The Innovations of the Phoenicians

As the Phoenicians are the first seafaring, trading people we have come across in our study of history, let's note a few things about sailing and trading in the ancient world. First, in sailing, the Phoenicians rarely sailed straight out into the middle of the sea. Instead, they hugged the coastline of the Mediterranean. That way, if a menacing storm struck their ship, the sailors would never have that far to swim to make it to land. Then, the Phoenicians established a series of trading posts across the ancient world. These trading posts were used as places of safe refuge for Phoenician sailing vessels. At such trading posts, they could gather supplies for longer voyages. The most famous of these trading posts would become the great city of **Carthage**, established on the coastline of North Africa circa 814 BC. Carthage's position gave its traders and seafarers exclusive access to the lands of the western Mediterranean and Sicily, places that had precious metals like tin or commodities like grapes and olives.

The Phoenicians established other colonies and trading posts to assist in their growing commercial network. Such sites were established in Spain (often called Tarshish), Sicily, and Sardinia, whose trading posts were often separated by a day's journey by sea at a distance of about 30 miles (Beck et al., 74). The Phoenicians and their Carthaginian descendants traded so much on the islands of Sicily and Sardinia, as well as the west coast of Italy, that the sea was just called the Tyrrhenian Sea, Tyre being one of the principal cities of Phoenicia.

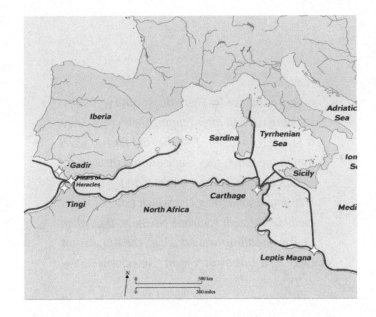

‖ TRADE ROUTES / WESTERN MEDITERANNEAN

Truth be told, the Phoenicians did not always hug the Mediterranean coastline. As related by the later Greek historian Herodotus, one Phoenician voyage set sail from the Erythraean Sea, an ancient term for the Gulf of Aden, where the Red Sea meets the Indian Ocean. Those sailors hugged the utterly-unknown coastline of Africa until they returned to the Mediterranean Sea three years later. Herodotus writes of their boldness:

Lastly, the Phoenicians built sturdy, powerful ships with the timber available to them. These ships were called

The first one we know of to have discovered this fact (about the shape of the African continent) was Nechos king of Egypt. After he had stopped excavation work on the canal, which extended from the Nile to the Arabian Gulf, he sent some Phoenicians off on boats with orders to sail around Libya and back through the Pillars of a Hercules onto the Mediterranean Sea and to return by that route to Egypt. And so the Phoenicians set out from the Erythraean Sea and sailed the Southern sea. Whenever autumn came, they would put in to shore at whatever region of Libya they happened to have reached in order to sow seeds. There they would wait for the abreast, and after reaping their crops, they would sail on again. This they did for two years, and in the third, they came around through the Pillars of Heracles and returned to Egypt. They mentioned something else which I do not find credible, through someone else may: that when they were sailing around Libya, the sun was on their right side as they went (Herodotus 261-262).

‖ **PHOENICIAN BIREME / ASSYRIAN RELIEF**

biremes, so named for their two (hence the *bi-*) banks of oars that gave biremes added speed and maneuverability. The bireme also had a massive ram fixed to its prow, the front of the ship, that could be used to ram enemy ships when necessary. Along with the bireme, the Phoenicians also invented the keel, a long wooden plank onto which the rest of the hull is built, and the process of caulking, the addition of sticky, tar-like substances like pitch between seams in the wood to prevent water from seeping in. These inventions are often attributed to the Phoenicians. The Phoenicians enjoyed a vaunted, well-deserved reputation for seamanship from the Bronze Age well up until the days of the Romans.

Then, the Phoenicians devised an alphabet to record commercial transactions. Just as in Sumer, the Phoenicians needed a quick, efficient way to record commercial transactions. Unlike in Sumer, whose priestly bureaucrats devised a pictographic writing system both difficult to learn and to write in, the Phoenicians developed the world's first **phonetic alphabet**. A phonetic alphabet is one where symbols are attached to sounds, the symbols being what we know of as letters, and the sounds being combined together until they form words we can recognize. The word *phonetic* comes from the Greek word for *sound* or *voice* and is only related to the word *Phoenicia* by coincidence. The Phoenicians then spread their writing system to their trading partners, many of whom adapted the script to their own language.

This new phonetic alphabet was much easier to learn than the cuneiform of the Sumerians, and the Phoenician, phonetic alphabet was more adaptable to the dialects of the peoples with whom the Phoenicians traded. The most famous example of this alphabet adoption is in the ancient Greeks, whose changes make the Phoenician alphabet look far more familiar to us and our own English alphabet. For instance, the word alphabet derives from the first two letters of the Phoenicians alphabet: *alef* and *beth*. The Greeks changed these letters to *alpha* and *beta*: from there, we get our English word, *alphabet*. The Phoenician alphabet spread throughout the Near East and influenced not only Greek but also Hebrew and Aramaic, languages that would become the most widely-spoken languages in the region (Mieroop 238).

In conclusion, the Phoenicians contributed many valuable things to world history. They invented powerful warships called biremes capable of sailing on the seas of the Mediterranean, along with shipbuilding components like the ship's keel and the use of caulk to keep ships watertight. They grew wealthy not merely by exploiting a natural resource—the murex shell—but by developing the ships and cultivating the spirit needed to bring that Tyrrenian purple dye to port cities willing to pay for it. In the process, the Phoenicians helped pioneer trade routes across the Mediterranean and thus helped integrate large, advanced economies across the Near East together into one intricate trade network. Then, to facilitate their own record-keeping, the Phoenicians developed a new alphabet that would be much easier to write and adapt than Sumerian cuneiform, an alphabet that influenced the English alphabet we use today.

In this way, the seafaring and adventurous spirit of the Phoenicians helps us to understand the idea of risk-taking and entrepreneurship. An entrepreneur takes a series of calculated risks to start their business, a new project, or some other venture whose outcome is ultimately uncertain. A sea voyage, not unlike the ones undertaken by the Phoenicians, is the perfect metaphor for such a venture, as these Phoenicians took a series of calculated risks to accomplish things few at the time believed to be possible.

✦ ✦ Reading Comprehension Questions

What was the land of ancient Phoenicia like? What advantages did they have, and what disadvantages?

....

....

....

What did the Phoenicians do that made them so successful?

....

....

....

What did the Phoenicians do (or invent) that helped support trade and commerce?

....

....

....

A Closer Look at the Phoenician Alphabet

LET US TAKE A CLOSER LOOK at the phonetic alphabet of the ancient Phoenicians. Like the Sumerians and Egyptians, the Phoenicians developed a writing system to keep accurate records of business dealings, but the Phoenician alphabet is much different from the pictographic writing systems of the ancient Sumerians and Egyptians. A pictographic writing system has pictures, or words that have a passing resemblance to pictures, which might work for relatively simple nouns like *bread* or *water*.

But, a pictographic writing system is exceedingly difficult for anyone to learn. In contrast, the phonetic alphabet of the ancient Phoenicians paired a symbol to a sound, and then could rearrange the sounds to represent words. Below are pictures of the Phoenician alphabet to help compare and contrast their alphabet with our own, and thus identify some stages in the development of a written language, the kind which we are reading today.

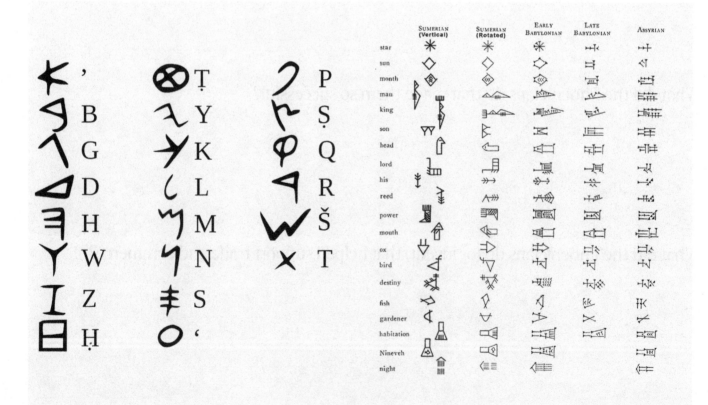

Look at the cuneiform script to the left. Why was cuneiform so much harder to learn?

What similarities do you find between the Phoenician alphabet and our own?

Could the ancient world have advanced, if they only had the cuneiform script in which to write?

UNDERWATER ARCHAEOLOGY

An archaeology excavates a mysterious finding at the Uluburun Shipwreck.

In 1982, sponge divers discovered these odd, dog-bone-shaped metal pieces. They are seemingly composed of different metals in ratios of 9 to 1–that is, for every piece of a certain metal, there are nine pieces of the other. What could this find have been?

A Closer Look:
The Uluburun Shipwreck

IN 1982 AD, A SPONGE DIVER operating off the coast of Turkey saw what he could only describe as "biscuits" on the bottom of the sea. He relayed this information to his captain, who passed the information on to archaeologists at the Institute of Nautical Archaeology. George Bass, the director of the institute, had spoken to captains in the eastern Mediterranean and asked them to look out for these "biscuits" as evidence of ancient, sunken shipwrecks. These "biscuits" were actually bronze ingots shaped into flat, oxhide-like shapes to prevent them from moving around during the voyage (Cline 73-75). That is, of course, the answer to the question on the previous page: the underwater archaeologists found copper and tin in the ratios needed to make bronze, which is itself composed of approximately ninety percent copper and ten percent tin. A team of underwater archaeologists soon began excavating the site in 1984. They have since uncovered a treasure trove of archaeological and historical information about the Late Bronze Age from this shipwreck off the coast of Uluburun, Turkey ("Grand Premonitory" in Turkish).

The shipwreck occurred sometime around 1300 BC, but the ship's home port is unknown. The artifacts recovered from the site give historians and archaeologists an incredible viewpoint into the commercial networks of the Late Bronze Age. The ship contained raw glass, large storage jars called *amphora* containing barley, a grain, and also terebinth resin. Terebinth resin is made from pistachio trees and used in perfume manufacturing in Greece. Some of these amphora jars presumably

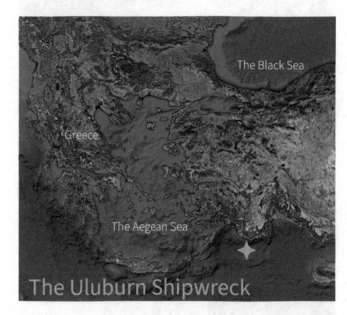

THE ULUBURUN SHIPWRECK / TURKISH COAST
Map from Google Earth

contained wine or oil. The ship also carried literal tons of precious metals, in odd ratios of nine tons of copper and one ton of tin.

For safety, underwater archaeologists worked in teams of two for only twenty minutes at a time. They removed objects from the seafloor with incredible care and advanced planning to help circumvent the dizzying, intoxication-like effects of working underwater at a depth of 140 to 170 feet below the surface. The next page features photos of the divers from the Institute of Nautical Archaeology recovering various artifacts from the shipwreck (Cline 73-77).

> **For teachers and teaching parents**: *Bronze is made from nine parts copper for every one part tin. Ships carrying the ingredients to make bronze carried them in these proportions.*

The Uluburun Shipwreck

‖ AN ARCHAEOLOGIST EXCAVATING BRONZE INGOTS

‖ CANAANITE STORAGE JARS, OF WHICH ALMOST 150 WERE FOUND ON BOARD THE SHIP

‖ BALLOONS TO HELP LIFT PRECIOUS OBJECTS FROM THE WRECKAGE

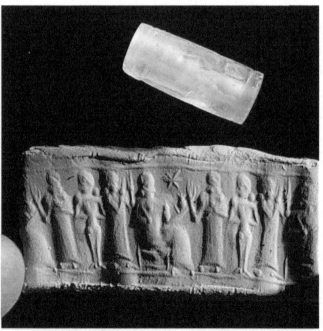

‖ A CYLINDER SEAL FOUND AT ULUBURUN

Photographs from the Institute for Nautical Archaeology.

What do archaeological discoveries like the Uluburun shipwreck tell us about the ancient world?

What do the goods found on board the ship tell us about trade and commerce in the ancient world?

Why did they find copper and ten in such odd ratios—ten parts copper to one part tin?

Writing Prompt

Writing is thinking, so we will spend considerable time this year writing and thinking about history. In the space provided, write a short essay answering the question: *What were the major innovations pioneered by the ancient, seafaring Phoenicians? Were their contributions to world history more or less significant those of ancient Sumer? Why or why not? Be sure to explain your reasoning with relevant examples, sound reasoning, and clear, complete sentences.*

Direct Instruction Review

The hardest part about history is memorizing all those facts, dates, and events. To make this process easier, we have included this short section called *Direct Instruction Review*. Direct Instruction (or DI) is a powerful pedagogical tool whereby teachers ask students a series of *call-and-response* questions, and students respond back with the aim of learning this material to *mastery*. Teacher's lines are in **bold**; student's lines in *italics*.

Who were the ancient Phoenicians? *The Phoenicians were a seafaring, commercial people on the eastern coast of the Mediterranean; their commercial networks knit together the far flung civilizations of the Late Bronze Age.*

Where is Phoenicia located? *Phoenicia is located on the east coast of the Mediterranean Sea.*

What kind of people were the Phoenicians? *They were seafaring people, meaning that they sailed across the Mediterranean carrying valuable trade goods.*

What were the main cities of the Phoenicians? *In the Bronze Age, the main Phoenician cities were Byblos and Ugarit; in later ancient history, the cities of Tyre and Sidon became the largest and most successful Phoenician ports.*

What kind of goods did they trade in? What kind of goods did they carry across the Mediterranean Sea? *The Phoenicians carried valuable commodities like cedar and a purple dye made from the murex snail.*

Why was Tyrrhenian purple so valuable? *The dye was so valuable because it took tens of thousands of murex snails to make one gram of dye, enough to dye the hem of only one garment.*

What innovations did the Phoenicians contribute to world history? *They helped develop trade routes along the Mediterranean coastline that linked together the economies of ancient Greece, Egypt, and Mesopotamia.*

What other innovations did the Phoenicians contribute to world history? *The bireme, a massive oar-powered ship with two banks of oars.*

What other innovations did the Phoenicians contribute to world history? *They contributed a phonetic alphabet, an alphabet in which symbols represent sounds, an alphabet just our own English alphabet.*

What can we learn from the ancient Phoenicians? *We can learn about the bold, intrepid nature of the human spirit, taking to the high seas to make or break our fortunes!*

Map Practice: The Phoenicians

Instructions: Carefully look over the maps below, which are identical to maps provided in the rest of this chapter aside from one crucial difference—they have blanks in the place of the name of a sea, region, or site. Fill in the appropriate blank with the term list provided above each map.

The Phoenicians: Bodies of water such as the Mediterranean, Aegean, Black, Adriatic Ionian, the Tyrrhenian; cities such as Leptis Magna, Carthage, Cyrene, Memphis, Byblos, Tyre, Sidon, Gadiz, Tingi; islands such as Crete, Cyprus, Sardina, and Sicily; and regions or landforms such as and the Pillars of Heracles, Egypt, North Africa, and Asia Minor

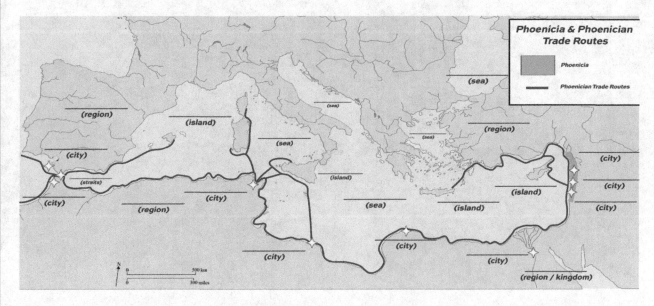

Want to study this map online? Type in the link below or scan the QR code to access an interactive diagram:
https://bit.ly/3okSogF

CHAPTER
10

The People of Israel

ROADMAP

+ Read a selection from the book of Genesis in the Hebrew Bible about the creation of the world and mankind.

+ Learn more about the background of the Hebrew Bible and the first books in the Hebrew Bible, known collectively as the Torah.

+ The growth of ancient Israel into a centralized state, on par with the other kingdoms of the Near East.

+ Practice our knowledge of maps and chronology, as well as our writing skills through reading comprehension questions and an essay.

THALES OUTCOME

Nº 11

Someone with **Dreams & Aspirations to Change the World** *produces plans to accomplish personal and educational aspirations.*

The people of Israel may be small compared to the other states and empires we have studied this year, but they have contributed some of the most important ideas in the Western canon.

A people must be big, important, and powerful to have an impact on world history. Explain your reasons why or why not this statement is true.

....

....

....

Genesis 1 / Moses, 14th to 12th century BC...

IN THE BEGINNING, God created the heavens and the earth. 2 Now the earth was formless and empty, darkness was over the surface of the deep, and the Spirit of God was hovering over the waters.

3 And God said, "Let there be light," and there was light. 4 God saw that the light was good, and he separated the light from the darkness. 5 God called the light "day," and the darkness he called "night." And there was evening, and there was morning—the first day.

6 And God said, "Let there be a vault between the waters to separate water from water." 7 So God made the vault and separated the water under the vault from the water above it. And it was so. 8 God called the vault "sky." And there was evening, and there was morning—the second day.

9 And God said, "Let the water under the sky be gathered to one place, and let dry ground appear." And it was so. 10 God called the dry ground "land," and the gathered waters he called "seas." And God saw that it was good.

11 Then God said, "Let the land produce vegetation: seed-bearing plants and trees on the land that bear fruit with seed in it, according to their various kinds." And it was so. 12 The land produced vegetation: plants bearing seed according to their kinds and trees bearing fruit with seed in it according to their kinds. And God saw that it was good. 13 And there was evening, and there was morning—the third day.

14 And God said, "Let there be lights in the vault of the sky to separate the day from the night, and let them serve as signs to mark sacred times, and days and years, 15 and let them be lights in the vault of the sky to give light on the earth." And it was so. 16 God made two great lights—the greater light to govern the day and the lesser light to govern the night. He also made the stars. 17 God set them in the vault of the sky to give light on the earth, 18 to govern the day and the night, and to separate light from darkness. And God saw that it was good. 19 And there was evening, and there was morning—the fourth day.

20 And God said, "Let the water teem with living creatures, and let birds fly above the earth across the vault of the sky." 21 So God created the great creatures

of the sea and every living thing with which the water teems and that moves about in it, according to their kinds, and every winged bird according to its kind. And God saw that it was good. 22 God blessed them and said, "Be fruitful and increase in number and fill the water in the seas, and let the birds increase on the earth." 23 And there was evening, and there was morning—the fifth day.

24 And God said, "Let the land produce living creatures according to their kinds: the livestock, the creatures that move along the ground, and the wild animals, each according to its kind." And it was so. 25 God made the wild animals according to their kinds, the livestock according to their kinds, and all the creatures that move along the ground according to their kinds. And God saw that it was good.

26 Then God said, "Let us make mankind in our image, in our likeness, so that they may rule over the fish in the sea and the birds in the sky, over the livestock and all the wild animals,[a] and over all the creatures that move along the ground."

27 So God created mankind in his own image,

in the image of God he created them;

male and female he created them.

28 God blessed them and said to them, "Be fruitful and increase in number; fill the earth and subdue it. Rule over the fish in the sea and the birds in the sky and over every living creature that moves on the ground."

29 Then God said, "I give you every seed-bearing plant on the face of the whole earth and every tree that has fruit with seed in it. They will be yours for food. 30 And to all the beasts of the earth and all the birds in the sky and all the creatures that move along the ground—everything that has the breath of life in it—I give every green plant for food." And it was so.

31 God saw all that he had made, and it was very good. And there was evening, and there was morning—the sixth day (World English Bible).

✦ ✦ **Reading Comprehension Questions**

Summarize the plot and, in your opinion, the moral of the opening chapters of Genesis.

....

....

....

....

How does this text appear to be different than the stories of the *Atrahasis Epic* and the *Enūma Eliš*?

....

....

....

Based on this brief reading, what seems to be man's purpose? What was he created for? What does it mean that both men and women were created in God's image?

....

....

....

Based on this creation story, the story that these people tell themselves about the creation of the world and man's purposes within it, what do you think life will be like in ancient Israel?

....

....

....

The People of Israel

THE HISTORY OF THE PEOPLE OF ISRAEL may be small compared to the other nations and empires we have studied so far this year. But few nations from the ancient Near East have even survived to the present day, much less had the impact that descendants of Abraham, the Jewish people, have had over the past 4,000 years. Nor has any other nation of the ancient Near East impacted and shaped the development of world history in general and Western history, in particular, the way the people of Israel have. The history and the religious tradition of the Jewish people have influenced the course of human history like no other writings available in the Western canon. Indeed, the people of Israel themselves are responsible for some of the most sublime and significant ideas in the Western canon. And it is to the people of Israel we now turn.

The Hebrew Bible

The Bible is our primary source of information about the people of Israel. In fact, the Hebrew Bible was long the only book that had survived from the ancient Near East and was available for people to read, so people knew about the Babylonian Empire or the Assyrian Empire through the lens of their dealings with the Hebrew people. Archaeological excavations in Syria, Israel, Egypt, and the surrounding deserts have also provided historians evidence to help us better understand the events in the Bible, although much remains to be discovered.

The word **Bible** comes from the Greek *biblia*, which simply means "books" and refers to a collection of books that are "sacred" or "set apart" to both the religious traditions of Judaism and Christianity. The complete 66 books of the Old and New Testament are *sacred* (set apart) in Christianity, whereas twenty-four of those books are sacred to the religion of Judaism. Those twenty-four books make up the Hebrew Bible, books that in Christianity are called the "Old Testament." The word **testament** is a near-synonym for the word *covenant*, a binding agreement between two parties with one party being of greater power than the other.

The Hebrew Bible has a unique organization to it and is a bit different from the bibles you may be familiar with, known by the acronym **TaNaK**. The term TaNaK refers to the threefold division of the Hebrew Bible into the *Torah,* the *Nevi'im,* and the *Ketuvim.* The **Torah**, Hebrew for "law" or "instruction," refers to the first five books of

The people of Israel may be small in comparison with the other peoples of the ancient Near East, but through their writings in the Bible, the Israelites have influenced the course of world history more than any other people we may study this year. Moreover, Israel intersects with that of the other empires, kingdoms, and states that have at one time or another ruled the wider Mediterranean world.

BIG IDEA

THE TORAH

Together, the first five books of the Hebrew and Christian Bible are called the Torah, a word derived from the Hebrew word for law, word, *and* instruction.

the Bible—namely, the books of Genesis, Exodus, Leviticus, Numbers, and Deuteronomy. The **Nevi'im**, or "the Prophets" and the books of Isaiah and Jeremiah to the book of Kings; and the **Ketuvim**, or the "Writings," that include books like Psalms, Proverbs, and Job.

The Bible is a massive collection of almost every type of book: historical narrative, poetry, called the Psalms; a group of wisdom literature in the form of proverbs and didactic plays not unlike other examples of wisdom literature from the ancient Near East; one philosophical treatise, prophetic literature, and legal writings. So what exactly makes the Bible so unique that this book was so influential when so many other works from the ancient Near East have been lost amidst the historical rubble?

The Worldview of the Bible: Monotheism

The Bible's worldview sets this particular book apart from other works of ancient Near Eastern literature. For one, the Bible is thoroughly shaped in and around the idea of monotheism. **Monotheism** is the idea that there is only one God, and in both the faith traditions of Judaism and Christianity, this God is the Creator of Heaven and Earth and all that dwells within them. The word *mono*, as you may have guessed, means "one," whereas the word *theism* comes from the Greek *theos*, meaning "god." Most of the cultures we have studied this year practiced polytheism and worshiped many gods, for the Greek prefix *poly* means "many." We should ask ourselves though: is monotheism really any different from polytheism, except that one tradition worships one god and the other many gods? And what does monotheism actually look like?

Vocabulary

Write down this vocabulary in your notebook. These terms will help you better learn and understand the material in this chapter.

Israel
The Bible describes the patriarch Jacob wrestling with God and after the match, he is renamed "Israel," or "he who wrestles with God"; the name refers to the descendants of Abraham, the Jewish people.

Bible
A collection of books that are sacred to the faith traditions of Judaism and Christianity.

Testament
A binding agreement between two parties, often with one party being of greater power than the other.

TaNaK
The term *TaNaK* refers to the division of the Hebrew Bible into the *Torah*, the *Nevi'im*, and the *Ketuvim*.

Torah
Torah, the Hebrew term for "law" or "instruction," refers to the first five books of the Bible that include the books of Genesis, Exodus, Leviticus, Numbers, and Deuteronomy. According to Jewish tradition, Moses wrote these books.

Simply put, **polytheism** is the belief in, and worship of, many gods. In the polytheistic world of the ancient Sumerians, Egyptians, Phoenicians, Assyrians, Babylonians, Greeks, and Romans, those polytheistic deities controlled the various forces of nature. These forces of nature could be both so terrifying and so hostile they made human flourishing practically impossible. Thunder, for example, is scary if one does not live in a strong, sturdy house. As a result, the god of thunder (Zeus for the Greeks, Jupiter for the Romans, and Thor for the Germanic peoples living further north) was typically the most powerful god in many polytheistic traditions. And those societies created an elaborate system of rituals and sacrifices to appease these gods and ensure plentiful rains, bountiful harvests, and protection from barbarian tribes. If they didn't, the gods may destroy everything those civilizations had built.

On the other hand, the ancient Hebrews believed in one God, a worldview called *monotheism*. In this framework, God is capitalized because the word is used as a name and thus, a proper noun. This God was the creator and was, at his essence, fundamentally good and fundamentally different from the world he created. This God was in control of nature but was not like the natural world. While God created people in his image, he is not inconsistent or irrational in the way that people can sometimes be. Actions such as floods and droughts are not the cause of random, fickle, mean-spirited deities like Ishtar or the storm god Adad, but because God has imparted an orderly rhythm and harmony to the natural world. Because of this order, there are natural causes for these events that, terrible though floods and earthquakes are, we as intelligent beings can come to understand and even prevent them.

If they happen in a somewhat-orderly fashion, we can understand why they happen and perhaps stop them. Subsequently, there is an order in the universe at large imparted by the Creator, that this Creator has allowed

THE NIGHT SKY
Photo by Klemen Vrankar

us to understand this order, and that he allows us to understand this order because he cares about humanity. And, as the ancient Israelites believed, this Creator actually spoke to them.

The early pages of the Bible include the book of **Genesis**, a word that appropriately means *beginnings*. Moses, the traditional author of Genesis, describes the world as being created by one purposeful, rational, all-powerful God who also created human beings in his image. In this way, each and every human being is endowed with an inherent dignity and worth that no one could take away, an idea most often called the **imago dei**. The Latin phrase *imago dei* means "in the image of God," and refers to the Judeo-Christian idea that human beings, being made in God's image, possess meaningful aspects of God's character like the ability to reason, make meaningful moral choices, and solve problems on a scale utterly unlike anything else in all creation. This view of humans, moreover, stands in contrast to the creation stories of the Sumerians and the Babylonians, both of whom believed that human beings were essentially created to be slaves, toiling on the canals and work projects of these ancient and mighty gods.

The pivotal moment in Genesis comes at the fall of the human race. As with other cultures, the Bible includes a

ADAM & EVE / FRESCO (4ᵀᴴ C. AD)

The earliest depictions of Adam and Eve from the Catacombs of Marcellinus and Peter in Rome.

story wherein everything went from "very good" to "very bad," a transition that came about because of the disobedience of the first human beings, Adam and Eve. Adam and Eve had been placed somewhere in a paradisiacal garden called Eden, and they had been told they may eat of every tree in that garden, all except for one tree: the Tree of the Knowledge of Good and Evil. Upon receiving advice from a talking snake (hint: don't talk to strangers), Adam and Eve decide to reject God's rules in favor of making their own, followed by their expulsion from paradise.

The expulsion of Adam and Eve from Eden begins the downward cycle of humanity into violence and hardship. First, there is violent fighting between their sons, Cain and Abel. Cain grows jealous of Abel's favor, and Cain kills him; Cain is driven out from his family and settles in a land called Nod, ironic because the word *Nod* in Hebrew means "wandering". There, Cain founds a city that he names after his son. From there, the fighting, violence, and bloodshed continue to spread across human settlements. There are so many terrible deeds that God decides to cleanse the earth through a terrifying, forty-day flood.

Only one man would survive—Noah—who builds a massive boat and carries with him his family and two of every animal so as to repopulate the earth once the flood subsides. In the next chapter, we will turn to the stories of Abraham, the Patriarchs, and the deliverance of the Israelites from Egypt, the moment when the people of Israel become a nation and enter the pages of history.

Vocabulary

Nevi'im

From the Hebrew word for "Prophets," *Nevi'im* refers to the prophetic books in the Hebrew Bible and include the works of I and II Kings, Isaiah, Jeremiah, among others.

Ketuvim

From the Hebrew word for "Writings," *Ketuvium* refers to books in the Bible that are neither prophetic in nature nor found in the Torah. They include works such as the book of Job, the Psalms, and Ecclesiastes.

Monotheism

From the Greek prefix *mono* and the Greek word *theos*, *monotheism* means the belief in only one God who, in Judaism and Christianity, is the creator of the world and everything in it.

Polytheism

The belief in many (the Greek prefix, *poly*) gods (the Greek word, *theos*) who are often personified by, and in control of, the forces of nature.

Genesis

Genesis is the first book of the Hebrew and Christian Bible, which was written by Moses according to Jewish tradition.

Imago Dei

From a Latin phrase meaning *in the image of God*, this phrase refers to the special creation of human beings by a good and wise Creator.

What contributions have the people of Israel made to human history?

How is the Hebrew Bible organized? (Hint: use the term TaNaK in your answer.)

What is monotheism? What is polytheism? How are they different?

Writing Prompt

Writing is thinking, so we will spend considerable time this year writing and thinking about history. In the space provided, write a short essay answering the question: *Compare and contrast the people of Israel with that of the cultures and peoples we have studied so far this year. Cite at least three broad categories of evidence that meaningfully separate the Israelites from the other peoples of the ancient Near East.*

Direct Instruction Review

The hardest part about history is memorizing all those facts, dates, and events. To make this process easier, we have included this short section called *Direct Instruction Review*. Direct Instruction (or DI) is a powerful pedagogical tool whereby teachers ask students a series of *call-and-response* questions, and students respond back with the aim of learning this material to *mastery*. Teacher's lines are in **bold**; student's lines in *italics*.

Who were the people of Israel? *The people of Israel are the descendants of Abraham, Isaac, and Jacob. They came to live in the land of Canaan, which today is known as Israel.*

Are there other names for the people of Israel? *Yes, we may use the terms descendants of Abraham, the Hebrews, and Jews to refer to the offspring of Abraham, Isaac, and Jacob.*

What kind of influence did the people of Israel have on world history? *The greatest influence the people of Israel have had is through their religious writings, collected together in the Hebrew and Christian Bible.*

And what is the Bible? *The word* Bible *comes from the Greek word for "book" and is a collection of books—sixty-six books in fact, written over a period of thousands of years.*

Why is the Bible important? *The Bible contains the writings sacred to the religious traditions of Judaism and Christianity and also serves as a primary source to help us understand the world of the ancient Near East.*

How is the Hebrew Bible organized? *The Hebrew Bible is divided into three parts, known by the acronym* TaNaK.

And what does TaNaK mean? *The acronym TaNaK stands for Torah, or the* Law, *the Nebi'im, or the* Prophets, *and the Ketuviim, or the* Writings.

What is the Torah, and what books are included in the Torah? *The term* Torah *means law, word, or instruction, and collectively refers to the first five books of the Bible.*

And what books are included in the Torah? *The Torah includes the books of Genesis, Exodus, Leviticus, Numbers, and Deuteronomy.*

What events does the book of Genesis record? *The book of Genesis means* beginnings, *and the book of Genesis includes the creation of the world, the creation of human beings, and the beginnings of the nation of Israel from Abraham.*

What may be the most important event recorded in the book of Genesis? *The creation of man, for God created man in his image, an act that gives each and every person—no matter who—a unique value and dignity no one else can ever take away.*

Map Practice: Ancient Israel

Instructions: Carefully look over the maps below, which are identical to maps provided in the rest of this chapter aside from one crucial difference—they have blanks in the place of the name of a sea, region, or site. Fill in the appropriate blank with the term list provided above each map.

Ancient Israel: Rivers such as the Nile and the Jordan; Mount Sinai; seas such as the Red Sea, the Dead Sea and the Mediterranean Sea; regions such as the Sinai Peninsula, the Nile Delta, and Canaan; and the cities of Jerusalem, Jericho, Memphis, Rameses, and Migdol.

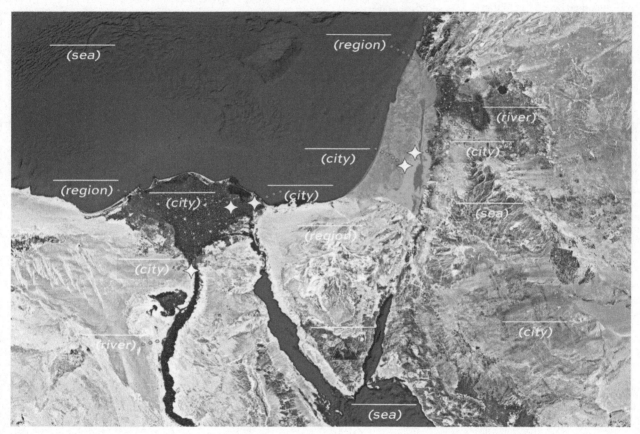

Timeline Practice / Ancient Israel

The hardest part about history is memorizing all those facts, dates, and events. To make this process easier, check out the timeline below—well, technically, there are *two* timelines. Some entries are missing dates, and others are missing the event that occurred on that date. With the information available from both timelines, fill in the missing blanks to get a better sense of the timeline for this chapter.

1786 to 1550 BC
The Second _____ Period in Egyptian history, marked by the rule of the _____, who may have welcomed Joseph's family into Egypt.

2004 BC
The collapse of the Sumerian city of ____-__.

1350 to 1225 BC
The late date for the _____, with _____ II being the likey pharaoh of the Exodus.

1204 BC
The composition of the _____ Stele, which lists the Israelites amongst conquered subjects in _____.

~ 2000 BC
According to _____, God calls Abraham to travel from Ur to the land of _____, a land God promises to give to the vast multitude of Abraham's descendants.

1446 to 1437 BC
The early date for the _____, the moment God delivers his people from slavery in Egypt, with the likely pharaoh being _____ III or _____ II.

1177 BC
The collapse of the _____ Age.

1010 to 970 BC
The reign of King _____, the first king over a united Israel.

_____ to _____ BC
The Second Intermediate Period in Egyptian history, marked by the rule of the Hyksos, who may have welcomed Joseph's family into Egypt.

_____ BC
The collapse of the Sumerian city of Ur-III.

_____ to _____ BC
The late date for the Exodus, with Ramses II being the likey pharaoh of the Exodus.

_____ BC
The composition of the Merneptah Stele, which lists the Israelites amongst conquered subjects in Canaan.

~ _____ BC
According to Genesis, God calls Abraham to travel from Ur to the land of Canaan, a land God promises to give to the vast multitude of Abraham's descendants.

_____ to _____ BC
The early date for the Exodus, the moment God delivers his people from slavery in Egypt, with the likely pharaoh being Thutmose III or Amenophis II.

_____ BC
The collapse of the Bronze Age.

_____ to _____ BC
The reign of King David, the first king over a united Israel.

SUMMIT OF MOUNT SINAI
Photo by Mohammed Moussa

SECTION III Bronze Age Civilizations

CHAPTER

The Exodus

ROADMAP

✦ Continue our study of the history of ancient Israel.

✦ Learn the seminal event in the Hebrew Bible—the Exodus—and the importance of the Exodus to the people of Israel.

✦ Study the Ten Plagues of Egypt, investigate who *might* have been the Pharaoh of the Exodus, and examine the Ten Commandments, the law code of the people of Israel.

✦ The growth of ancient Israel into a centralized state, on par with the other kingdoms of the Near East.

✦ Practice our knowledge of maps and chronology, as well as our writing skills through reading comprehension questions and an essay.

THALES
OUTCOME

Nº 14

Someone who displays **Gratitude** *recognizes the advantages of his/her environment.*

The Exodus may be the defining event in the history of Israel. The book of Exodus describes how God uses his servant Moses to free the people of Israel from their slavery in the land of Egypt. Later, God gave Moses the Ten Commandments, the ten laws that Israel should follow if they are to live long in the land of Canaan, the land God promises to give to them. In this way, the book of Exodus demonstrates the idea of *Gratitude*, in that the people of Israel owe their freedom and prosperity to God and should obey his laws from a spirit of gratitude.

The Patriarchs to the Exodus

THE HISTORY OF THE PEOPLE OF ISRAEL takes place against the backdrop of the ancient Near East, beginning with ancient Sumer. Towards the close of the second millennium BC, the city-states of ancient Sumer were ruled by warlords like Sargon of Akkad and later overrun by barbarian tribes like the Gutians. The Sumerian city of Ur took the reins of leadership for a brief period and became exceptionally wealthy from its control of the trade routes into and out of Sumer. It is during this time, the dynasty of Ur-III, to be exact, that a man named Abraham was "called out" of the city of Ur before the final demise of Sumerian civilization.

In the twilight years of Sumerian civilization, a wealthy man named Abraham was told in mysterious but no un-certain terms to leave the city of Ur. The Bible describes the scene in the following way:

> Now the Lord said to Abram, "Go from your country and your kindred and your father's house to the land that I will show you. And I will make of you a great nation, and I will bless you and make your name great, so that you will be a blessing. I will bless those who bless you, and him who dishonors you I will curse, and in you all the families of the earth shall be blessed." So Abram went, as the Lord had told him, and Lot went with him. Abram was seventy-five years old when he departed from Haran. And Abram took Sarai his wife, and Lot his brother's son, and all their possessions that they had gathered, and the people that they had acquired in Haran, and they set out to go to the land of Canaan," (Gen 12:1-5).

So who was Abraham? From what we can glean from the Bible, **Abraham** was a member of an ethnic and linguistic group known as **Semitic** people. This partic-ular ethnic group is named for an ancestor of Abraham named Shem. According to the biblical story, Shem was one of the three sons of Noah, the individual whom God told to build an ark to survive a catastrophic worldwide flood, and Shem's descendants are collectively known as Semitic peoples. They include Hebrews, Phoenicians, Arabian tribes, and the Amorites (in Babylon), amongst other ethnic and linguistic groups.

BIG IDEA

There are many strains of classical education, some of which are more distinctively religious or non-religious than others. But the Bible occupies a central place in every brand of classical education for its unparalleled influence on Western thought and culture. Genesis 1-11 forms the very bedrock of that influence.

Vocabulary

Israel

The name given, collectively, to the descendants of Abraham, Isaac, and Jacob. In Hebrew, the name *Israel* means "one who strives with God" and is derived from an alternate name for Jacob, the grandson of Abraham. The names Hebrews, Israelites, and Jews may be used interchangeably with the term *people of Israel*.

Abraham

Abraham is often called the *father* of the Jewish people. God calls Abraham and tells him to leave his homeland of Ur and journey to Canaan; in Canaan, God promises to bless Abraham with a great nation of descendants.

Semitic People

An ethnic group from the ancient Near East named for Shem, the ancestor of Abraham. It included the Hebrews, Phoenicians, Arabian tribes, and the Amorites, amongst other tribes and people-groups.

Canaan

A region on the east coast of the Mediterranean Sea between the larger and more powerful states of Mesopotamia and Egypt.

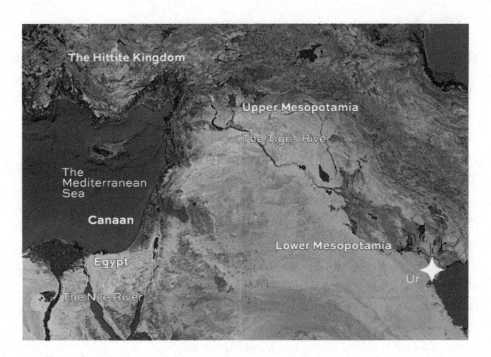

❙ MAP OF THE ANCIENT NEAR EAST

The Sumerians, meanwhile, are an ethnic group distinct from that of the Semitic peoples of the ancient Near East. Still, Abraham would have been familiar with Sumerian customs and traditions since he lived in Ur. Abraham's time living in Ur may account for some of the similarities between the events of Genesis 1-11 and that of ancient Sumerian mythology even if the Sumerian stories generally paint a very different picture of man (created to be a servant) and of the flood (sent to destroy a troublesome and annoying humanity). Regardless, when God calls Abraham, Abraham leaves Ur. He travels north and then south to the land of **Canaan**, a region on the Mediterranean Sea located between the lands of Egypt and Mesopotamia.

Then, God promised Abraham a son. Yet, Abraham would spend decades waiting for the fulfillment of this promise until, at last, after years of waiting, Abraham and his wife Sarah had a son named Isaac. The name Isaac is related to the Hebrew word for "laughter." (Sarah laughed when told that she, an older woman, would have children.) Isaac had children of his own, twins named Jacob and Esau. Jacob himself had twelve children who would, in turn, would become the twelve tribes of the nation of Israel. Thus, the first three generations of the people of Israel—namely, Abraham, Isaac, and Jacob—are known as the **Patriarchs**, a term that literally means *ruling fathers* but more specifically refers to the founders of the nation of Israel. But first, during the lifetime of Jacob, a terrible famine gripped the lands of the ancient Near East, forcing Jacob and his family to journey to the only land that still had any grain: Egypt.

The Israelites in Egypt

The "great nation of descendants" God promised to Abraham comes through Abraham's grandson, Jacob. The book of Genesis relates how Jacob fell in love with a distant relative named Rachel. Jacob wanted to marry Rachel, but Jacob was tricked by Rachel's father, Laban, into marrying Rachel's older but (in Jacob's eyes) less attractive sister, Leah. Jacob ended up marrying both sisters and subsequently had eleven children. It is these children who gave rise to the later twelve tribes of Israel: Judah, Dan, Reuben, Simeon, Levi, Naphtali, Gad, Asher, Issachar, Zebulun, and Benjamin, as well as Manasseh and Ephraim, the sons of Joseph who, because of Joseph's role in saving Jacob's entire family, received a double portion of the inheritance.

Some of these names, such as the tribe of Judah, may be very familiar to you. For those of you who know ancient history, you know that the name *Judah* is the source of the name of the Roman province of Judea. Moreover, the name "Judea" is the source of our more-modern designations for the people of Israel: the Jews, the religion of Judaism, and the Jewish people. Moreover, both the biblical king David and Jesus of Nazareth, a religious teacher whom Christians believe to be the Messiah foretold in the Hebrew Bible, come from the tribe of Judah.

The names of other tribes, however, you may not recognize at all. That is because they were conquered by the Assyrian king Shalmaneser V in 722 BC. In that year, Shalmaneser V sacked their capital city at Samaria. He deported almost its entire population, moved them to various parts of the Assyrian Empire, and forced them to intermarry with other peoples of the ancient Near Eastern world. Those tribes have been completely erased from the pages of world history—but, that is a story for another unit.

For now, let us return to the time of the Patriarchs, for it is during Jacob's lifetime that the (ever-increasing) people of Israel migrate into the land of Egypt. The story is that of Jacob's eleven sons, Jacob favored one son named **Joseph** above all the others. This favoritism drove Joseph's brothers mad with jealousy, and they sold the young boy to slave traders en route to Egypt. Joseph would spend time both as a slave and as a prisoner in Egypt. But Joseph had the unique ability to interpret dreams, and this gift attracted the attention of **Pharaoh**, the king of Egypt. The nameless Pharaoh had a dream of skinny cows eating healthy cows, a dream that Joseph correctly interpreted as predicting a famine that would soon swallow up the whole of the ancient Near East. Pharaoh appointed Joseph in charge of the granaries, and Joseph's leadership allowed the Egyptians to survive the famine. In time, Joseph would become the second-in-command of all of Egypt, rising from a slave to Egypt's most powerful official.

As a result, when Jacob sent his sons to Egypt to buy grain, they had to buy that grain directly from Joseph, the brother they themselves had sold into slavery. Joseph was in a position to save his family from starvation, which he gladly did. Joseph said to his brothers, "You meant [selling me into slavery] for evil, but God meant it for good," (Gen 50:20). The biblical story describes God bringing great good out of Joseph's suffering because, by such hardship, Joseph was in the position to offer his brothers and their families a place in Egypt. Jacob and his sons then relocate to the Nile Delta and live in the town of Goshen until the famine ends.

But, where do these particular events fit in with the narrative of ancient Near Eastern and ancient Egyptian history?

Joseph's rise may have coincided with the arrival of the Hyksos in Egypt. The **Hyksos** were a Semitic group of chariot-driving warriors who ruled Egypt during the Second Intermediate Period in Egyptian history. The Hyksos invaded Egypt circa 1663 and ruled from their

Vocabulary

‖ A HYKSOS SHEPHERD / 19ᵀᴴ BC

capital at Avaris in the Nile Delta (Bauer 179-180). You may remember we know precious little about the Hyksos except that they drove chariots, used compound bows, and came from somewhere near Canaan (Stearns 30). The 3ʳᵈ-century BC Egyptian historian Manetho describes the Hyksos as "invaders of obscure race [who] marched in confidence of victory against our land... burned our cities ruthlessly, razed to the ground the temples of gods, and treated all the natives with a cruel hostility," (Bauer 179).

In reality, the reign of the Hyksos might not have been as terrible as Manetho described. The Hyksos adopted Egyptian customs and continued using Egyptian for their record-keeping (Bauer 180; Stearns 30). They may not have destroyed as many cities and temples as Manetho relates. Most important-ly, they may have allowed Joseph's family to settle in the Nile Delta simply because they were Semitic in origin like the Hyksos.

But the native Egyptians hated the presence of the Hyksos in their land. The pharaoh Amosis (or Ahmose, who reigned from 1552-1527) drove the Hyksos from the Nile Delta and re-established Egypt's dominance over their own land. Amosis established the famed New Kingdom Egypt, a period when Egypt be-came an aggressive military power.

Thus, when the Bible speaks of "a new king over Egypt, [one] who did not know Joseph," they may have been referring to a pharaoh from this new dynasty (Exodus 1:8). That "new king" may have regarded the Israelites with suspicion and fear, and thus took steps to remove any possible threat the Israelites might pose to the Egyptian people. And so, Pharaoh, king of Egypt,

MAP OF NEW KINGDOM EGYPT

enslaved the descendants of Joseph, forcing them into massive building projects. The descendants of Abraham, Isaac, and Jacob, would live as slaves in the land of Egypt for the next four hundred years.

The Israelites as Slaves in Egypt

The book of Exodus, the second book of the Hebrew and Christian Bible, describes some of the most significant events in the life of the people of Israel. The word **Exodus** refers to the deliverance of the people of Israel from their slavery in Egypt. The word *Exodus* comes from two Greek words: the preposition *ex*, meaning "out of" and *odus*, meaning 'way." Thus, the *Exodus* is literally *the way out* of the people of Israel from their centuries-long period as slaves in the land of Egypt. This event is recorded in the book of Exodus, written by the prophet **Moses**, the second book in the Torah.

Moreover, the Exodus is the defining moment for the people of Israel, the starting point for their history as a nation, and the event to which so much of Jewish religion, culture, and identity refer back. The Exodus opens with the Israelites languishing as slaves in the land of Egypt but ends as the Israelites have been freed and are making their way to the land of Canaan, the land God promised to give to the descendants of Abraham. Exodus also includes the giving of the Ten Commandments, the ten rules by which the Israelites were to govern themselves if they were to live long in this new promised land.

The book of Exodus opens with the ascension of this "new king over Egypt." This new king, known only by the title "Pharaoh", from the Egyptian word for "Big House", the residence in which the king resided, then took steps to

Vocabulary

The Exodus

The word *Exodus* refers to the deliverance of the people of Israel from their slavery in Egypt; the word *Exodus* comes from two Greek words: *ex*, meaning "out of" and *odus*, meaning "way." Thus, *Exodus* refers to the Jewish people literally *going out* of their slavery in Egypt.

Moses

The leader of the Exodus, the author of the Torah, the first five books of the Bible, and a prophet who, in the book Exodus, spoke to and relayed God's instructions to Israel.

Pogrom

A pogrom is an attempt to destroy an entire people, acts that are often directed against the people of Israel.

Prophet

A figure who, in the Bible, would speak to and relay the instructions of God to the people of Israel.

The Ten Plagues

A series of devastating natural events that God, through Moses, brought on Egypt which convinced Pharaoh to release the Israelites from their slavery in Egypt.

The Ten Commandments

The Ten Commandments are the ten rules that God gave to Moses and the people of Israel. They included prohibitions against murder, theft, and idolatry. The Ten Commandments are also known as the Mosaic law.

subjugate and enslave the Hebrews. Pharaoh forced the Hebrew people to build the massive store cities of Pithom and Raamses in the Nile Delta. These sites were part-training grounds, part barracks, and part weapons-manufacturing centers close to the border with Syria-Palestine. That way, the Pharaoh might always have a force ready to either extend or defend Egypt's borders. Later in Egyptian history, the pharaoh Ramses II launched his campaign against the Hittites from the store city of Raamses.

Then, the Pharaoh commanded that all of the Hebrew baby boys be killed. Sadly, this order is the first instance of a **pogrom**, an attempt by an unjust and cruel government to destroy the people of Israel, with the last and most horrific of such pogroms being the Holocaust World War II. As with other such attempts, Pharaoh undertook this pogrom with the hope of extinguishing the people of Israel from the land of Egypt. The 1st-century Jewish historian Josephus relates that this pogrom was directed at exterminating one Hebrew boy "born to the Israelites, who, if he were reared, would bring the Egyptian dominion low, and would raise the Israelites" (77).

Now, at this undetermined date during the age of New Kingdom Egypt, the Hebrews had been reduced to a state of terrible servitude, building storehouses for Pharaoh and toiling in the land of Egypt (Exodus 12:40-41; Isserlin 50). In total, the Hebrews remained in Egypt for 430 years from the time of Joseph to the time of the Exodus.

The Exodus

The book of Exodus starts with the people of Israel enslaved in Egypt. God calls a **prophet**, a figure who in the Bible would speak with God and relayed instructions from God (the word Torah, after all, means "law" or "instruction") named Moses, who helped bring about the release of the Israelites from their toil.

Moses himself narrowly escaped the Pharaoh's pogrom. Many of the Hebrew midwives, women who helped assist in the delivery of babies, did not go along with Pharaoh's decree. On top of that, Moses' mother also hid her baby in a basket in the Nile, where Pharaoh's daughter would find the baby boy Moses. Finding the baby Moses to be an exceptionally beautiful child, Pharaoh's daughter decided to adopt the child as her own, even hiring Moses' mother to be the boy's nursemaid. From then on, Moses grew up in Pharaoh's palace and received the kind of education given to an Egyptian prince.

One day, when Moses was a young man, he took a walk outside the palace. He saw an Egyptian overseer striking a Hebrew slave. At this sight, Moses grew incensed and, unable to control his emotions, struck down the Egyptian. Afraid that others would find out about what

BIG IDEA

Moses' birth is similar to that of myths in which a ruler marked for future greatness narrowly escapes destruction: Cyrus the Great, Romulus and Remus, and many Greek heroes have similar backstories. The story is also similar to that of Sargon of Akkad, whose mother placed him in a basket in the Euphrates, a story that Moses' mother, for instance, may have imitated to save her boy. It does not mean that any of these events are any "less true" because of shared events and themes between them, but it is helpful to know of them beforehand.

he had done, Moses fled from Egypt and moved to the land of Midian. Midian was a desolate region located on the Sinai Peninsula. Moses married into a local family and became a shepherd, tending sheep and raising a family. There Moses stayed for years, a time period long enough that Pharaoh died while the Israelites continued to groan under their servitude. But one day Moses would see something that would bring him back to Egypt.

The Exodus

Moses saw a bush "burning, yet it was not consumed", and heard the voice of God speaking to him (Exodus 3:2-3): One would think Moses would return to Egypt in glory, full of confidence, and at the head of a large army. But Moses related how nervous he was, saying that he was not important enough to perform such a task (Exodus 3:11), that no one would listen to him or believe that God had spoken to him (Exodus 4:1), and lastly that Moses was simply not an eloquent public speaker (Exodus 4:10). In short, Moses was just a bad fit for the task that God had in mind for him. To all of these concerns, God promised to stand with Moses and even provide Moses' brother to help him speak in public if needed and provide a series of miraculous signs to free the Israelites from their slavery.

These signs culminate in the **Ten Plagues**, a series of devastating natural events that God, through Moses, brought down upon the land of Egypt. These Ten Plagues showcased God's power over and against the gods of Egypt until Pharaoh finally released the people of Israel from their bondage. At the conclusion of the Ten Plagues, Pharaoh, king of Egypt, finally relented. He permitted Moses to bring the people of Israel out of Egypt and into the desert to worship God. But Pharaoh changed his mind and instead pursued the Israelites into the desert, catching up to them at the shores of the Red Sea. The Israelites were terrified and complained

that Moses had brought them out of Egypt to destroy them but, according to Exodus, God miraculously parted the waters of the Red Sea. That way, the Israelites could walk across it "as if on dry land". When Pharaoh followed them into the waters, God brought the waters crashing down on them and drowned Pharaoh and all his army.

At this point, the Israelites are freed from their slavery. But, they have not yet made it into the promised land of Canaan. God directed Moses and the people of Israel to Mount Sinai, upon which God gave Moses **the Ten Commandments**, the ten rules by which the Israelites were to govern their lives if they were to live long in the land of Canaan. These rules included prohibitions against murder, theft, and idolatry, the worship of other gods. The Ten Commandments contain the rules to govern the Israelites' dealings with each other, such as the prohibitions against fraud and coveting, as well as rules governing their relationship with the God who freed them from Egypt. These laws include the right worship of God and prohibitions against using the Lord's name in vain. But then, according to the biblical story, the Israelites spent forty years in the desert as a punishment for complaining against God and rejecting the command to enter into the promised land of Canaan (the Israelites were scared of the size of the inhabitants there). The book of Deuteronomy, the last book of the Torah, found the Israelites ready to enter into the land of Canaan after forty long years of living in tents in the desert.

For this chapter, we have three special investigations and a primary source analysis. The first is a Closer Look at the Ten Plagues of Egypt and how each plague may have been directed against one of the Egyptian gods. Second is a Closer Look at the Pharaoh of the Exodus to try and find the identity of the otherwise-unnamed Pharaoh. Last is a primary source analysis of the Ten Commandments.

How does the story of Joseph and the other sons of Jacob "fit" into the history of ancient Egypt? Why might the Hyksos have been more likely to help the Hebrew people, and the new Egyptian pharaohs less likely to help them?

Why does Pharaoh command that all the Hebrew boys be destroyed? How does Moses escape such a terrifying fate?

What were the Ten Plagues, and what were they intended to demonstrate to the people of Israel? To the people of Egypt?

Closer Look: The Ten Plagues of Egypt

The Ten Plagues of Egypt range from turning the Nile to blood to bringing clouds of locusts, frogs, and gnat upon the land of Egypt. Each plague seems calculated to show that the gods of ancient Egypt, including Pharaoh, who believed that he himself was a god, are fake, helpless deities. These plagues culminated in the destruction of the firstborn sons of all of the people of Egypt, up to and including Pharaoh. At this point, Pharaoh finally relented and lets the people of Israel go. From here, we will examine each of the Ten Plagues of Egypt and how they may have occurred in response to one particular Egyptian god or practice.

The Ten Plagues

Plague	Text of Exodus	Relevance for Egyptian Mythology (if applicable)	Photo (if applicable)
1st Plague / The Nile River to Blood	*Moses and Aaron did so, as God commanded; and he lifted up the rod, and struck the waters that were in the river, in the sight of Pharaoh, and in the sight of his servants; and all the waters that were in the river were turned to blood. The fish that were in the river died. The river became foul. The Egyptians couldn't drink water from the river. The blood was throughout all the land of Egypt.* (Exodus 7:17-19).	Egypt's prosperity depended upon the smooth, steady rising and falling of the Nile River each year. The king of Egypt performed a series of rituals to help ensure that the Nile would deposit the nutrient-rich topsoil needed for intensive agriculture. The Egyptians identified several deities with the Nile, including Khnum (*right*), Hapi, and Osiris, for whom the "Nile was [his] bloodstream" (Hill and Walton 115).	

The Ten Plagues (Continued)

Plague	Text of Exodus	Relevance for Egyptian Mythology (if applicable)	Photo (if applicable)
2nd *Plague* / *Frogs*	*If you refuse to let [my people] go, behold, I will plague all your borders with frogs. 3 The river will swarm with frogs, which will go up and come into your house, and into your bedroom, and on your bed, and into the house of your servants, and on your people, and into your ovens, and into your kneading troughs,* (Exodus 8:2-3).	The Egyptians worshiped a fertility goddess named Heqet, who had the head of a frog. The Egyptians worshiped several different fertility deities (like Heqet, *right*) to ensure that the land would produce enough food for the people of Egypt to live on and that Egyptian families would be blessed with children. The idea of a "swarm" of frogs turns this fertility goddess upon its head.	
3rd *Plague* / *Gnats*	*...and Aaron stretched out his hand with his rod, and struck the dust of the earth, and there were lice on man, and on animal; all the dust of the earth became lice throughout all the land of Egypt,* (Exodus 8:17).		
4th *Plague* / *Flies*	*... if you will not let my people go, behold, I will send swarms of flies on you, and on your servants, and on your people, and into your houses. The houses of the Egyptians shall be full of swarms of flies, and also the ground they are on,* (Exodus 8:21).		
5th *Plague* / *A plague of flies*	*For if you refuse to let them go, and hold them still, behold, Yahweh's hand is on your livestock which are in the field, on the horses, on the donkeys, on the camels, on the herds, and on the flocks with a very grievous pestilence,* (Exodus 9:2-3).	Livestock was crucial to an ancient, agricultural society, and the Egyptians worshiped many different deities connected to cows: Hathor, a goddess with the head of a cow, and the Apis bull, a manifestation of Ptah, a god also associated with artisans.	

The Ten Plagues (*Continued*)

Plague	Text of Exodus	Relevance for Egyptian Mythology (if applicable)	Photo (if applicable)
6th Plague / Boils	*Yahweh said to Moses and to Aaron, "Take handfuls of ashes of the furnace, and let Moses sprinkle it toward the sky in the sight of Pharaoh. It shall become small dust over all the land of Egypt, and shall be boils and blisters breaking out on man and on animal, throughout all the land of Egypt." (Exodus 9:8-9).*		
7th Plague / Hail	*Now therefore command that all of your livestock and all that you have in the field be brought into shelter. The hail will come down on every man and animal that is found in the field, and isn't brought home, and they will die, (Exodus 9:19).*	Hailstorms would have destroyed the crops of the Egyptians, an area guarded over by Neper, the Egyptian god of grain.	
8th Plague / Locusts	*Or else, if you refuse to let my people go, behold, tomorrow I will bring locusts into your country, and they shall cover the surface of the earth, so that one won't be able to see the earth. They shall eat the residue of that which has escaped, which remains to you from the hail, and shall eat every tree which grows for you out of the field, (Exodus 10:4-6).*	Pharaoh was also responsible for the agricultural productivity of Egypt year in and year out.	
9th Plague / Darkness	*Yahweh said to Moses, "Stretch out your hand toward the sky, that there may be darkness over the land of Egypt, even darkness which may be felt." Moses stretched out his hand toward the sky, and there was a thick darkness in all the land of Egypt for three days. They didn't see one another, and nobody rose from his place for three days; but all the children of Israel had light in their dwellings, (Exodus 10:21-23).*	Egyptians worshiped a variety of solar deities that included Amun, Ra, and Horus (right), whereas the pharaoh was the divine embodiment of these solar deities while he was alive on earth. The idea that the God of the Hebrews could blot out the sun and cover the land in darkness makes it apparent that the pharaoh does not have any such power over the sun (or any other force of nature).	

The Ten Plagues (*Continued*)

Plague	Text of Exodus	Relevance for Egyptian Mythology (if applicable)	Photo (if applicable)
10th Plague / The Death of the Egyptian First Born	*About midnight I [the Lord] will go out into the middle of Egypt, and all the firstborn in the land of Egypt shall die, from the firstborn of Pharaoh who sits on his throne, even to the firstborn of the female servant who is behind the mill, and all the firstborn of livestock. There will be a great cry throughout all the land of Egypt, such as there has not been, nor will be any more...(Exodus 11:4-6).*	The Egyptians worshiped Pharaoh as a god, the representative of the sun-god Horus while Pharaoh was alive and identified with Osiris, the god of the underworld, once he died. The death of the Egyptian firstborn, as well as the other 10 Plagues of Egypt, showcases that the pharaoh is not a god among gods but a mortal man.	

✦ Closer Look Questions

Which of these plagues would have been the hardest to endure? Explain your reasoning.

What is the purpose behind the 10 Plagues? Why these plagues in particular, and not others?

Why send these plagues at all? Are these plagues justified in light of Pharaoh's refusal to let the Hebrew people go?

Could there be any naturalistic reasons that may account for the plagues? An earthquake? A volcanic eruption, etc.?

Closer Look: Who was the Pharaoh of the Exodus?

PHARAOH MAY BE ONE of the central characters in the book of Exodus, but Moses never refers to him by name. Instead, Moses called him only by the title *Pharaoh*, which means "big house." This is as if we referred to the President as the *White House* instead of their first and last name. Given that Moses grew up in the palace of Pharaoh, he not only knew Pharaoh's identity but also numerous personal details about Pharaoh's life and background. So why doesn't Moses provide his readers with Pharaoh's real name? And who might the pharaoh of the Exodus actually be?

Let's go ahead and weigh the candidates for the Pharaoh of the Exodus.

Pharaoh #1 / Thutmose III

We have two candidates for the Pharaoh of the Exodus based on the date of the Exodus. The first date is known as *the early date* when the Exodus could have taken place from 1446 to 1437 BC. These dates are based on the construction of Solomon's Temple in Jerusalem. According to I Kings 6:1, that construction began in the fourth year of Solomon's reign in a year which was 480 years after the Exodus (Hill and Walton 106). That could place the Exodus somewhere between, with some margin for error, between 1446 to 1437 BC, a period when the energetic conqueror Thutmose III ruled as Pharaoh.

That makes our first candidate for Pharaoh of the Exodus Thutmose III, who ruled from 1479 to 1429 BC. As pharaoh, Thutmosis was a brilliant military general. He

THUTMOSIS III / 1479 – 1429 BC

would have had need for the kind of store cities that the Hebrews built. Note also the similarity between the name Thut*mosis*, "Thoth is born" and *Moses*, so named because he was drawn "out of the water" (Exodus 2:10).

Pharaoh #2 / Tutankhamun or Ramses II

The dates in I Kings 6:1 could be symbolic and metaphorical, rather than real, literal dates. That makes the range of other possible dates from 1350 to 1225 BC. This view is based more on the geographical details of Exodus, such as the references to the building of Pithom and Raamses in the Nile Delta. That would make the pharaoh of the Exodus either Tutankhamun (reign, 1362 to 1352 BC) or, more likely, Ramses II (reign, 1304 to 1237 BC). The store cities of Pithom and Raamses were built by the Egyptian pharaoh Seti I and his successor, Ramses II (Cline 89-90). The Jewish historian Josephus identified the Egyptian princess who rescued Moses as "Thermuthis," who may have been the daughter of Seti I (79). Ramses II also lost a son under tragic circumstances, circumstances that coincide with the events described in the book of Exodus.

Moreover, this date fits better with other archaeological evidence for the period, for the 13th century BC was a period of chaos and devastation as the Late Bronze Age came to a close. Subsequently, the Exodus' chaotic events were just one chaotic event occurring in a whole series of earthquakes, famines, and barbarian invasions flaring up across the Mediterranean world. Thus, the deliverance of the Hebrew people may have coincided with other epoch-ending, cataclysmic events occurring all over the ancient Mediterranean world.

‖ **RAMSES II / 1304 - 1237 BC**

Pharaoh #3 / There was no Pharaoh

There was no Pharaoh because there was no Exodus. One explanation is that the Hebrew people needed a founding myth to help explain their origins and their beginnings as a people. As a result, Moses (or a group of people that may or may not have included Moses) took several different traditions and stitched them together to create such a tradition. It is as if the Exodus were a myth in the same way we might view the story of Romulus and Remus, a myth told to tell the origins of Rome. In other words, the Exodus may have been a much simpler affair if it even happened at all but in all regards, the people of Israel composed the story of the Ten Plagues, a heart-hardened Pharaoh, and the parting of the Red Sea to give themselves a story that would bring the descendants of Abraham together as one nation. But is that the only way to read the evidence—or lack thereof—available to us?

Recall that the Exodus is the foundation story for the people of Israel, the moment when they are delivered from bondage, assembled into a nation, and inherit the land of Canaan promised to their forefather Abraham. Despite the central place that the Exodus plays in the life of the people of Israel, and the awe-inspiring events depicted in the book of Exodus, there is actually little to no archaeological evidence for the Exodus event. Nor is there any textual evidence for the Ten Plagues of Egypt or the parting of the Red Sea outside of the Bible itself. One additional possible explanation with which student historians must grapple is that the events of the Exodus did not happen either the way they are portrayed or that they did not even happen at all. Indeed, how should we view such an important historical event, if we can't find any historical evidence to corroborate what is written in the pages of Exodus?

The lack of evidence requires careful work on the part of the student historian. There are always limits to what we can know about the past and what we can discover through textual study and archaeology. Despite the importance of the Exodus to the biblical narrative, the events of the Exodus do not seem to have been of the kind that would have left remains available to archaeologists to study thousands of years later. For instance, the Israelites lived in tents in the desert for forty years, tents they carried into the promised land. Such tents would have biodegraded into the literal sands of Sinai had they left behind the tents anyway (Cline 92). The lack of evidence for the Exodus may just be normal, given the limits of what we can learn from the archaeological record.

Lastly, the two possible candidates for the pharaoh of the Exodus may provide a clue for the lack of textual support outside the Bible. The early date of the Exodus points to Thutmose III as pharaoh and the late date to Ramses II, and both pharaohs actually spent considerable time altering or manipulating the textual record describing various events of their reigns.

For example, when Thutmose III began pharaoh, he undertook a campaign to make his aunt Hatshepsut, who reigned as a (male) pharaoh from 1490-1468 BC, disappear from the historical record (Cline 28). Hatshepsut ruled in Thutmose's place, a fact he so deeply resented he erased her name or visage from official relief carvings, inscriptions, and public monuments that Hatshepsut had commissioned during her reign. That Thutmose III was unsuccessful in this endeavor (we do know a lot about Hatshepsut) speaks to the large numbers of high officials, bureaucrats, and mortuary priests still loyal to Hatshepsut for her lavish gifts to them. They did not wholeheartedly comply with Thutmose III's order to extirpate her from the textual record. Ramses II also embellished the events of the Battle of Qadesh. If you look through his mortuary temples, the pyramid drawings make it appear as if he won the battle when, in reality, he had fought it to a draw. Both pharaohs attempted to alter the textual record to make themselves appear as grander, more powerful, more exalted pharaohs. It may be entirely possible that Pharaoh—whoever he may have been—and the rest of the Egyptian religious establishment chose not to write about, speak about, or in any way acknowledge the presence of the Hebrews in Egypt (aside from the sheer hatred we see of their Semitic relatives, the Hyksos). On one level, this intentional silence makes some sense. The 10 Plagues demonstrated just how little power Pharaoh or his officials truly had, a reality that few pharaohs would ever want to acknowledge by commissioning a relief carving or a public monument. As a result, we may know so little about the Exodus from the perspective of the Egyptians because the Egyptians chose to ignore the event and move on (Bauer 236).

But the Exodus is the defining moment for the people of Israel. In the Exodus, Israel's people cease to be an isolated and fragmented collection of tribes and become a real nation. The events of the Exodus provide a powerful "founding story" to bind together these people into a cohesive and dynamic nation under the direction of a God who not only rules the universe but also moved to save his people from slavery when they could not save themselves. Moreover, the people of Israel have celebrated the Exodus events every year since in the holiday of Passover by reading the Torah and sharing in the Passover meal as outlined in Exodus 12:43-50 and 13:3-16.

We may never know specific details about the Exodus, such as the precise date for the Exodus event, Pharaoh's real name and identity, and how the plagues happened. But the story of God moving to save his people from harrowing slavery, and the implications one can draw from the Exodus narrative, have profoundly influenced the course of world history in general and the Western tradition in particular. That is because the Exodus really serves as the starting point for the influence that the Hebrews have had on the course of human events ever after.

Who are the candidates for the pharaoh of the Exodus and what is the evidence for and against these individuals?

Why is there so little evidence for the Exodus outside of the Bible, both from the Egyptian textual record and from the findings of archaeology?

Primary Source Analysis / The Law

RECALL THAT PRIMARY SOURCES are documents (or similar artifacts) created at or very near the time of the event under investigation. They are a record created around the time of the event the historian is studying, and they can include the chronicles of great kings, letters, poems, songs, diaries, historical artifacts, even paintings.

Title: The Ten Commandments

Author & Date: According to Jewish and church tradition, Moses wrote the first five books of the Bible collectively known as the Torah. The Torah includes the books of Genesis, Exodus, Leviticus, Numbers, and Deuteronomy. The Ten Commandments actually appear in two books of the Torah: first in Exodus, following the events at the Red Sea. The second time comes in the book of Deuteronomy, in a kind of speech that Moses gives near the end of his life and just as the Israelites are about to enter into the promised land of Canaan. The date of the composition of the Torah depends on the date of Exodus, which could have occurred sometime during the 15th to the 13th centuries.

Description: The Ten Commandments are the ten words, the ten rules, the ten laws God gave to his people, Israel. These rules focus on the way the God of Israel would be worshiped by his people, as well as rules for their conduct once they enter into the land of Canaan, the land God promised to give to their forefathers. In the book of Exodus, God gave the Ten Commandments to his servant, Moses, who then delivered them to the people on Israel written on tablets of stone. God gives these rules after he has already redeemed from their slavery in Egypt, and he gave these

TEN COMMANDMENTS, JEKUTHIEL SOFER
Amsterdam Esnoga synagogue (1768 AD)

laws for the good of the Israelites once they enter into Canaan, a land flowing with milk and honey. If the Israelites follow them, they will enjoy God's blessing in the land He has promised to give to them.

The Ten Commandments appear in the proceeding pages, followed by a helpful chart to organize the Ten Commandments, reading comprehension, and a writing prompt. Text comes from the World English Bible.

¹⁹ Exodus 19: *Moses on Mount Sinai*

1 In the third month after the children of Israel had gone out of the land of Egypt, on that same day they came into the **wilderness of Sinai**. 2 When they had

departed from **Rephidim**, and had come to the wilderness of Sinai, they encamped in the wilderness; and there Israel encamped before the mountain. 3 Moses went up to God, and **Yahweh** called to him out of the mountain, saying, "This is what you shall tell the house of Jacob, and tell the children of Israel: 4 'You have seen what I did to the Egyptians, and how I bore you on eagles' wings, and brought you to myself. 5 Now therefore, if you will indeed obey my voice and keep my covenant, then you shall be my own possession from among all peoples; for all the earth is mine; 6 and you shall be to me a kingdom of priests and a holy nation.' These are the words which you shall speak to the children of Israel."

7 Moses came and called for the elders of the people, and set before them all these words which the Lord commanded him. 8 All the people answered together, and said, "All that Yahweh has spoken we will do."

Moses reported the words of the people to Yahweh. 9 Yahweh said to Moses, "Behold, I come to you in a thick cloud, that the people may hear when I speak with you, and may also believe you forever." Moses told the words of the people to Yahweh. 10 Yahweh said to Moses, "Go to the people, and **sanctify them** today and tomorrow, and let them wash their garments, 11 and be ready for the third day; for on the third day Yahweh will come down in the sight of all the people on Mount Sinai. 12 You shall set bounds to the people all around, saying, 'Be careful that you don't go up onto the mountain, or touch its border. Whoever touches the mountain shall be surely put to death. 13 No hand shall touch him, but he shall surely be stoned or shot through; whether it is animal or man, he shall not live.' When the trumpet sounds long, they shall come up to the mountain."

14 Moses went down from the mountain to the people, and sanctified the people; and they washed their clothes. 15 He said to the people, "Be ready by the third day."

16 On the third day, when it was morning, there were thunders and lightnings, and a thick cloud on the mountain, and the sound of an exceedingly loud trumpet; and all the people who were in the camp trembled. 17 Moses led the people out of the camp to meet God; and they stood at the lower part of the mountain. 18 All of Mount Sinai smoked, because Yahweh descended on it in fire; and its smoke ascended like the smoke of a furnace, and the whole mountain quaked greatly. 19 When the sound of the trumpet grew louder and louder, Moses spoke, and God answered him by a voice. 20 Yahweh came down on Mount Sinai, to the top of the mountain. Yahweh called Moses to the top of the mountain, and Moses went up.

21 The Lord said to Moses, "Go down, warn the people, lest they break through to Yahweh to gaze, and many of them perish. 22 Let the priests also, who come near to the Lord, sanctify themselves, so that the Lord God may not break out on them."

23 Moses said to the Lord, "The people can't come up to Mount Sinai, for you warned us, saying, 'Set bounds around the mountain, and sanctify it.'"

24 The Lord said to him, "Go down! You shall bring Aaron up with you, but don't let the priests and the people break through to come up to the Lord, lest he break out against them."

25 So Moses went down to the people, and told them.

²⁰ Exodus 20: *The Ten Commandments*

1 God spoke all these words, saying, 2 "I am the Lord your God, **who brought you** out of the land of Egypt, out of the house of bondage.

Vocabulary

Sinai

According to Jewish and Christian tradition, God gives the Ten Commandments to Moses on top of Mount Sinai, a small mountain on the Sinai Peninsula. The Sinai Peninsula is a relatively-small triangle-shaped piece of land connecting Africa to Asia. Some historians and biblical scholars suggest the giving of the Ten Commandments might have taken place elsewhere, with various mountains on the Arabian Peninsula suggested as an alternative.

Rephidim

The location of the site called *Rephidim* is unknown but may be somewhere on the Sinai or the Arabian Peninsula.

...wilderness of Sinai

Moses uses the word *wilderness* is often used as a symbol for the kind of life lived apart from God, a world full of hardship and struggle.

Yahweh

Yahweh is the name God uses to describe himself; the name derives from the Hebrew verb *to be*.

...sanctify them

The word *sanctify* means to "make holy" or "to set something apart for a noble use".

...who brought you

Notice how God begins the Ten Commandments reminding the Israelites how he has already saved them from slavery.

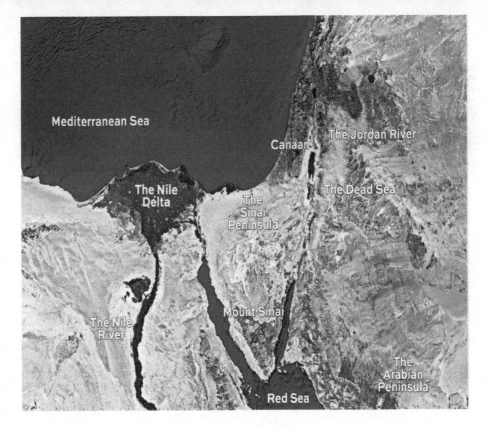

‖ **SINAI PENINSULA AND SURROUNDING AREAS**

3 "You shall have **no other gods** before me.

4 "You shall not make for yourselves an **idol**, nor any image of anything that is in the heavens above, or that is in the earth beneath, or that is in the water under the earth: 5 you shall not bow yourself down to them, nor serve them, for I, Yahweh your God, am a jealous God, visiting the iniquity of the fathers on the children, on the third and on the fourth generation of those who hate me, 6 and showing loving kindness to thousands of those who love me and keep my commandments.

7 "You shall not misuse the name of the Lord your God, for Yahweh will not hold him guiltless who misuses his name.

8 "Remember **the Sabbath day**, to keep it holy. 9 You shall labor six days, and do all your work, 10 but the seventh day is a Sabbath to Yahweh your God. You shall not do any work in it, you, nor your son, nor your daughter, your male servant, nor your female servant, nor your livestock, nor your stranger who is within your gates; 11 for **in six days** Yahweh made heaven and earth, the sea, and all that is in them, and rested the seventh day; therefore Yahweh blessed the Sabbath day, and made it holy.

12 "Honor your father and your mother, that your days may be long in the land which Yahweh your God gives you.

13 "You shall not murder.

THE COMMANDMENTS IN HEBREW

The photo above comes from the Dead Sea Scrolls, *written around the* 1st c. AD.

14 "You shall not commit adultery.

15 "You shall not steal.

16 "You shall not give false testimony against your neighbor.

17 "You shall not covet your neighbor's house. You shall not covet your neighbor's wife, nor his male servant, nor his female servant, nor his ox, nor his donkey, nor anything that is your neighbor's."

18 All the people perceived the thunderings, the lightnings, the sound of the trumpet, and the mountain smoking. When the people saw it, they trembled, and stayed at a distance. 19 They said to Moses, "Speak with us yourself, and we will listen; but don't let God speak with us, lest we die."

20 Moses said to the people, "Don't be afraid, for God has come to test you, and that his fear may be before you, that you won't sin." 21 The people stayed at a distance, and Moses came near to the thick darkness where God was.

22 Yahweh said to Moses, "This is what you shall tell the children of Israel: 'You yourselves have seen that I have talked with you from heaven. 23 You shall most certainly not make gods of silver or gods of gold for yourselves to be alongside me. 24 You shall make an altar of earth for me, and shall sacrifice on it your burnt offerings and your peace offerings, your sheep and your cattle. In every place where I record my name I will come to you and I will bless you. 25 If you make me an altar of stone, you shall not build it of cut stones; for if you lift up your tool on it, you have polluted it. 26 You shall not go up by steps to my altar, so that you may not be exposed to it.'

Vocabulary

...no other gods

The Israelites are to worship no other gods (such as those of the Egyptians or the Canaanites). Often, this commandment is interpreted in light of the relationship God wants to have with his people, Israel, similar to that of a parent and child. Moreover, many peoples in the ancient world worshiped their gods by hurting themselves or innocent people—something the God of Israel does not want the Israelites to do in worshiping him.

...idol

A statue made of wood or said to represent or embody a particular god or goddess. In the ancient world, such objects were worshiped by people who believed they could channel the god or goddess of whom it was a representation. Only Jews and Christians did not engage in this practice.

...the Sabbath Day

The Sabbath is a day of rest, wherein the ancient Israelites and modern-day people who hold to the religious traditions of Judaism and Christianity refrain from working.

...in six days Yahweh

The commandment to honor the Sabbath is rooted in creation and the opening pages of Genesis. The Sabbath is in contrast to the peoples of the ancient world who often worked for weeks on end until the end of a harvest season, followed by months of inactivity.

The Ten Commandments

The word *commandment* comes from the Hebrew word *torah*, meaning "rule," "word," or "instruction." Each of the ten commandments is a word of instruction to the people of Israel who, if they follow these commandments, would enjoy God's blessings whilst they lived in the land of Canaan. Use the chart below to help organize the text of the Ten Commandments and summarize the meaning of each one.

Commandment	Text of Exodus	Student Summaries
1st Commandment	You shall have no other gods before me v. 3	
2nd Commandment	You shall not make for yourselves an idol, nor any image of anything that is in the heavens above, or that is in the earth beneath, or that is in the water under the earth. v. 4	

The Ten Commandments (*Continued*)

Commandment	Text of Exodus	Student Summaries
3rd Commandment	You shall not misuse the name of Yahweh your God. v. 7	
4th Commandment	Remember the Sabbath day, to keep it holy. 9 You shall labor six days, and do all your work, 10 but the seventh day is a Sabbath to the Lord your God. v. 8-10.	
5th Commandment	Honor your father and your mother, that your days may be long in the land which Yahweh your God gives you. v. 12	
6th Commandment	You shall not murder. v. 13	

The Ten Commandments (*Continued*)

Commandment	Text of Exodus	Student Summaries
7th Commandment	You shall not commit adultery. v. 14	
8th Commandment	You shall not steal. v. 15	
9th Commandment	You shall not give false testimony against your neighbor. v. 16	
10th Commandment	You shall not covet your neighbor's house. You shall not covet your neighbor's wife, nor his male servant, nor his female servant, nor his ox, nor his donkey, nor anything that is your neighbor's. v. 17	

Why do the Ten Commandments begin with a reminder about the Exodus? i.e., I am the Lord your God, who brought you out of slavery in Egypt...

....

....

....

....

....

....

If you were to divide the Ten Commandments into two groups or two categories of laws, what would these categories be? How would you organize the Ten Commandments?

....

....

....

....

....

....

What do the Ten Commandments imply about God and his relationship with the people of Israel in particular, and also with humanity in general? What does the God of the Bible seem to care about most?

Of the Ten Commandments, which one of them would be the hardest to keep? Explain your reasoning.

The Israelites in the Land

AT LONG LAST, the people of Israel have entered into the land of Canaan. **Canaan** sits on the eastern coastline of the Mediterranean Sea (sometimes called the "Great Sea"). There is a coastal plain running east, a series of elevated hills suitable for raising sheep and other livestock even further east, and a desert country in the south, called the "Negeb." Then, in the east, separating Israel from the Arabian Desert, are the Sea of Galilee, the Jordan River Valley, and the Dead Sea, so-named because of its high salt content (nothing grows in it) and its incredibly low elevation point (1,412 feet below sea level). Unlike Egypt, the region of Canaan does not have a river system suitable for sustained, intensive agriculture, which left the Israelites at the mercy of the rains. Still, once established, the Israelite settlements slowly and steadily grew.

But of course, there were people already living in Canaan. The peoples of Canaan lived in small, scattered kingdoms which had been conquered by the Egyptians, and the Canaanite kings served as vassals to the Egyptian pharaoh. The book of Joshua and Judges describes the entrance of the Israelites into the land of Canaan as a kind of conquest, with the Israelites going to war against the land's original inhabitants. The authors depict this conquest as a kind of act of judgment on the peoples of Canaan for generations of violence and wild, riotous living. Some letters in the Amarna archives, the former capital city of Akhenaten, have survived from these Canaanite kings. These kings request aid and assistance from Pharaoh against the *Habiru*, a name that could refer to escaped slaves or roving bands of marauders. Or, because the name *Habiru* sounds so similar to the word *Hebrew* that perhaps the Canaanite

kings were referring to the invasion of the Hebrews after the Exodus.

Beyond what is in the biblical book of Joshua and Judges, It is difficult to construct a timeline from the textual and archaeological evidence from approximately 1250 to 1000 BC. The ancient Near East was in a period of the so-called Dark Ages: trade routes had collapsed, literacy rates plummeted, and the scribal activity needed to shed light on the everyday events had all but disappeared. The archaeological evidence may be hard to find, but some of these archaeological artifacts are immensely helpful to us student historians investigating this period.

The first and most prominent example of this archaeological evidence comes in the Merneptah Stele, dated to around 1204 BC. The pharaoh Merneptah had built a stele, a massive Near Eastern billboard to celebrate his defeat of various enemies in the land of Canaan. Amongst those enemies, he includes the Egyptian term for "Israel," alongside an Egyptian symbol (called a "glyph") for "people." This artifact shows that the Israelites were living in the land of Canaan, albeit as isolated tribes, by at least 1204 BC when the stele was created (Cline 5-7).

The Bible refers to this period as that of the **Judges**. The name derives from the book of Judges which chronicles this period when the twelve tribes of Israel lived largely independently of each other (Isserlin 67). Frequently, the Israelites would ignore the terms of God's covenant and live however they wanted. The author of Judges attributes this kind of living to the lack of a good, godly king to help the Israelites stay faithful to the Ten Com-

Vocabulary

Canaan

The land promised to Abraham and his descendants. This region sits on the east coast of the Mediterranean Sea, and the land's original inhabitants were vassals of the king of Egypt.

Judges

A book in the Bible that describes the first few centuries when Israel lived in the land of Canaan. These judges were military leaders that led the Israelites into battle for short periods of time.

Saul

The first king of a united Israel. Approximately, his reign lasted from 1037 to 1010 BC.

David

The second, but far more successful king over a united Israel. Under David's reign, Israel becomes a more centralized state on par with the other kingdoms of the ancient Near East. Approximately, his reign was from 1010 to 970 BC.

Solomon

The son of David, who enriches the Kingdom of Israel through trade and diplomacy. While Solomon is fabled for his wisdom, he breaks many of the *rules for kings*, and the kingdom unravels after his death. Approximately, his reign was 970 to 931 BC.

‖ THE MERNEPTAH STELE (~ 1204 BC)

mandments: "in those days there was no king in Israel. Everyone did what was right in his own eyes," (Judges 21:25). When they broke the Mosaic Covenant, the book of Judges describes God as permitting the neighboring tribes like the Moabites and Philistines to attack Israel as a kind of judgment against Israel's own wild, riotous living. The tribes of the Israelites would come together for mutual defense and serve under the authority of a common military leader, whom the Bible calls *judges* (Hebrew, *shophet*) to repel the invaders. This cycle continued until the Israelites asked for a king.

The First Kings: Saul, David, and Solomon

A king could be bad news. As the biblical prophet Samuel warns the Israelites, a king could oppress the people of Israelites, forcing them into military service or menial labor. But the Israelites are insistent and ask for a king, and God responds by giving the people of Israel one bad king named **Saul**, followed by one much better, albeit still flawed, king named David. Saul is a warrior, but he lacks self-control and is prone to jealousy. Soon, he is replaced by an upstart shepherd boy named David.

The figures of David and Solomon are some of the most interesting figures from the Bible. **David** was originally a shepherd, the youngest son in a large family, and largely unimpressive in his appearance and prowess. But God had chosen him to succeed Saul as king because David was a "man after God's own heart," (1 Samuel 13:14). David proved himself as a warrior against a towering Philistine warrior named Goliath, taking the giant down with a sling and a stone; once king, David successfully removes the Philistines as a threat to Israel's peace and prosperity; and as king, he conquers the city of Jerusalem and establishes this hill-top fortress as his capital city. Under King David, the people of Israel have gone from a scattered group of tribes to a centralized state, a kingdom on a level similar to that of the other kingdoms of the ancient Near East. When David died, his son Solomon became king in his place.

As king, **Solomon** was famous for his wisdom, the wealth and prosperity he brought to the kingdom of Israel, and the monumental building projects Solomon completed. For his wisdom, Solomon was credited for writing thousands of "proverbs," short maxims that tell a general truth. For that wealth and prosperity, Solomon sponsored overseas expeditions to lands in Africa to bring back exotic goods like spices, aromatic woods, and precious stones (I Kings 10:11-13). Because the land of Israel sits between the larger states of Egypt, Assyria, and Babylon, Israel served as a convenient trading post and entry point for merchant caravans traveling back and forth between these larger, more prosperous trading partners. That location and the trade routes that passed through Israelite territory made Israel relatively wealthy for a state of its size.

It was with this wealth that Solomon constructed a massive temple in Jerusalem, Israel's capital city. Solomon began building this temple in the 4th year of his reign, approximately 966 BC.

The Temple of Solomon was a massive, monumental building project on par with the other examples of monumental architecture at which we have looked so far this year. The temple itself was made of stone, adorned with cypress and cedar imported from Phoenicia, and overlaid with gold and bronze. The interior of the Temple was filled with gold implements, lamp stands, beautiful pillars and relief carvings, and a massive basin for ceremonial washings. The remains of the Ten Commandments were stored in the Ark of the Covenant, a wooden chest overlaid with gold, which itself was kept in an inner sanctuary known as the Most Holy Place. The building project required a labor force of an unprecedented scale in ancient Israel. This labor force included specialized craftsmen, some of whom came from abroad, and around 30,000 manual laborers Solomon tasked with the project (1 Kings 5:13). This large-scale activity is all the more unprecedented because up until now, Israel had little need for labor specialization nor the money to pay for massive building projects.

Solomon may have been a wise king who enriched Israel, but the kingdom begins to unravel after Solomon's death. Solomon broke many of the laws in the *rules for kings*, purchasing huge numbers of horses for cavalry, gaining huge amounts of gold through trade and commerce, and marrying literally hundreds of foreign wives. Solomon did these things as a means of securing alliances with other countries, but it also introduced the kind of polytheistic religious worship that the Ten Commandments forbade. Moreover, building projects like the Temple in Jerusalem required huge amounts of money, money that must be collected from the people in the form of higher and higher taxes.

After Solomon's death, several of the northern tribes of Israel rebelled against Solomon's son, Rehoboam. The tribes asked Rehoboam to reduce their tax burden and when he refused, they split away from Jerusalem and formed their own kingdom with their own capital at Samaria. For the next three hundred years, the northern Kingdom of Israel and the southern Kingdom of Judah operated as separate political units, sometimes fighting with each other and sometimes standing together against the more powerful countries of the ancient Near East. For to the east of Israel and Judah, the powers of

Assyria and Babylon were growing and looking to add to their vast dominions the people of Israel. To that story, and the fate awaiting the ancient Hebrews, we will turn in later chapters.

✦ Reading Comprehension Questions

What was the land of Canaan like?

Who was David? What did he do to push the story of the Israelites further?

Who was Solomon? What were his most significant accomplishments?

Writing Prompt

Writing is thinking, so we will spend considerable time this year writing and thinking about history. In the space provided, write a short essay answering the question: *How did the people of Israel go from one person—Abraham—to a great nation of descendants and a country of their own? What happened that they might become a nation of their own? How do the events of the Exodus and the Ten Commandments factor into this story? Be sure to explain your answer with relevant examples, sound reasoning, and clear, complete sentences.*

Direct Instruction Review

The hardest part about history is memorizing all those facts, dates, and events. To make this process easier, we have included this short section called *Direct Instruction Review*. Direct Instruction (or DI) is a powerful pedagogical tool whereby teachers ask students a series of *call-and-response* questions, and students respond back with the aim of learning this material to *mastery*. Teacher's lines are in **bold**; student's lines in *italics*.

Who were the people of Israel? *The people of Israel are the descendants of Abraham, Isaac, and Jacob. They came to live in the land of Canaan, which today is known as Israel.*

What kind of influence did the people of Israel have on world history? *The greatest influence the people of Israel have had is through their religious writings, collected together in the Hebrew and Christian Bible.*

What events does the book of Genesis record? *The book of Genesis means* beginnings, *and the book of Genesis includes the creation of the world, the creation of human beings, and the beginnings of the nation of Israel from Abraham.*

What was the Exodus? *The Exodus is the deliverance of the people of Israel from their bondage in the land of Egypt.*

What does Exodus mean in Greek? *The word* Exodus *comes from the Greek words* ex, *meaning "out of," and* odus, *meaning "way," so that the Exodus is literally the Israelites coming out of Egypt and into the land of Canaan.*

Why were the Israelites even in Egypt to begin with? *A terrible famine struck the ancient Near East, and so the sons of Jacob went down to Egypt to buy grain and eventually settled there.*

Why did a nameless Pharaoh enslave the people of Israel? *We cannot know, but we think that Pharaoh felt threatened by so large a group of foreigners living inside the borders of Egypt.*

Who led the Exodus? *The God of the Bible called a shepherd named Moses, a man who had miraculously survived being placed in the Nile and had grown up in the palace with Pharaoh.*

How did God free the people of Israel from their slavery? *God sent a series of plagues to showcase his power, plagues that included turning the Nile to blood, sending hordes of gnats, locusts, and frogs, and blotting out the sun.*

And were the Israelites ever freed? *Yes! Moses led the people of Israel out of Egypt to the Red Sea, which God parted to save the Israelites from the Egyptians.*

Timeline Practice / Ancient Israel and the Exodus

The hardest part about history is memorizing all those facts, dates, and events. To make this process easier, check out the timeline below—well, technically, there are *two* timelines. Some entries are missing dates, and others are missing the event that occurred on that date. With the information available from both timelines, fill in the missing blanks to get a better sense of the timeline for this chapter.

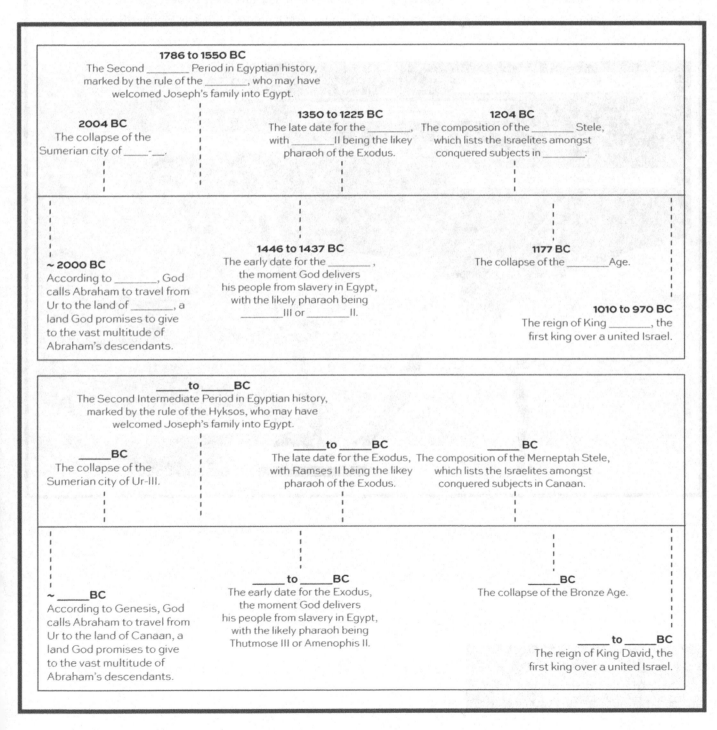

1786 to 1550 BC
The Second _____ Period in Egyptian history, marked by the rule of the _____, who may have welcomed Joseph's family into Egypt.

2004 BC
The collapse of the Sumerian city of ____-__.

1350 to 1225 BC
The late date for the _____, with _____ II being the likely pharaoh of the Exodus.

1204 BC
The composition of the _____ Stele, which lists the Israelites amongst conquered subjects in _____.

~ 2000 BC
According to _____, God calls Abraham to travel from Ur to the land of _____, a land God promises to give to the vast multitude of Abraham's descendants.

1446 to 1437 BC
The early date for the _____, the moment God delivers his people from slavery in Egypt, with the likely pharaoh being _____ III or _____ II.

1177 BC
The collapse of the _____ Age.

1010 to 970 BC
The reign of King _____, the first king over a united Israel.

_____ to _____ BC
The Second Intermediate Period in Egyptian history, marked by the rule of the Hyksos, who may have welcomed Joseph's family into Egypt.

_____ BC
The collapse of the Sumerian city of Ur-III.

_____ to _____ BC
The late date for the Exodus, with Ramses II being the likely pharaoh of the Exodus.

_____ BC
The composition of the Merneptah Stele, which lists the Israelites amongst conquered subjects in Canaan.

~ _____ BC
According to Genesis, God calls Abraham to travel from Ur to the land of Canaan, a land God promises to give to the vast multitude of Abraham's descendants.

_____ to _____ BC
The early date for the Exodus, the moment God delivers his people from slavery in Egypt, with the likely pharaoh being Thutmose III or Amenophis II.

_____ BC
The collapse of the Bronze Age.

_____ to _____ BC
The reign of King David, the first king over a united Israel.

Map Practice: The Land of Canaan

Instructions: Carefully look over the maps below, which are identical to maps provided in the rest of this chapter aside from one crucial difference—they have blanks in the place of the name of a sea, a region, or a site. Fill in the appropriate blank with the term list provided above each map.

The Land of Canaan: Seas such as the Mediterranean Sea, the Dead Sea, and the Red Sea; regions such as Canaan, the Sinai Peninsula, the Nile Delta, and the Arabian Desert; landforms such as Mount Sinai; and rivers such as the Nile and the Jordan.

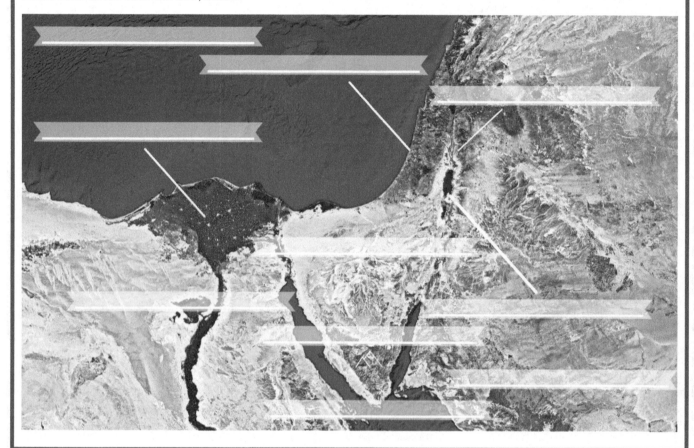

Want to study this map online? Type in the link below or scan the QR code to access an interactive diagram:
https://bit.ly/3okSogF

THE PHOENICIAN COAST
Photo by Ramy Kabalan

CHAPTER

The (First) Collapse

ROADMAP

✦ Learn about the potential causes of the collapse of the Bronze Age.

✦ Examine the criteria as to what exactly constitutes a *collapse*, as well as the commercial, cultural, and economic consequences concerning the collapse of the Bronze Age.

✦ Practice our knowledge of maps and chronology, as well as our writing skills through reading comprehension questions and an essay.

THALES
OUTCOME

№ 4

A **Truth Seeker** *critiques a variety of truth statements and/or observations through research and scientific methodology.*

Circa 1200 BC, the world of the Bronze Age suffered a devastating collapse with many of its cities never to be inhabited again, and yet, no one knows exactly *what caused* this collapse. A Truth Seeker wants to know why such events happen and evaluates the best evidence available while acknowledging we can never know for certain why events occurred the way they did.

CHAPTER 12 The (First) Collapse ✦ 279

What exactly is a collapse, *and what can cause a civilization to collapse?*

The Causes / The End of the Bronze Age

THE WORD *COLLAPSE* BRINGS to mind a house of cards coming down on itself. A city or a state that has grown too big to support itself in one or a number of factors, factors that will be discussed in this chapter, bring that civilization crashing down. We have already studied the collapse of ancient Sumer, which happened when a group of barbarians sacked Sumerian cities—but the collapse of the Late Bronze Age is different. That is because we are not dealing with one city or even one region, but many cities and kingdoms—the Hittites, the Phoenicians, Babylon and Assyria, New Kingdom Egypt—and they all came crashing down at roughly the same time. So, what was the world of the Late Bronze Age even like, and what happened to bring it all down?

The Late Bronze Age

The Bronze Age lasted from approximately 3,300 BC to 1,200 BC. The world of **the Late Bronze Age** was a world of wealthy and powerful states, knit together by huge commercial networks. Kingdoms like the Hittites and the Egyptians were at their peak in power and influence, and they participated in a kind of club with other kingdoms that were as powerful and influential as themselves. Historians refer to this "club" as the **Club of Great Powers**, as the kings and princes of Egypt, the Hittites, Assyria, Babylon, Mitanni (a state that stretched along the western reaches of the Euphrates River), and to an extent, a new player—Mycenaean Greece.

The rulers of these kingdoms had far more in common with each other than they did with the people over whom they ruled. Kings and princes exchanged correspondence, asked for advice and for aid, and gave lavish gifts to each other as a show of friendship between these kingdoms—just like a club. One can compare the world of the Late Bronze Age to that of modern, twentieth-century Europe, where Europe's Five Great Powers—Great Britain, France, Russia, Germany, and the Austro-Hungarian Empire—also interacted in high-level diplomacy and high-stakes rivalry. These states fought each other in World War I, but their rulers were even related to each other: Kaiser Wilhelm II of Germany and King George V of England shared the same grandmother in Queen Victoria, and Tsar Nicholas II of Russia and King George V of England were

Vocabulary

Write down this vocabulary in your notebook. These terms will help you better learn and understand the material in this chapter.

The Late Bronze Age

The Late Bronze Age refers to the last thousand or so years of the Bronze Age, characterized by huge trading networks and international diplomacy. The Bronze Age lasted until approximately 1200 BC when the period collapsed suddenly and without warning.

Club of Great Powers

A network of the great states of the Late Bronze Age that traded lavish gifts with each other; engaged in both warfare and diplomacy; and included Egypt, Mitanni, Babylon, and the Hittites.

Bronze

A metal alloy composed of nine parts of copper to every one part of tin. Because the components needed to make bronze were rarely, if ever, found in the same place, complicated trade networks developed across the ancient world to transport bronze.

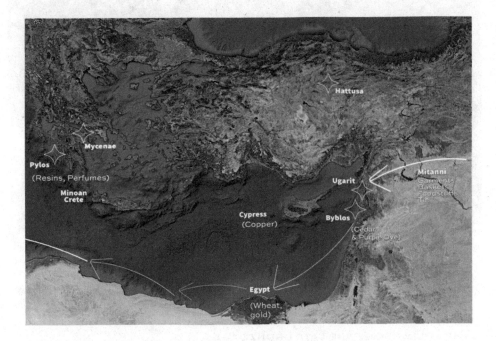

TRADING ROUTES IN THE MEDITERRANEAN WORLD
Map by Google Earth

actually cousins. More widespread, the Russian tsars and aristocrats actually preferred speaking French over their native Russian. The rulers of the Late Bronze Age lived in a similar world and were the ruling elites of that world, and they found it was easier to talk to each other than it was to talk to the common people living in Egypt, Hatti, or Babylon. They exchanged letters in the ancient, scholarly language of cuneiform, and gave gifts that showed their respect to one another.

The king of Egypt was always the most "popular" member of the club because, as Pharaoh, he was always the richest and most powerful. Egypt had the Nile River valley, containing some of the most abundant and productive farmland in the world, and pharaohs like Thutmosis III and Ramses II had conquered regions that held gold mines. That gave Egyptian pharaohs lots of gold to give as gifts to nearby rulers to solidify that friendship. And local rulers weren't ashamed to ask for more gold, which they said was "as plentiful as dirt" in the land of Egypt (Cline 57).

But goods like wheat and gold, as well as the important metals of copper and tin to make **bronze**, had to get from one city to another. Cities like the Phoenician trading ports of Ugarit and Byblos brought goods from one city to another. Merchants from Phoenicia operated huge trading networks that typically followed the coastline of the Mediterranean and the Aegean Sea. These trade networks were especially important for making bronze since the elements needed to make bronze—copper and tin—were rarely found in the same place.

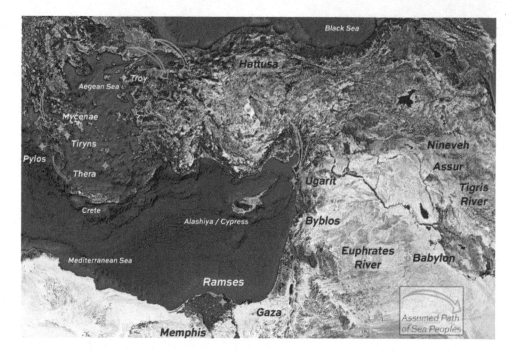

THE COLLAPSE OF THE LATE BRONZE AGE

Map by Alexikoua

Copper might be found in the island of Cyprus, whereas tin came from as far west as Tarshish (an ancient name for Spain) or as far east as Afghanistan. If a kingdom like the Hittites or the Egyptians wanted to make bronze, they needed middlemen like the Phoenicians to bring them the metals they needed. The Phoenicians also traded luxury goods like gold (which came from Egypt), resins, spices, perfumes, and wine in their ships. These trade networks stretched from Afghanistan to the Balkans, tied these states together in the bands of commerce, and helped each of them to flourish in a way that none of them could have done on their own.

But then, from approximately 1225 to 1175 BC (with the definitive year coming at 1177 BC), the states of the Late Bronze Age all suffered a system-wide collapse. Typically, when a civilization collapses, whole cities and regions are destroyed and for multiple reasons, they do not reappear. The people who lived in those regions do not rebuild their society, although some new civilization may arise to take its place. Often, in such a collapse, the trade networks that helped sustain a relatively high standard of living disappear, and the people left alive do not have the stamina or the resources to rebuild their once-thriving civilization.

In the collapse of the Late Bronze Age, only New Kingdom Egypt survived the destruction (Mieroop 209, 212; Cline 150). This destruction ranged from port cities like Ugarit to powerful, highly-militarized states like the Hittites, and even the far-off palace centers in Mycenaean Greece—all gone, and all in a little under half a century. So what happened, and who caused this widespread destruction?

Vocabulary

The Sea Peoples
A mysterious group of marauders and invaders from (presumably) Greek islands in the Aegean and the western Mediterranean; they are often blamed for the collapse of the Late Bronze Age.

The Aegean Sea
A sea hemmed in by the Greek mainland and the west coast of Anatolia.

Ramses III
An Egyptian pharaoh who, in 1177, claims to have defeated the Sea Peoples and kept them from destroying Egypt. He reigned from 1186 to 1155 and is the last significant pharaoh of New Kingdom Egypt.

Mycenaean Greece
A period in Greek history that lasted from approximately the 18th century to the 11th century BC; Mycenaean Greece is so-named for the city of Mycenae, home of the famous Greek warrior Agamemnon.

What was the world of the Late Bronze Age like? (Hint: use the term Club of Great Powers in your answer).

Who was in the Club of Great Powers, and how did the members of the "club" interact with each other?

Why did vast, international, complicated trading networks arise in the ancient Mediterranean world?

The foreign countries made a conspiracy in their islands. All at once the lands were removed and scattered in the fray. No land could stand before their arms: from Hatti, Qode, Carchemish, Arzawa (western Anatolia), and Alashiya (Cyprus) on, being cut off at one time.

A camp was set up in Amurru. They desolated its people, and its land was like that which has never come into being. They were coming forward toward Egypt, while the flame was prepared before them. Their confederation was the Peleset, Tjeker, Shekelesh, Denyen, and Weshesh, lands united. They laid their hands upon the land as far as the circuit of the earth, their hearts confident and trusting: "Our plans will succeed!"

The Collapse of the Bronze Age

The collapse of the Late Bronze Age is often been blamed on **the Sea Peoples**, a group of mysterious sea-borne raiders that came from somewhere in the Aegean Sea. **The Aegean Sea** is the sea separating the Greek mainland from Anatolia.

The name *Sea Peoples* comes from the text above, written by the Egyptian New Kingdom pharaoh **Ramses III**. At his grand mortuary temple at Medinet Habu, located near Luxor in modern Egypt, Ramses III records that, in 1177, raiders from the islands north and west of Egypt arrived and tried to destroy Egypt. They made a "conspiracy in their islands" and arrived in lands across the Mediterranean like *Hatti* (the Kingdom of the Hittites), *Arzawa*, the west coast of Anatolia, *Alashiya*, modern-day Cyprus, and New Kingdom Egypt. Only New Kingdom Egypt survived the onslaught, and only because of Ramses III's leadership. So who were the people referenced in this text?

The peoples identified in this text have most often been identified with the Greek-speaking peoples living to the west and north of Egypt. The peoples mentioned in this passage and elsewhere at Medinet Habu include:

Denyen: Greeks, possibly the same Danoi used by Homer in The Iliad.

The Ekwesh: These may be more Greek marauders, but their exact identity is unknown.

Lukka: Peoples living in western Anatolia, who may be related to the later states of Lycia and Lydia.

Peleset: These may be the Philistines, who are identified in the Bible as "colonists from Crete."

Shekelesh: These may be native Sicilian peoples.

The Sherden: These may be peoples from the island of Sardinia or people of western Anatolia in and around the future city of Sardis.

The Teresh: These may be Tyrrhenians or even Etruscans from the Italian peninsula.

The Tjeker: These may be Mycenaean Greeks.

Weshesh: This tribe has not been identified with any tribe or people with any real certainty.

The keywords in each description is *may be*. The names of the Sea Peoples look similar enough to the names of other historical groups we know with greater certainty, but we do not know whether or not the groups mentioned by Ramses III are really the same as later groups of Greek-speaking peoples (Mieroop 217). Could the Sea Peoples have been raiders and marauders from Greece?

In the Late Bronze Age, the Greek world was dominated by the city of **Mycenae**. The Greek mainland also had its own system of palaces, ones similar in size and function to those at Babylon, Hattusa, and in New Kingdom Egypt. These palaces were located at Mycenae, Tiryns, and Pylos, and each palace was deeply interconnect-

Vocabulary

Write down this vocabulary in your notebook. These terms will help you better learn and understand the material in this chapter.

The Collapse of the Bronze Age

The Bronze Age lasted until approximately 1200 BC, when the period collapsed suddenly and without warning. the causes of this collapse range from the destructive raids of the Sea Peoples to volcanic eruptions and earthquakes.

RAMSES II DEFEATING THE SEA PEOPLES
Drawing made from a much larger wall painting at Ramses III's palace at Medinut Habu

ed with the economy of the ancient Near East. That way, the ruling elites at Mycenae or the craftsmen at Pylos could obtain the copper and tin for bronze and ingredients for making perfume. These Sea Peoples may have come from Greece, and they may have filled the "seven ships of the enemy," setting sail from some unknown island in the Aegean or the northern reaches of mainland Greece. Palaces in mainland Greece were also destroyed, so the Sea Peoples may have come from other areas on the periphery of Greece, not the palaces at Tiryns or Mycenae. Then these raiders would sail onto some other hapless city in Phoenicia, Egypt, or anywhere else in the Mediterranean they dared to roam. And in the ensuing chaos, the Sea Peoples brought down the entire Bronze Age one palace center at a time.

Whoever the "Sea Peoples" were, they get most of the blame for the collapse of the Late Bronze Age. In addition to the battles in the Nile river delta circa 1177, these "Sea Peoples" may have also destroyed the city of Hattusa, the capital city of the Hittites, circa 1200, for it was also destroyed suddenly and violently at around the same time. And these Sea Peoples may have also destroyed the prominent Phoenician port-city of Ugarit in 1190 and the nearby city of Emar circa 1185 (Mieroop 206-207).

That these cities bear evidence of violent destruction such as scorch marks, hidden hoards of precious items, and arrowheads indicate that the cities may have fallen to invaders (Cline 151). Here is a letter found in a kiln at the city of Ugarit, as if it were just waiting to be baked before the city was destroyed:

ARCHAEOLOGICAL RUINS: GIBALA-TELL TWEINI & THE WALLS OF UGARIT

Photo from David Kaniewski, et. al (2011)

The tone of the letter appears both rushed and frantic as if the enemy ships were bearing down on the writer at the time of the letter's composition. At first read, it looks as if the letter was written just before the city was destroyed.

> *My father, now the ships of the enemy have come. They have been setting fire to my cities and have done harm to the land. Doesn't my father know that all of my infantry and [chariots] are stationed in Khatte, and that all of my ships are stationed in the land of Lukka [in Anatolia, usually identified with Lycia]?*
>
> *They have not arrived back yet, so the land is thus prostrate. May my father be aware of this matter. Now the seven ships of the enemy which have been coming have done harm to us. Now if other ships of the enemy turn up, send me a report somewhere, so that I will know,* (Cline 9).

The identity of the Sea Peoples is shrouded in even more mystery when compared with the textual evidence. For instance, Classical Greek sources describe the invasion of the Dorians, a group of Greek settlers from northern Greece that migrated into the Peloponnesian peninsula and conquered much territory there.

Some historians even speculate that the Sea Peoples and the Greek warriors at Troy, the ones immortalized in Homer's *Iliad* and *Odyssey*, are really one and the same. After all, the *Iliad*'s great warrior king Agamemnon came from Mycenae and wise Nestor from Pylos. Thus, it is possible that the literary events of the *Iliad* could have played out against the historical events of the Late Bronze Age. That the collapse of the Bronze Age occurred during the "late date" for the Exodus adds another player to the general destruction: the Israelites, fleeing Egypt, destroyed some (but not all) of these cities and regions (Cline 127-132). Could some or all of the Sea Peoples have been either the Dorians, the Homeric warriors at Troy like Agamemnon and Odysseus, or even the Israelites?

And of course, some states were not attacked by peoples from the sea at all. The states of Assyria and Babylon were threatened not by the Sea Peoples at all, but by desert tribes like **the Arameans and the Chaldeans** (Mieroop 209-217). Perhaps these tribes took advantage of the general, worldwide chaos to carve out states for themselves in Syria and the Kassite dynasty in Babylon (Mieroop 194, 209). The Arameans and the Chaldeans lived in the desert, so they most certainly did not "make a conspiracy in their islands" before ravaging Lower Mesopotamia. So if we can't blame the Sea Peoples for everything, what else could have the collapse of the Bronze Age?

THE AEGEAN SEA & THE ISLAND OF THERA

A volcano on the island of Thera (modern-day Santorini) erupted circa 1600 BC; map from Google Earth

Causes for the Collapse: Ecological Disasters

At times, an event like an earthquake, a volcanic eruption, or a drought may destroy an entire civilization. But such events are rare, and even more rare is that *one* earthquake or *one* eruption destroys multiple civilizations spread across a huge geographical area. But, historians and geologists still offer a series of ecological disasters happening in a sequence as enough to bring about the end of Bronze Age.

Case in point: the eruption on the island of **Thera**, circa 1,600. The volcanic eruption on Thera in the Aegean (the modern-day island of Santorini) is of particular importance to our narrative. Such events usually provide a useful chronological reference point for many other events happening during a particular historical period, with the eruption at Thera occurring as early as 1628 or as late as 1500 BC (Cline 93). That the volcano eruption occurred much earlier than the collapse of the Bronze Age is not surprising: volcanoes spew out immense clouds of ash that affect global climate patterns, global temperatures, and crop harvests around the world and for long periods of time following an eruption.

Historians have tried to connect the eruption at Thera a number of events around the collapse of the Bronze Age. Some of them include the Exodus: the billowing ash from the volcano, for instance, could have provided the darkness in the 9th Plague of the Ten Plagues of Egypt. Also, the eruption could have destroyed homes and farmland, and thus forced the Sea Peoples to flee their homes. If the Sea Peoples originally came from Mycenaean Greece, then perhaps the volcanic eruption caused such ecological disaster that the Sea Peoples fled and looked for new opportunities abroad—opportunities in Egypt, Syria, and the

SANTORINI / AERIAL VIEW
Photo by Sidvics

Hittite New Kingdom.

The other possible contenders include **ecological disasters** like droughts, famines, and earthquakes. Such disasters happening in relatively-short succession hurt one state and kept them from contributing to the Mediterranean economy. Remember that a trading network—like one stretching from Afghanistan to Spain—is a delicate thread. If one pulls on enough "threads," the entire network may break. If a volcano hurts crop yields for a long period of a time, and if an earthquake destroys a port city there, cities and regions far removed from these problems will suffer, too. When too many actors are removed from the international market, the system cannot continue and falls apart.

In economics, the laws of supply and demand dictate that producers make only as many goods as they can sell and if the "market" for resins, spices, or woolen fabrics disappears, those goods will eventually disappear, too. In this way, it is not necessarily one cause but a series of causes that contribute to the effect of the end of the Bronze Age (Mieroop 202-203). As a result, perhaps not one but a number of different ecological disasters could have contributed to the collapse of the Bronze Age.

Causes for the Collapse: Popular Uprisings

The last and perhaps the most interesting explanation for the collapse of the Bronze Age may be rooted in the very organization of Bronze Age society. In brief, cities across the Near East may have seen a series of popular uprisings, moments when the large, lower classes rise up and destroy the people and the institutions that had mistreated them.

Recall that the international scene was made up of a "club" of Great Powers. This club included New Kingdom Egypt, the Hittite New Kingdom, the Mesopotamian states of Assyria and Babylon, and a host of smaller but dynamic players in Phoenicia and Mycenaean Greece. The rulers of these states were the only ones in the "club," and they excluded their own people from "membership" in the club. The rulers of each state, too, had more in common with each other than with the people they ruled over. Kings and princes distanced themselves even further by building massive, isolated palace centers either at the center of a city or on its outskirts (Mieroop 194). When rulers become so isolated from their people, disaster often follows.

In such cases, the ruling elites look at their subjects just like that—as subjects. The common people become more of a means to an end of building up the power of the state and contributing to the comfort of the ruling classes. The ruling classes in Egypt and abroad even had ice for their drinks, carried down from the mountains, and packed in straw for safe transport. In such cases, the people can only take so much until they rise up and rebel against their overbearing masters.

The wealthy lifestyle enjoyed by the elites of the ancient Near East needed a massive network of farmers and craftsmen to support them. To sustain such trading networks, these palace cultures depended on the labor of a large class of workers labeled by historians simply as "dependents." These individuals wove woolen garments, made baskets, toiled in mines, fetched water, or performed other difficult tasks for little pay—or no pay at all if the workers were slaves. If they were not slaves, many of these depends had fallen into serious debts. These societies had little to no social mobility or oppor-

Vocabulary

Ecological Disasters
Events such as earthquakes, famines, and volcanic eruptions that often influence the course of human events.

Habiru
Groups of wandering nomads who may have composed part of the Sea Peoples and thus contributed to some, but not all, of the destruction. The name *habiru* also sounds eerily similar to *Hebrew*.

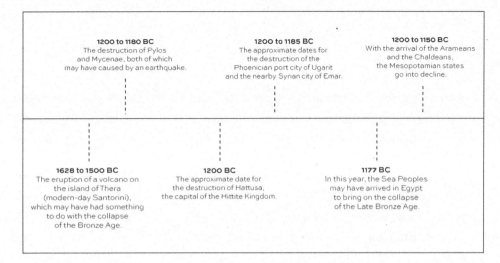

1200 to 1180 BC	1200 to 1185 BC	1200 to 1150 BC
The destruction of Pylos and Mycenae, both of which may have caused by an earthquake.	The approximate dates for the destruction of the Phoenician port city of Ugarit and the nearby Syrian city of Emar.	With the arrival of the Arameans and the Chaldeans, the Mesopotamian states go into decline.

1628 to 1500 BC	1200 BC	1177 BC
The eruption of a volcano on the island of Thera (modern-day Santorini), which may have had something to do with the collapse of the Bronze Age.	The approximate date for the destruction of Hattusa, the capital of the Hittite Kingdom.	In this year, the Sea Peoples may have arrived in Egypt to bring on the collapse of the Late Bronze Age.

TIMELINE / COLLAPSE OF THE BRONZE AGE
Dates from Cline and Mieroop

tunities for economic betterment, and these poor farmers often fled cities or estates where they had no real opportunities for a meaningful, rewarding life.

Most often, these dependents and slaves ran away. They headed for the city-states in Phoenicia which, being thriving ports, had more economic freedoms and opportunities for social advancement. Remember, too, that peace treaties of the Late Bronze Age—like the Treaty of Qadesh between the Hittites and the Egyptians—included treaties for returning runaway captives known collectively as the **habiru**. The *habiru* were groups of (perceived) wandering nomads and escaped slaves, and their owners took every means necessary to bring them back (Mieroop 211).

Local leaders had to return the *habiru* immediately to their country of origin, as mentioned in the diplomatic correspondence found at Amarna in Egypt (Mieroop 179). The name *habiru* also sounds eerily similar to *Hebrew*, so some historians associate references to *habiru* in letters to the movement of the Israelites after the Exodus.

Local rulers desperately needed the labor of each farmer or peasant to bring in the harvest each year. If these individuals ran away, the agricultural productivity of a state like the Hittites or Assyria declined accordingly. That decline could not happen.

So when the Bronze Age started to fall in the years surrounding 1200 BC, did these groups of disaffected, exploited individuals join forces with the invaders?

For years, scholars thought this side switch had happened to the Hittite capital of Hattusa. There, the city's temples and palaces were destroyed, but the homes of seemingly-normal people had been left standing. It was as if the looters and rioters had turned their focus solely on the institutions—the palace and the temple—which had mistreated them. Such a scenario reminds us of the importance of treating all individuals with dignity and respect, and that the elites can often game the system by means of the political control they exercise.

But this narrative, too, has been cast in doubt by new historical evidence. Now, scholars can read and understand Hittite writings, and these writings suggest that the Hittite royal family and their administrators simply abandoned Hattusa. They found the capital too hard to govern effectively and they just left. Groups of marauders invaded the city but found it empty, perhaps destroying the temples and palaces out of frustration (Mieroop 220). So where do we go from here, and how do we understand what happened at the end of the Bronze Age?

Conclusion & Summary

To summarize, there is often no single "cause" of a collapse. We want to find such a cause either out of the desire to know why things happened they did and perhaps to avoid whatever that one thing was. But it seems as if the Bronze Age was brought down by several interdependent factors that together weakened each of the member states in the Club of Great Powers. Those states weakened until they could no longer contribute to the international commercial network that had developed during the Late Bronze Age. At a certain point, the damage became so great that the whole international system came crashing down.

Certainly, no one wants to live through a collapse. The period around which one period "ends" is often filled with riots, famines, droughts, earthquakes, and other violent epoch-ending events. All such events are typically detrimental to human flourishing. Then, there is the reality that life will not be the same as it was at some point back in the past when times were "good." We may not want to live through such times, and we cannot control what times we live through, but we can decide how we will live during our time. We can glean two important consequences from the nature of a "collapse," the two most famous being the Bronze Age collapse circa 1177 BC and that of the Roman Empire circa 476 AD. The first consequence is "dark," so dark the preceding periods in both 1100-900 BC and 500-1300 AD are known (unfairly) as the "Dark Ages," while the second consequence is far *brighter* and far more optimistic. For out of the ashes of one great era arises a new civilization that takes the best elements of the old world and builds something new, dynamic, vibrant, and beautiful. Let's turn to these consequences, both the good and the bad, the dark and the bright consequences, now.

Other civilizations have faced similar ruin to that of the Bronze Age and its system-wide collapse. Sometimes, this collapse happens to a host of external threats such as warfare and barbarian invasions; other times, changes in the environment make it all but impossible for a large, once-thriving civilization to survive; and other times, the rulers of a particular kingdom make choices that lead to their downfall.

Who were the Sea Peoples? From where did they come originally come?

What ecological disasters occurred, and how might these disasters have contributed to the fall of the ancient Near East?

What is a "popular uprising," and why might have such an uprising occurred across the ancient Near East?

The Consequences / The End of the Bronze Age

FOLLOWING THE COLLAPSE of the Bronze Age, the entire Near East entered into a time of "so-called Dark Ages," (Mieroop, 3-7). The term **Dark Ages** refers to the relative lack of books and writings. You see, textual evidence and primary sources shed light on a historical era. The term *Dark Ages* was originally coined by the Italian poet Petrarch, who labeled the period between the fall of the Roman Empire and the rise of the Renaissance as a period of superstition and thus a time of great darkness. In contrast, the Romans and the Florentines of Petrarch's time were filled with the beautiful light of writing, scholarship, and poetry. But why might a period of darkness follow the collapse of a once mighty and thriving civilization? What accounts for the noticeable lack of education, scholarship, and literature following the end of one great civilization like the Roman Empire, or the collapse of an entire historical era like the Late Bronze Age?

The "Dark" Consequences

Think back to the palace centers, the central institution of the Late Bronze Age. The palaces were the royal residences of a king and a large network of scholars, scribes, and bureaucrats. Those scholars learned cuneiform and mathematics to keep records of commercial transactions, and the palaces had to train such individuals to help them keep records. That way, these well-educated scribes could help record and direct the economic activities of their states. When the Bronze Age collapsed, there was no more money available to pay scribes to record such transactions. Nor was there any need, since economic activity had collapsed and there were no more worthwhile commercial transactions for scribes to record (Mieroop 213).

And of course, once these scribes could read and write, they could write works other than the records of buying and selling sheep. Such scribes often composed cuneiform hymns and poems in honor of the gods or even long, epic poems like the *Epic of Gilgamesh*. *Gilgamesh* may have circulated orally throughout the ancient Near East for generations, but literate scribes wrote down the epic on clay tablets during the Late Bronze Age, somewhere around 1300-1000 BC (this was the version found in the celebrated library of the Assyrian king Ashurbanipal).

Thus, the period following a collapse seems very "dark." The textual record practically disappears from 1100 to 900 BC, a period historians refer to as **the Greek Dark Ages** to distinguish Mycenaean Greece from the Archaic and Classical periods that come after the Dark Ages. In such periods historians have no sources to shed light on the historical events happening during those two centuries. This is the "fair" definition of the term "Dark Ages" because such an age is dark only because the textual record is practically non-existent.

Without institutions to train new scribes, there would be no written records of either commercial activity or great works of literature. Each state had to focus on survival, so they neglected the arts, literary works, or large building projects. These examples of "high culture" require lots of money, lots of time, and lots of safety from external threats like barbarians or ecological disasters. If a king is focused on finding enough grain to feed his people, he most likely does not have the money to commission luxurious grave goods with which to be buried, either (those grave goods disappeared, too). Instead, people focus on the difficult process of survival and rebuilding—and in those efforts, a new, dynamic

Vocabulary

Dark Ages

A period in which there is relatively-little textual evidence that helps later historians understand the events of that era.

The Greek Dark Ages

A period that lasted from approximately 1100 to 900 BC.

The *Iliad* and the *Odyssey*

Homer's *Iliad* and Homer's *Odyssey* are two epic poems that may be the most famous poems in the Western canon. These works were composed towards the end of the Dark Ages, but focus on events that happened around the end of the Bronze Age.

Homer

A blind poet credited with composing the epic poems *Iliad* and the *Odyssey*, both of which describe events that occurred during the Bronze Age. Homer lived during the 8th c. BC.

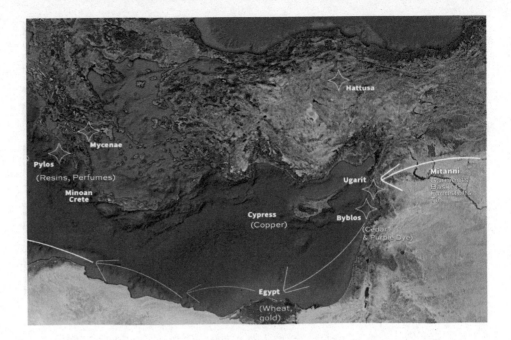

TRADING ROUTES IN THE MEDITERRANEAN WORLD

Map by Google Earth

civilization emerges from the ashes of the old.

Thus, these ages seem "dark" only because we do not have beautiful artifacts of human culture like poetry, paintings, or monumental building projects that metaphorically brim with light and wonder. And we do not have them because no one had the money or the time to create such wonderful works. But if those are the "dark" consequences, what about the "brighter," more optimistic ones? What "bright" consequences can we possibly find amidst the ruins of the Late Bronze Age?

The "Bright" Consequences

First, a host of new tribes and peoples entered the international scene that helped shape the world we live in today. The world we have inherited owes much to the ancient Phoenicians, of whom we have already learned so much, as well as the ancient Greeks and Israelites. The Phoenicians, Greeks, and Israelites may have been present in the Bronze Age, but without the Egyptians or the Hittites holding them back, they accomplished more in the Iron Age than in the Bronze Age. Without highly-militarized states like the Egyptians and the Hittites, these new players could spread their positive cultural influences across the Mediterranean world. So what ideas did they bring with them?

Such ideas included the Phoenician alphabet (see right) and ideas of Phoenician commerce. While some Phoenician cities were destroyed and never inhabited again, others flourished and extended their commercial networks to the western Mediterranean. The Phoenician city of Tyre founded the port city of Carthage towards the end of the Dark Ages in the 800s-BC, and the founding of Carthage highlights the kind of trade networks the Phoenicians had been operating at the literal ends of the Mediterranean world. The demise of great and powerful states

RUINS OF TROY VIIa / HISARLIK, TURKEY

Archaelogical excavations, like those at Troy VIIa, a "layer" of historical settlement at this particular site in the 13th c. BC, help verify that at least some of the events of the Trojan War happened. Photo by Alexikoua

like Egypt and the Hittites gave "private actors, who did not rely on great states for their support but were based in mercantile cities" in Cyprus and Phoenicia allowed these merchants to flourish (Mieroop 216). Private individuals could operate more freely and engage in commerce more readily without the presence of the state trying to control (and tax) their movements.

Further west in Greece, we'll see the beginnings of the Greek literary tradition culminating in Homer's *Iliad* and *Odyssey*. These epic poems describe the legendary Trojan War, a ten-year-long struggle between the Mycenaean Greeks and the city of Troy, located in northwestern Anatolia. The fabled events of the Trojan War may have even occurred against the backdrop of the ancient Near East, as some of the Hittite kings wrote of insurrections in northwestern Anatolia that were close, so close, to the archaeological sites believed to be ancient Troy (Cline 35). Hittite texts referring to the *Ahhiyawa* and *Wilusa* could be referring to the Achaeans, a name for the Greeks, and the city of Troy itself, respectively.

Indeed, while Homer describes events that seemingly occurred during the Late Bronze Age, certain details—such as the kind of armor and fighting practices—belong to the world of the Greek Dark Ages. And while the kind of poetic, oral, bardic tradition, of which the blind poet Homer is its greatest example, existed before the collapse of the Bronze Age, this kind of oral poetry flourished during the Dark Ages. The palaces that remained may have been smaller in size and reduced in power, but they still needed entertainment. Such entertainment they found in itinerant poets wandering from palace to palace and praising the deeds of heroes like Odysseus, Achilles, and Agamemnon, who had long since passed.

Lastly, there are the Israelites, of whom we will examine in greater detail in later chapters. Thus far, we have only seen the Israelites at sporadic, haphazard moments in our narrative: the journey of Abraham from Ur (Ur-III, to be exact)

Vocabulary

The Trojan War

A period in Greek history that lasted from approximately the 18th century to the 11th century BC; Mycenaean Greece is so-named for the city of Mycenae, home of the famous Greek warrior Agamemnon.

The Exodus

The word *Exodus* refers to the deliverance of the people of Israel from slavery in Egypt.

Camel

A relative of the horse, camels are uniquely-equipped to carry goods and people across the desert. They were domesticated towards the end of the Bronze Age.

Iron

A metal that is stronger than bronze, can be sharpened and resharpened as needed, and is found practically everywhere on earth. As a result, iron would replace bronze at the end of the Bronze Age and thus usher in the Iron Age.

and the presence of the Israelites in Egypt. But it is at the close of the Dark Ages that the Israelites emerge onto the international scene and, despite their relatively small size, have had by far the greatest impact on the Western canon. For the foundational moment for the people of Israel, the event in which a loose and disaffected band of Abraham's descendants, becomes a nation is set against the backdrop of the Bronze Age: **the Exodus,** the deliverance of the people of Israel from slavery in Egypt. If the Exodus occurred in the 12th c. BC, then it occurred during the chaotic backdrop of the Bronze Age collapse. The simple but profound idea of monotheism and the literary tradition of the ancient Israelites would profoundly shape almost every aspect of the course and contours of the Western tradition.

Developments in technology also occurred. Technology may be good or bad, depending on how we use it—and we ought to use it to promote human flourishing. The camel, for instance, was domesticated in the decades surrounding the collapse of the Bronze Age. **Camels** could be used to carry goods across deserts in merchant caravans over long distances, and the domestication of the camel allowed peoples on the Arabian peninsula to trade with the cities and civilizations on their periphery like Mesopotamia and Egypt (Mieroop 219).

More importantly, though, we see the use of a new metal, one found practically everywhere: **iron**. The Bronze Age was predicated on the forging of bronze tools and weapons, bronze being an alloy made from copper and tin. These metals were rarely found in the same location and with the trade routes having disappeared, they could not be readily obtained to make bronze. Iron had been in use for millennia, but in the twelfth and eleventh centuries, individuals found out how to "alloy iron with charcoal from the furnace during the smelting process" to make steel, a far stronger metal than bronze (Mieroop 216). Iron was superior to bronze since it could make stronger weapons and tools. Moreover, bronze cannot be sharpened once its cutting edge has lost its edges; iron, meanwhile, could be sharpened and resharpened as much as needed.

The use of iron would give rise to the Iron Age. While iron was more readily available and could produce tools needed for farming and other essential activities (a good thing), iron could also be used to make stronger and stronger weapons (a bad thing). Those stronger weapons and the ability of new and powerful states to mass-produce them would contribute to the rise of the world's first real empires: the Neo-Assyrian Empire, the Babylonian Empire, and the Persian Empire. It is to these great and ancient states that we will turn to in a later volume, for these states belong not to the age of Bronze but of Iron.

BIG IDEA

The period following the collapse of a once-great civilization may be full of massive social upheaval, chaos, and confusion, but the human spirit finds ways of adapting to such chaos and endures no matter the circumstances. While it may sound boring and unoriginal, there is always hope—and our study of history helps to show that hope.

Why does literacy and scholarship tend to disappear following the end of one era and the beginning of another? In other words, what makes an age so "dark"?

....

....

....

....

What new actors emerged on the international scene during the collapse of the Bronze Age, and what ideas did they bring with them?

....

....

....

....

What advances in technology occurred during the Dark Ages? Were these advances good or bad?

....

....

....

....

Writing Prompt

Writing is thinking, so we will spend considerable time this year writing and thinking about history. In the space provided, write a short essay answering the question: *Why did the Bronze Age collapse? Was it a series of ecological disasters or the raids of the Sea People? Be sure to explain your answer with relevant examples, sound reasoning, and clear, complete sentences.*

Direct Instruction Review

The hardest part about history is memorizing all those facts, dates, and events. To make this process easier, we have included this short section called *Direct Instruction Review*. Direct Instruction (or DI) is a powerful pedagogical tool whereby teachers ask students a series of *call-and-response* questions, and students respond back with the aim of learning this material to *mastery*. Teacher's lines are in **bold**; student's lines in *italics*.

How long did the Bronze Age last? *The Bronze Age lasted from around 4,000 BC to 1,200 BC.*

What was the world of the Late Bronze Age like? *The world of the Bronze Age was a world of powerful states like Egypt and the Hittites, a world of diplomacy and gift-giving, and international trade.*

When did the Bronze Age collapse? *The world of the Bronze Age collapsed in and around the year 1200 BC.*

Why did the Bronze Age collapse? *We do not know exactly why the Bronze Age collapsed but we think it may have been because of invaders, disasters, or uprisings.*

Who were the invaders that may have caused the end of the Bronze Age? *In and around the year 1200 BC, the Sea Peoples arrived in the eastern Mediterranean, destroying many cities and regions and settling down.*

Who were the Sea Peoples? *We do not know who they were but they have come from Greece, since Ramses III mentions place-names that may have been Greek.*

What else may have caused the end of the Bronze Age? *A volcanic eruption at Thera may have ruined harvests and crop yields for years, as well as earthquakes, famines, droughts, and other similar natural disasters.*

And what was the third possibility for bringing about the end of the Bronze Age? *The common people in places like Hattusu and elsewhere may have risen up and destroyed the rulers and the institutions that had taken advantage of them for so long.*

What followed after the collapse of the Bronze Age? *A period known as the "Dark Ages" is so named because of the lack of written sources available to us from that period.*

Why was this period so "dark"? *If society collapses, it no longer has the money needed to support education, learning, and scholarship; instead, all resources are geared toward survival.*

What were some of the "bright" consequences of the fall of the Bronze Age? *We see new ideas and new people coming to the forefront of history including the commercial spirit of the Phoenicians, the literature of the Greeks, and the religious ideas of the Israelites.*

Timeline Practice / The Collapse of the Bronze Age

The hardest part about history is memorizing all those facts, dates, and events. To make this process easier, check out the timeline below—well, technically, there are *two* timelines. Some entries are missing dates, and others are missing the event that occurred on that date. With the information available from both timelines, fill in the missing blanks to get a better sense of the timeline for this chapter.

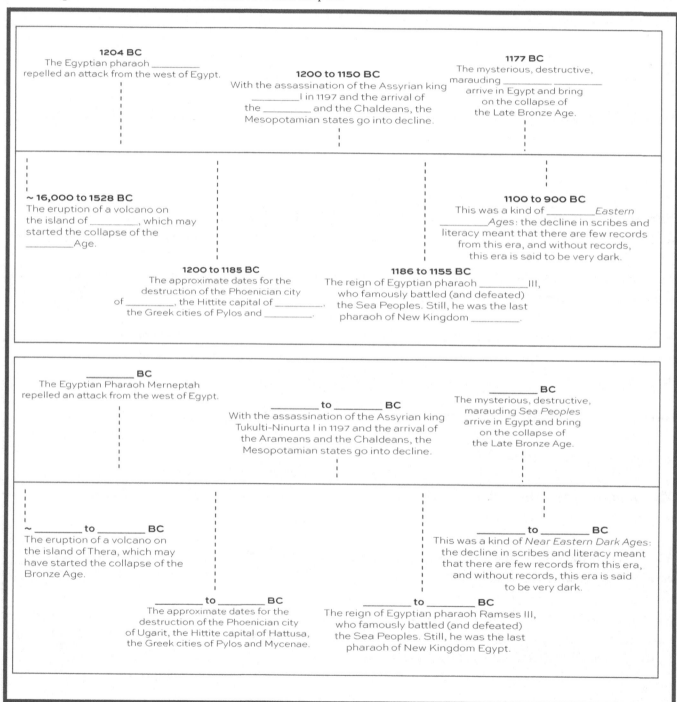

1204 BC
The Egyptian pharaoh _____ repelled an attack from the west of Egypt.

1200 to 1150 BC
With the assassination of the Assyrian king _____ I in 1197 and the arrival of the _____ and the Chaldeans, the Mesopotamian states go into decline.

1177 BC
The mysterious, destructive, marauding _____ _____ arrive in Egypt and bring on the collapse of the Late Bronze Age.

~ 16,000 to 1528 BC
The eruption of a volcano on the island of _____, which may started the collapse of the _____ Age.

1100 to 900 BC
This was a kind of _____ *Eastern* _____ *Ages*: the decline in scribes and literacy meant that there are few records from this era, and without records, this era is said to be very dark.

1200 to 1185 BC
The approximate dates for the destruction of the Phoenician city of _____, the Hittite capital of _____, the Greek cities of Pylos and _____.

1186 to 1155 BC
The reign of Egyptian pharaoh _____ III, who famously battled (and defeated) the Sea Peoples. Still, he was the last pharaoh of New Kingdom _____.

_____ BC
The Egyptian Pharaoh Merneptah repelled an attack from the west of Egypt.

_____ to _____ BC
With the assassination of the Assyrian king Tukulti-Ninurta I in 1197 and the arrival of the Arameans and the Chaldeans, the Mesopotamian states go into decline.

_____ BC
The mysterious, destructive, marauding *Sea Peoples* arrive in Egypt and bring on the collapse of the Late Bronze Age.

~ _____ to _____ BC
The eruption of a volcano on the island of Thera, which may have started the collapse of the Bronze Age.

_____ to _____ BC
This was a kind of *Near Eastern Dark Ages*: the decline in scribes and literacy meant that there are few records from this era, and without records, this era is said to be very dark.

_____ to _____ BC
The approximate dates for the destruction of the Phoenician city of Ugarit, the Hittite capital of Hattusa, the Greek cities of Pylos and Mycenae.

_____ to _____ BC
The reign of Egyptian pharaoh Ramses III, who famously battled (and defeated) the Sea Peoples. Still, he was the last pharaoh of New Kingdom Egypt.

Map Practice: Collapse of the Bronze Age

Instructions: Carefully look over the maps below, which are identical to maps provided in the rest of this chapter aside from one crucial difference—they have blanks in the place of the name of a sea, region, or site. Fill in the appropriate blank with the term list provided above each map.

Collapse of the Bronze Age: Rivers such as the Tigris and the Euphrates; seas such as the Mediterranean, the Black, and the Aegean; cities such as Memphis, Ramses, Gaza, Hattusa, Byblos, Ugarit, Nineveh, Assur, Babylon, Pylos, Tiryns, Mycenae, and Troy; and islands such as Thera, Crete, and Cyprus.

Works Cited

Bauer, Susan Wise. *The History of the Ancient World: from the Earliest Accounts to the Fall of Rome*. W.W. Norton, 2007.

Beck, Roger B., et al. *World History: Patterns of Interaction*. Houghton Mifflin Harcourt Pub. Co., 2012.

Chisholm, Lawrence James and Zupko, Ronald. "Measurement System". Encyclopedia Britannica, 19 Nov. 2018, https://www.britannica.com/science/measurement-system. Accessed 26 July 2022.

Cline, Eric H. *1177 B.C.: The Year Civilization Collapsed*. Princeton University Press, 2021.

Diamond, Jared M. *Guns, Germs, and Steel: the Fates of Human Societies*. Norton, 2011.

Josephus, Flavius, William Whiston. *Josephus: The Complete Works*. Thomas Nelson, 2004.

Leeming, David and Margaret Leeming. *A Dictionary of Creation Myths*. Oxford University Press, 1994.

Editors of Encyclopaedia. "mina". Encyclopedia Britannica, 26 Apr. 2018, https://www.britannica.com/science/mina-unit-of-weight. Accessed 26 July 2022.

Hill, Andrew E., and John H. Walton. *A Survey of the Old Testament*. Zondervan Pub. House, 2009.

Isserlin, B. S.J. *The Israelites*. Thames and Hudson, 1998.

King, L., translator. "The Code of Hammurabi." The Avalon Project at Yale University, 1 Feb. 2008, https://avalon.law.yale.edu/ancient/hamframe.asp. Accessed 26 July 2022.

Leonard, Austen Henry, *Enuma Elis*, 1849.

Lovgren, Stefan. "King Tut Died From Broken Leg, Not Murder, Scientists Conclude." National Geographic, 1 Dec. 2006, https://www.nationalgeographic.com/history/article/king-tut-died-from-broken-leg--not-murder--scientists-conclude. Accessed 11 Apr. 2022. "DNA Identifies Tutankhamun's Parents."

Mark, Joshua J. "The Atrahasis Epic: The Great Flood and the Meaning of Suffering." The Atrahasis Epic: The Great Flood and the Meaning of Suffering. Ancient History Encyclopedia, 2011. Web. 10 Oct. 2016. <http://www.ancient.eu/article/227/>.

Mieroop, Marc Van De. *A History of the Ancient Near East: Circa 3000 - 323 BC*. Blackwell Publishing, 2006.

Mieroop, Marc Van De. *A History of Ancient Egypt*. Blackwell Publishing, 2021.

Pritchard, J. B. *Ancient Near Eastern Texts Related to the Old Testament*. Princeton University Press, 1969.

Stearns, Peter N., and William L. Langer. *The Encyclopedia of World History: Ancient, Medieval, and Modern, Chronologically Arranged*. Houghton Mifflin, 2001.

Stein, Burton, and David Arnold. *A History of India*. Wiley-Blackwell, 2010.

Tanner, Harold Miles. *China: A History*. Hackett Pub. Co., 2010.

Works Cited

The Epic of Atrahasis." The Epic of Atrahasis. Livius.org, 1 May 2007. Web. 8 July 2015. <http://www.livius.org/asat/
atrahasis/atrahasis.html>.

Photography Credits

Cover

The Standard of Ur, Peace side is available in the public domain and is accessible at <https://en.wikipedia.org/wiki/Standard_of_Ur#/media/File:Standard_of_Ur_-_peace_side.jpg>.

Table of Contents

The photo in the Table of Contents is of the Temple of Karnak, is available via a Creative Commons license, was made by user Diego Delso, and is accessible at <http://commons.wikimedia.org/wiki/File:Templo_de_Karnak,_Luxor,_Egipto,_2022-04-03,_DD_170-172_HDR.jpg>.

Section I

The photo of the library at Trinity College in Dublin, Ireland is available via an Unsplash license, was made by user Giammarco Boscaro, and is accessible at <https://unsplash.com/photos/zeH-ljawHtg>.

Chapter 1: The Study of History

The photo of the library at Wells Cathedral is available via an Unsplash license, was made by user Annie Spratt, and is accessible at <https://unsplash.com/photos/A-G8FsDDQC0>.

The photo of Seven Wonders of the Ancient World by Marten van Heemskerck is available in the public domain and is accessible at <https://en.wikipedia.org/wiki/Maarten_van_Heemskerck#/media/File:Pharos_of_Alexandria.jpg>.

The photo of the liberal arts is available in the public domain and is accessible at <https://en.wikipedia.org/wiki/Liberal_arts_education#/media/File:Hortus_Deliciarum,_Die_Philosophie_mit_den_sieben_freien_Künsten.JPG>.

The photo of the walls of Troy is available via a Creative Commons license, was made by user CherryX on September 27, 2012, and is accessible at <https://en.wikipedia.org/wiki/Troy#/media/File:Walls_of_Troy_(2).jpg>.

The photo of the walls of Troy II is accessible via a Creative Commons license, was made by user Carole Raddato on April 17, 2011, and is accessible at <https://en.wikipedia.org/wiki/Troy#/media/File:Troy_(Ilion),_Turkey_(7446526244).jpg>.

The photo of the layers of settlement of Troy is accessible via a Creative Commons license, was made by user Winstonza on May 4, 2012, and is accessible at <https://en.wikipedia.org/wiki/Troy#/media/File:Layers_of_Troy.JPG>.

The walls of Troy I is available via a Creative Commons license, was made by Dennis Jarvis on October 20, 2005, <https://en.wikipedia.org/wiki/Troy#/media/File:Turkey-2941_(2216425111).jpg>.

The photo of Herodotus of Halicarnassus is available via a Creative Commons liencse from the Metropolitan Museum of Art and is accessible at <https://en.wikipedia.org/wiki/Herodotus#/media/File:Cropped-removebg-herodotus-historian.png>.

The photo of Pompeii and Vesuvius is available via a Creative Commons license, was made by user ElfQrin on November 28, 2015, and is accessible at <https://en.wikipedia.org/wiki/Pompeii#/media/File:Theathres_of_Pompeii.jpg>.

The map of the world from Ptolemy is available in the public domain and is accessible at <https://en.wikipedia.org/wiki/Ptolemy%27s_world_map#/media/File:PtolemyWorldMap.jpg>.

Photography Credits

The photo of the world map from Gerard van Schagen, 1689, is available in the public domain and is accessible at <https://en.wikipedia.org/wiki/Map#/media/File:World_Map_1689.JPG>.

The map from the CIA World Fact Book (2016) is available in the public domain and is accessible at <https://en.wikipedia.org/wiki/Map#/media/File:Map_of_the_world_by_the_US_Gov_as_of_2016.svg>.

The map of the world created by Islamic cartographer Muhammad al-Idrisi's Tabula Rogeriana (1154) is available in the public domain and is accessible at <https://en.wikipedia.org/wiki/Map#/media/File:TabulaRogeriana_upside-down.jpg>.

The illustration of the first page of the *Histories* is available in the public domain and is accessible at <https://en.wikipedia.org/wiki/Histories_(Herodotus)#/media/File:Dedication_page_for_the_Historiae_by_Herodotus_printed_at_Venice_1494.jpg>.

The map showcasing the spread of agriculture across the world is available in via a Creative Commons license, was made by user Joe Roe on November 29, 2010, and is accessible at <https://en.wikipedia.org/wiki/Neolithic_Revolution#/media/File:Centres_of_origin_and_spread_of_agriculture.svg>.

Chapter 2: The Neolithic Revolution

The photo of Ciucas Peak in Romania is available via an Unsplash license, was made by user David Marcu, and is accessible at <https://unsplash.com/photos/78A265wPiO4>.

The photo of stone tools from the Museum of Toulouse is available via a Creative Commons license, was made by user Didier Descouens on May 31, 2010, and is accessible at <https://en.wikipedia.org/wiki/Stone_tool#/media/File:Hache_222.1_Global_fond.jpg>.

The map showcasing the spread of hunter-gatherers is available in the public domain and is accessible at < https://en.wikipedia.org/wiki/Hunter-gatherer#/media/File:World_in_2000_BC.svg>.

The map showcasing the spread of agriculture is available via a GNU license and is accessible at <https://commons.wikimedia.org/wiki/File:Centres_of_origin_and_spread_of_agriculture.svg>.

The photo of a horse at Lascaux is available via a Creative Commons license, was made by user Jack Versloot on May 1, 2008, and is accessible at <https://en.wikipedia.org/wiki/Lascaux#/media/File:Lascaux_II.jpg>.

The photo of a megaloceros at Lascaux is available in the public domain and is accessible at at <https://en.wikipedia.org/wiki/Lascaux#/media/File:Lascaux,_Megaloceros.jpg>.

The photo of a horse at Lascaux is available in the public domain and is accessible at at <https://en.wikipedia.org/wiki/Lascaux#/media/File:Lascaux2.jpg>.

The photo of a man and a bull at Lascaux is available via a Creative Commons license, was made by user I, Peter80 on May 20, 2005, and is accessible at <https://en.wikipedia.org/wiki/Lascaux#/media/File:Lascaux_01.jpg>.

The photo of a horse and oxen at Lascaux is available in the public domain and is accessible at at <https://en.wikipedia.org/wiki/Lascaux#/media/File:Lascaux_painting.jpg>.

The photo of oxen at Lascaux is available in the public domain and is accessible at at <https://en.wikipedia.org/wiki/Lascaux#/media/File:Lascaux-IV_01.jpg>.

Photography Credits

The map included in this chapter was mde using Google Earth and Photoshop.

Section II

Chapter 3: Ancient Sumer

The photo of Bodleian Library is available via an Unsplash license, was made by user Tim Wildsmith, and is accessible at <https://unsplash.com/photos/obCmqLSXetM>.

The Standard of Ur, Peace side is available in the public domain and is accessible at <https://en.wikipedia.org/wiki/Standard_of_Ur#/media/File:Standard_of_Ur_-_peace_side.jpg>.

The map of ancient Sumer is available via a Creative Commons license, was made on April 1, 2020, and is accessible at <https://en.wikipedia.org/wiki/Sumer#/media/File:Sumer_map.jpg>.

The photo of a cylinder seal from Uruk is available via a Creative Commons license, was made by user Marie-Lan Nguyen, and is accessible at <https://en.wikipedia.org/wiki/Sumer#/media/File:Uruk_King_priest_feeding_the_sacred_herd.jpg

The illustration of a shadoof and a person using it is available in the public domain and is accessible at < https://commons.wikimedia.org/wiki/File:Shaduf2.jpeg>.

The photo of a Sumerian necklace and attire is available via a Creative Commons license, was made by user JMiall on June 13, 2010, and is accessible at <https://en.wikipedia.org/wiki/Sumer#/media/File:Reconstructed_sumerian_headgear_necklaces_british_museum.JPG

The ziggurat of Ur is available in the public domain and is accessible at <https://commons.wikimedia.org/wiki/File:Ziggurat_of_ur.jpg>.

The photograph of the Blau Monuments is available in the public domain and is accessible at <https://en.wikipedia.org/wiki/Sumer#/media/File:Blau_Monuments_(front).jpg>.

The illustration of the Warka Vase is available via a Creative Commons license, was made by Jennifer Mei on October 14, 2012, and is accessible at <https://en.wikipedia.org/wiki/Warka_Vase#/media/File:Warka_Vase1.jpg>.

The photo of the Warka Vase is available via a Creative Commons license, was made by Osama Shukir Muhammad Amin on May 25, 2020, and is accessible at <https://en.wikipedia.org/wiki/Warka_Vase#/media/File:Warka_vase_(360).jpg>.

The photo of the Adda seal is available in the public domain and is accessible at <https://en.wikipedia.org/wiki/List_of_Mesopotamian_deities#/media/File:Ea_(Babilonian)_-_EnKi_(Sumerian).jpg>.

The photo of cuneiform symbols is available in the public domain and is accessible at <https://en.wikipedia.org/wiki/Cuneiform#/media/File:Cuneiform_evolution_from_archaic_script.jpg>.

The photo of cuneiform symbols is available in the public domain and is accessible at <https://en.wikipedia.org/wiki/Cuneiform#/media/File:Cuneiform_pictographic_signs_(vertical).jpg>.

The photo of a cuneiform tablet at the Metropolitan Museum of Art is available in the public domain and is accessible at <https://www.metmuseum.org/art/collection/search/327384>.

Photography Credits

The photo of the Blau Monuments is available in the public domain and is accessible at <https://en.wikipedia.org/wiki/Cuneiform#/media/File:Blau_Monument_British_Museum_86260.jpg>.

The photo of early cuneiform writings is available in the public domain and is accessible at <https://en.wikipedia.org/wiki/Cuneiform#/media/File:Archaic_cuneiform_tablet_E.A._Hoffman.jpg>.

The photo of a clay bulla and tokens is available in the public domain and is accessible at <https://en.wikipedia.org/wiki/Cuneiform#/media/File:Accountancy_clay_envelope_Louvre_Sb1932.jpg>.

The photo of the tablet of the poem of Inanna and Ebib is available at the Ancient History Encyclopedia, was made by Daderot on March 13, 2023, and is accessible at <https://www.worldhistory.org/image/17173/tablet-of-the-poem-inanna-and-ebih/>.

The photograph of the Great Ziggurat at Ur is available via a Creative Commons license, was made by user Hardnfast on September 20, 2005, and is accessible at <https://en.wikipedia.org/wiki/Sumer#/media/File:Ancient_ziggurat_at_Ali_Air_Base_Iraq_2005.jpg

The map of ancient Sumer is available via a Creative Commons license, was made on April 1, 2020, and is accessible at <https://en.wikipedia.org/wiki/Sumer#/media/File:Sumer_map.jpg>.

The photo of the lexical list is available via a Creative Commons license, was made by user Marie-Lan Nguyen on February 16, 2009, and is accessible at <https://en.wikipedia.org/wiki/Lexical_lists#/media/File:Sumerian-akkadian_lexicon_Louvre_AO7662.jpg>.

The Kassite Cylinder Seal (16th c - 12th c.) is available via a Creative Commons license, was made on March 27, 2019, and is accessible at <https://en.wikipedia.org/wiki/Kassites#/media/File:Kassite_cylinder_seal_impression,_ca._16th–12th_century_BC.jpg>.

Chapter 4: The Rise and Fall of Ancient Sumer

The Standard of Ur, War side is available in the public domain and is accessible at <https://en.wikipedia.org/wiki/Standard_of_Ur#/media/File:Standard_of_Ur_-_War.jpg>.

The illustration of the Vulture Stele is available in the public domain and is accessible at <https://en.wikipedia.org/wiki/Stele_of_the_Vultures#/media/File:Stele_of_the_vultures_(war).jpg>.

The Victory Stele of Naram-Sin available via a Creative Commons license, was made by Rama on October 24, 2007, and is accessible at <https://en.wikipedia.org/wiki/Naram-Sin_of_Akkad#/media/File:Victory_stele_of_Naram_Sin_9068.jpg>.

The photo of the mask of Sargon is available in the public domain and is accessible at <https://en.wikipedia.org/wiki/Sargon_of_Akkad#/media/File:Sargon_of_Akkad_(1936).jpg>.

The illustration of the Vulture Stele is available in the public domain and is accessible at <https://en.wikipedia.org/wiki/Stele_of_the_Vultures#/media/File:Stele_of_the_vultures_(war).jpg>.

Chapter 5: Babylon & Assyria

The massive basalt stele of the Code of Hammurabi is available via a Creative Commons license, was made by user Mbzt on January 1, 2011, and is accessible at <https://en.wikipedia.org/wiki/Hammurabi#/media/File:P1050763_Louvre_code_Hammurabi_face_rwk.JPG>.

Photography Credits

The drawing of Marduk is available in the public domain and is accessible at <https://en.wikipedia.org/wiki/Marduk#/media/File:Marduk_and_pet.jpg>.

The ruins of the White Temple at Uruk are available via a Creative Commons license, was made by user tobeytravels on August 3, 2020, and is accessible at <https://en.wikipedia.org/wiki/Sumer#/media/File:White_Temple_ziggurat_in_Uruk.jpg>.

The map of Mesopotamia is available in the public domain and is accessible at <https://en.wikipedia.org/wiki/Mesopotamia#/media/File:Ancient_Egypt_and_Mesopotamia_c._1450_BC.png>.

The picture of the Code of Hammurabi is available via a Creative Commons license, was made by user Mbzt on June 16, 2016, and is accessible at <https://en.wikipedia.org/wiki/Code_of_Hammurabi#/media/File:F0182_Louvre_Code_Hammourabi_Bas-relief_Sb8_rwk.jpg>.

The drawing of Assur by Austen Henry Layard https://en.wikipedia.org/wiki/Assyria#/media/File:Ashur_symbol_Nimrud.png>.

The photograph of the Assyrian seal and its image of Marduk and his dragon is available in the public domain and is accessible at <https://en.wikipedia.org/wiki/Marduk#/media/File:Image_from_page_39_of_"Ancient_seals_of_the_Near_East"_(1940).jpg>.

The photo of the Ishtar Gate in Berlin is available via a Creative Commons license, was made by user Raffaele Pagani on August 20, 2019, and is accessible at <https://en.wikipedia.org/wiki/Ishtar_Gate#/media/File:Mushkhusshu,_il_drago-serpente_raffigurato_sulla_porta_di_Ishtar_-_Pergamon_Museum,_Berlin.jpg>.

The photo of Neo_Assyrian Seal featuring Marduk slaying Tiamat is available via a Creative Commons license, was made by user Ben Pirard on July 19, 2006, and is accessible at <https://en.wikipedia.org/wiki/Enūma_Eliš#/media/File:Tiamat.JPG>.

The map of Kassite Babylonia is available via a Creative Commons license, was made by user MapMaster on March 3, 2008, and is accessible at <https://en.wikipedia.org/wiki/Kassites#/media/File:Kassite_Babylonia_EN.svg>.

The portrait of Hammurabi is available via a Creative Commons license, was made by user Serge Ottaviani on April 24, 2013, and is accessible at <https://en.wikipedia.org/wiki/Hammurabi#/media/File:Royal_portrait_-_Hamurabi_-_King_of_Babylon_-1900_before_JC_-.JPG

Chapter 6: Ancient Egypt

The photo of the Great Pyramids of Giza is available via an Unsplash license, was made by user Leonardo Ramos, and is accessible at <https://unsplash.com/photos/CJ4mbwSK3EY>.

The photo of Osiris, Isis, and Horus is is available via a Creative Commons license, was made by user Rama on June 22, 2019, and is available at <https://en.wikipedia.org/wiki/Osiris#/media/File:Jewel_Osiris_family-E_6204-IMG_0641-gradient.jpg>.

The photo of the First Cataract on the Nile River is available via a Creative Commons license, was made by March Ryckaert on March 12, 2012, and is accessible at <https://en.wikipedia.org/wiki/Cataracts_of_the_Nile#/media/File:Nile_First_Cataract_R03.jpg>.

The Nile Delta as seen from space https://en.wikipedia.org/wiki/Nile#/media/File:Nile_River_and_delta_from_orbit.jpg>.

The map of Upper and Lower Egypt with names of historic nomes is available via a Creative Commons license, was made by Jeff Dahl, and is accessible

Photography Credits

at <https://upload.wikimedia.org/wikipedia/commons/0/08/Upper_Egypt_Nomes.png>.

The photo of the pharaoh Khafre, enthroned with Horus, is available via a Creative Commons license, was made by user Djehouty on March 29, 2016, and is accessible at <https://commons.wikimedia.org/wiki/File:Ägyptisches_Museum_Kairo_2016-03-29_Chephren_03.jpg>.

The photo of the Scorpion King Macehead is available via a Creative Commons license, was made by Udimu on May 16, 2010, and is accessible at <https://en.wikipedia.org/wiki/Scorpion_II#/media/File:Kingscorpion.jpg>.

The photo of the Red Crown of Egypt is available via a Creative Commons license, was made by user Käyttäjä:kompak on May 2, 2005, and is accessible at <https://en.wikipedia.org/wiki/Lower_Egypt#/media/File:Deshret.svg>.

The photo of the White Crown of Egypt is available via a Creative Commons license, was made by user Käyttäjä:kompak on May 2, 2005, and is accessible at <https://en.wikipedia.org/wiki/Hedjet#/media/File:Hedjet.svg>.

The photo of the Narmer Palette is available in the public domain and is accessible at <https://en.wikipedia.org/wiki/Narmer_Palette#/media/File:Narmer_Palette.jpg>.

The photo of the Step Pyramid of Djoser is available via a Creative Commons license, was made by user File Upload Bot on March 13, 2012, and is accessible at <https://commons.wikimedia.org/wiki/File:Egypt-12B-021_-_Step_Pyramid_of_Djoser.jpg>.

The photo of the Great Pyramids of Giza is available via an Unsplash license, was made by user Shotaro Hamasaki, and is accessible at <https://unsplash.com/photos/pLkYJ5ZBh58>.

The photo of the Great Pyramids of Giza is available via an Unsplash license, was made by user Steffen Gundermann on October 2, 2019, and is accessible at <https://unsplash.com/photos/PtGvu2P-Gco>.

The artwork of the diagram of the Great Pyramid is available via a Creative Commons license, was made by user Flanker on May 18, 2015, and is accessible at <https://en.wikipedia.org/wiki/Great_Pyramid_of_Giza#/media/File:Great_Pyramid_S-N_Diagram.svg>.

The artwork of the diagram of the Seated Scribe is available via a Creative Commons license, was made by the user Rama on October 3, 2018, and is accessible at <https://en.wikipedia.org/wiki/The_Seated_Scribe#/media/File:The_seated_scribe-E_3023-IMG_4267-gradient-contrast.jpg>.

The image of the Papyrus of Hunefer from 1300 BC is available in the public domain and is accessible at <https://en.wikipedia.org/wiki/Book_of_the_Dead#/media/File:The_judgement_of_the_dead_in_the_presence_of_Osiris.jpg>.

The map of the six cataracts of the Nile is available via a Creative Commons license, was made by user Mark Dingemanse on April 17, 2005, and is accessible at <https://en.wikipedia.org/wiki/Cataracts_of_the_Nile#/media/File:Nubia_today.png>.

The photo of the Canopic Jars is available in the public domain and is accessible at <https://en.wikipedia.org/wiki/Canopic_jar#/media/File:Egyptian_-_A_Complete_Set_of_Canopic_Jars_-_Walters_41171,_41172,_41173,_41174_-_Group.jpg>.

The photo of the mummy of Ramesses II is available in the public domain and is accessible at

Photography Credits

<https://en.wikipedia.org/wiki/Ramesses_II#/media/File:Mummy_of_Ramesses_II_-_02.JPG>.

The photo of the steps of mummification is available via a Creative Commons lciense, was made by user SimplisticReps on July 15, 2020, and is accessible at <https://en.wikipedia.org/wiki/Mummy#/media/File:Mummification_simple.png>.

The illustration of hieroglyphics is available in the public domain and is accessible at <https://en.wikipedia.org/wiki/Egyptian_hieroglyphs#/media/File:Comparative_evolution_of_Cuneiform,_Egyptian_and_Chinese_characters.jpg>.

Chapter 7: Middle & New Kingdom Egypt

The photo of Abu Simbel is available via an Unsplash liense and was made by user AussieActive on August 8, 2017, and is accessible at <https://unsplash.com/photos/oTRD-P4nU8Q>.

The image of the Papyrus of Hunefer from 1300 BC is available in the public domain and is accessible at <https://en.wikipedia.org/wiki/Book_of_the_Dead#/media/File:The_judgement_of_the_dead_in_the_presence_of_Osiris.jpg>.

The illustration of Mentuhotep II is available in the public domain and is accessible at <https://en.wikipedia.org/wiki/Mentuhotep_II#/media/File:MentuhotepII.jpg>.

The photo of Hatshepsut was donated to Wikipedia by the Metropolitan Museum of Art and is accessible at <https://en.wikipedia.org/wiki/Hatshepsut#/media/File:Seated_Statue_of_Hatshepsut_MET_Hatshepsut2012.jpg>.

The photograph of Thutmosis III is available in the public domain and is accessible at <https://en.wikipedia.org/wiki/Thutmose_III#/media/File:TuthmosisIII-2.JPG>.

The photo of the Valley of the Kings is available via a Creative Commons license, was made by user Nikola Smolenski on July 24, 2008, and is accessible at <https://en.wikipedia.org/wiki/Valley_of_the_Kings#/media/File:Valley_of_the_Kings_panorama.jpg>.

The photo of the Akhenaten & Nefertiti worshipping Aten, the sundisk, is available via Creative Commons license, was made by the user Neoclassicism Enthusiast on December 20, 2014, and is accessible at <https://en.wikipedia.org/wiki/Akhenaten#/media/File:Relief_depicting_Akhenaton_and_Nefertiti_with_three_of_their_daughters_under_the_rays_of_Aton_01_(cropped).jpg>.

The bust of Nefertiti is available via a Creative Commons license, was made by user Philip Pikart on November 8, 2009, and is accessible at <https://en.wikipedia.org/wiki/Nefertiti#/media/File:Nofretete_Neues_Museum.jpg>.

The photo of Abu Simbel is available in the public domain and is accessible at <https://en.wikipedia.org/wiki/Abu_Simbel#/media/File:Abu_Simbel_Temple_May_30_2007.jpg>.

The photo of the Egyptian striking down a Hittite soldier is available via a Creative Commons license, was made by user Iocanus on September 17, 2009, and is accessible at <https://en.wikipedia.org/wiki/Battle_of_Kadesh#/media/File:Treaty_of_Kadesh.jpg>.

The photo of Tutankhamun's mask is available via a Creative Commons license, was made by user Roland Unger on January 1, 2016, is accessible at <https://en.wikipedia.org/wiki/Tutankhamun#/media/File:CairoEgMuseumTaaMaskMostlyPhotographed.jpg>.

Photography Credits

The photo of Howard Carter and the mummy of Tutankhamun is available in the public domain and is accessible at <https://en.wikipedia.org/wiki/Tutankhamun#/media/File:Tuts_Tomb_Opened.JPG>.

The photo of Ay and Tutankhamun is available in the public domain and is accessible at <https://en.wikipedia.org/wiki/Ay_(pharaoh)#/media/File:Opening_of_the_Mouth_-_Tutankhamun_and_Aja.jpg>.

The photo of the peace treaty between the Hittites and the Egyptians is available via a Creative Commons license on May 5, 2020, and is accessible at <https://en.wikipedia.org/wiki/Battle_of_Kadesh#/media/File:Egypt_Abou_Simbel6.jpg>.

Section III

The photo of Livraria Lello, Porto, Portugal is available via an Unsplash license, was made by user Ivo Rainha, and is accessible at <https://unsplash.com/photos/0rzUepBXHN0>.

Chapter 8: The Hittites

The photo of Cappadocia, Turkey is available via an Unsplash license, was made by user Daniela Cuevas, and is accessible at <https://unsplash.com/photos/t7YycgAoVSw>.

The photo of the Lion's Gate at Hattusa is available via a Creative Commons license, was made by user Carole Raddato on March 31, 2016, and is accessible at <https://en.wikipedia.org/wiki/Hattusa#/media/File:Lion_Gate,_Hattusa_13_(cropped).jpg>.

The photo of the Hittite gods of the underworld is available via a Creative Commons license, was made by user Klaus-Peter Simon on September 12, 2002, and is accessible at <https://en.wikipedia.org/wiki/Hattusa#/media/File:Yazilikaya_B_12erGruppe.jpg>.

The photo of the lion's gate at Mycenae is available via a Creative Commons license, was made by user JoyofMuseums on August 30, 2018, and is accessible at <https://en.wikipedia.org/wiki/Lion_Gate/#/media/File:Lion_Gate_-_Mycenae_by_Joy_of_Museums.jpg>.

Chapter 9: The Phoenicians

The photo of the Lebanese coastline is available via an Unsplash license, was taken by Kassem Mahfouz, and is accessible at <https://unsplash.com/photos/mUYCiaoGfdg>.

The photo of the Lebanese coastline is available via a Creative Commons license, was made by user Rodrigo on January 6, 2010, and is accessible at <https://en.wikipedia.org/wiki/Phoenicia#/media/File:Phoenician_trade_routes_(eng).svg>.

The map of Phoenicia and Phoenician towns is available via a Creative Commons license, was made by user Kordas on May 20, 2008, and is accessible at <https://en.wikipedia.org/wiki/Phoenicia#/media/File:Phoenicia_map-en.svg>.

The map of Phoenicia and Phoenician trading routes is available via a Creative Commons license, was made by user Rodrigo on January 6, 2010, and is accessible at <https://en.wikipedia.org/wiki/Phoenicia#/media/File:Phoenician_trade_routes_(eng).svg>.

The photo of a murex shell is available via a Creative Commons license, was made by user Dennis Hill on June 22, 2004, and is accessible at <https://en.wikipedia.org/wiki/Murex#/media/File:Murex_pecten_shell_3.jpg>.

The photo of a murex shell is available via a Creative Commons license, was made by user M. Violante on March 18, 2007, and is accessible at <https://

Photography Credits

en.wikipedia.org/wiki/Tyrian_purple#/media/
File:Haustellum_brandaris_000.jpg>.

The Assyrian warship is from the British Museum, is available via a Creative Commons license, and was created on August 13, 2005, and is accessible at <https://en.wikipedia.org/wiki/Bireme#/media/File:AssyrianWarship.jpg?/>.

The illustration of the Phoenician alphabet is available via the public domain and is accessible at <https://en.wikipedia.org/wiki/Phoenician_alphabet#/media/File:Phoenician_alphabet.svg>.

The photos from the Uluburun shipwreck is available from the Institute of Nautical Archaeology and is available at <https://nauticalarch.org/projects/uluburun-late-bronze-age-shipwreck-excavation/>.

Chapter 10: The People of Israel

The photo of Israel at night is available via an Unsplash license, was made by user Akhil Lincoln, and is accessible <https://unsplash.com/photos/dSeQCOh_q7o>.

The photo of the Torah is available via an Unsplash license, was made by user Tanner Mardis and is accessible at <https://unsplash.com/photos/xUXGHzhIbN4>.

The photograph of Mount Ararat is available via an Unsplash license, was taken by user Daniel Born, and is accessible at <https://unsplash.com/photos/iy-VCSsTajA>.

The photograph of the night sky is available via an Unsplash license, was taken by user Klemen Vrankar, and is accessible at <https://unsplash.com/photos/lcT_p8kLCsc>.

The fresco of Adam and Eve is available in the public domain and is accessible at <https://en.wikipedia.org/wiki/Adam_and_Eve#/media/File:Adam_&_Eve_02.jpg>.

Chapter 11: The Exodus

The photo of the summit of Mount Sinai is available via a Creative Commons license, was made by user Mohammed Moussa on September 12, 2013, and is accessible at <https://en.wikipedia.org/wiki/Mount_Sinai#/media/File:Mount_Moses.jpg>. Gianmarco and is accessible at <https://unsplash.com/photos/zeH-ljawHtg>.

The depiction of a Hyksos shepherd is available in the public domain and is accessible at <https://en.wikipedia.org/wiki/Hyksos#/media/File:Painting_of_foreign_delegation_in_the_tomb_of_Khnumhotep_II_circa_1900_BCE_(Detail_mentioning_"Abisha_the_Hyksos"_in_hieroglyphs).jpg>.

The map of the ancient Near East is available via the public domain and is accessible at <https://en.wikipedia.org/wiki/Ancient_Near_East#/media/File:Ancient_Orient.png>.

The map of New Kingdom Egypt is available via a Creative Commons license, was made by user Andrei Nacu, Jeff Dahl on July 7, 2008, and is accessible at <https://en.wikipedia.org/wiki/New_Kingdom_of_Egypt#/media/File:Egypt_NK_edit.svg

The drawing of Pharaoh, king of Egypt, is available via a Creative Commons license, was made by user Jeff Dahl on December 31, 2007, and is accessible at <https://en.wikipedia.org/wiki/Pharaoh#/media/File:Pharaoh.svg>.

The drawing of Khnum is available via a Creative Commons license, was made by user Jeff Dahl on January 3, 2008, and is accessible at <https://

Photography Credits

en.wikipedia.org/wiki/Khnum#/media/File:Khnum. svg>.

The photo of Heqet is available via a Creative Commons license, was made by user Roland Ungeron on August 24, 2000, and is accessible at <https://en.wikipedia.org/wiki/Heqet#/media/ File:DendaraMamisiKhnum-10.jpg>.

The photo of the Apis Bull is available in the public domain and is accessible at <https://en.wikipedia.org/ wiki/Apis_(deity)#/media/File:Api_or_Hapi_(Apis,_ Taureau_Consacré_a_la_Lune),_N372.2.jpg>.

The photo of Horos is available via a Creative Commons license, was made by user Jeff Dahl on December 26, 2007, and is accessible at <https:// en.wikipedia.org/wiki/Horus#/media/File:Horus_ standing.svg>.

The photo of Neper is available via a Creative Commons license, was made by user Heshbion on September 4, 2019, and is accessible at <https:// en.wikipedia.org/wiki/Neper_(mythology)#/media/ File:Nepri_(neper).png>.

The photo of the pharaoh Khafre, enthroned with Horus, is available via a Creative Commons license, was made by user Djehouty on March 29, 2016, and is accessible at <https://commons.wikimedia.org/ wiki/File:Ägyptisches_Museum_Kairo_2016-03-29_ Chephren_03.jpg>.

The photo of Ramses II as a child is available as copyrighted free use and is accessible at <https:// en.wikipedia.org/wiki/Ramesses_II#/media/ File:Ramesses_II_as_child.jpg>.

The image of the Ten Commandments is available in the public domain and is accessible at <https:// en.wikipedia.org/wiki/Ten_Commandments#/media/ File:Decalogue_parchment_by_Jekuthiel_Sofer_1768. jpg>.

The image of the Ten Commandments in Hebrew (1768) is available in the public domain and is accessible at < https://en.wikipedia.org/wiki/Ten_ Commandments#/media/File:4Q41_2.png>.

The portrait of Moses by Rembrandt is available in the public domain and is accessible at < https:// en.wikipedia.org/wiki/Moses_Breaking_the_Tablets_ of_the_Law#/media/File:Rembrandt_Harmensz._van_ Rijn_079.jpg>.

The engraving of Solomon by Gustave Doré is available via a Creative Commons license, was made by user Yitzilitt on July 7, 2021, and is accessible at <https:// en.wikipedia.org/wiki/Solomon#/media/File:King_ Solomon_in_Old_Age_higher-contrast_version.png>.

The engraving of Solomon by Gustave Doré is available via a Creative Commons license, was made by user Yitzilitt on July 7, 2021, and is accessible at <https:// en.wikipedia.org/wiki/Solomon#/media/File:King_ Solomon_in_Old_Age_higher-contrast_version.png>.

The photo of the Merneptah Stele is available via a Creative Commons license, was made by user Webscribe on March 15, 2003, and is accessible at <https://en.wikipedia.org/wiki/Merneptah_Stele#/ media/File:Merenptah_Israel_Stele_Cairo.jpg>.

Chapter 12: The (First) Collapse

The photo of the Lebanese coast is available via an Unsplash license, was made by Ramy Kabalan, and is accessible at <https://unsplash.com/photos/mF4_ MHgp4ps>.

The map of the Late Bronze Age Collapse is available via a Creative Commons license, was made by user Alexikoua on October 16, 2013, and is accessible at

Photography Credits

< https://en.wikipedia.org/wiki/Sea_Peoples#/media/File:Invasions,_destructions_and_possible_population_movements_during_the_Bronze_Age_Collapse,_ca._1200_BC.png>.

The drawing of Ramses III defeating the Sea Peoples is available in the public domain and is accessible at <https://en.wikipedia.org/wiki/Sea_Peoples#/media/File:Seevölker.jpg>.

The photo of the archaeological site at Ugarit is available via a Creative Commons license, was made by user David Kaniewski, et al, on May 11, 2019, and is accessible at <https://en.wikipedia.org/wiki/Ugarit#/media/File:Harbour_town_Gibala-Tell_Tweini_and_the_Sea_People_destruction_layer.jpg>.

The photo of Santorini is available via a Creative Commons license, was made by user Sidvics on August 22, 2018, and is accessible at <https://en.wikipedia.org/wiki/Santorini#/media/File:Santorini_-_Grecia_-_Vista_Aerea_del_promontorio_di_Ancient_Thira_-_agosto_2018.jpg>.

The photo of the south gate of Troy VIIa is available via a Creative Commons license, was made by user Sidvics on August 22, 2018, and is accessible at <https://en.wikipedia.org/wiki/Late_Bronze_Age_Troy#/media/File:Turkey-2956_(2217219986).jpg>.

The photo of the cuneiform tablet EA 288 is available via a Creative Commons license, was made by user Einsamer Schütze on June 28, 2011, and is accessible at <https://en.wikipedia.org/wiki/Amarna_letter_EA_289#/media/File:Vorderasiatisches_Museum_Berlin_019.jpg>.

Glossary of Terms

A

Abraham: Often called the father of the Jewish people. God calls Abraham and tells him to leave his homeland of Ur and journey to Canaan; in Canaan, God promises to bless Abraham with a great nation of descendants.

Aegean Sea: A sea hemmed in by the Greek mainland and the west coast of Anatolia.

Agriculture: The purposeful cultivation of certain foods solely for human consumption and flourishing.

Ahmose: The founder of Egypt's New Kingdom, reigning from 1550 to 1525 BC.

Akhenaten: A New Kingdom pharaoh who tried to establish an entirely new religion in Egypt, one devoted to the sun disk Aten. He reigned from 1351 to 1334 BC.

Amorite: The Amorites were a tribe from Mesopotamia, Syria, and Canaan of Semitic origin, who settled in Sumer in and around the third millennium BC. Figures like Shamshi-Adad of Assyria and Hammurabi of Babylon may have Amorite roots.

Anatolia: A peninsula surrounded by the Aegean, the Black Sea, and the Mediterranean; the region is also referred to as Asia Minor. Today it corresponds to the Republic of Turkey.

Arzawa: A small state in southwestern Anatolia, whose trading and political connections with Mycenaean Greece allowed Hittite influence to embed itself into Greek culture.

Assyria: Located on the Tigris River, Assyria was the dominant kingdom in Upper Mesopotamia.

Aten: Aten was the sun disk, whose worship Akhenaten tried to force upon the rest of Egypt.

B

Babylon: Located on the Euphrates River, Babylon was the dominant kingdom in Lower Mesopotamia.

Bible: A collection of books that are sacred to the faith traditions of Judaism and Christianity.

Bireme: A Phoenician warship with two banks of oars and a ram at its prows used for hitting enemy ships.

Bronze: A metal alloy composed of nine parts of copper to every one part of tin. Because the components needed to make bronze were rarely, if ever, found in the same place, complicated trade networks developed across the ancient world to transport bronze.

Bureaucrats: The well-educated, literate members of a society charged with keeping its records.

Byblos: Along with Ugarit, Byblos was one of the principal cities of Bronze Age Phoenicia.

C

Camel: A relative of the horse, camels are uniquely-equipped to carry goods and people across the desert. They were domesticated towards the end of the Bronze Age.

Canaan: A region on the east coast of the Mediterranean Sea between the larger and more powerful states of Mesopotamia and Egypt. The land promised to Abraham and his descendants. This region sits on the east coast of the Mediterranean Sea, and the land's original inhabitants were vassals of the king of Egypt.

Carthage: The most successful of the trading posts founded by the people of Phoenicia to aid in their overseas voyages.

Glossary of Terms

Cataracts: The falls of the Nile River, which mark the southernmost penetration of Egyptian power into Nubia.

Cedar: An aromatic, sweet-smelling wood valued as a building material by kings of the ancient world; this wood was readily available in Syria and Phoenicia.

Chronology: The arrangement of dates and events according to a rational, normally linear fashion.

City-State: An independent commercial center responsible for drafting and maintaining its own laws, infrastructure, military, and other services we might expect of modern-day states.

Civilization: A society that enjoys a high degree of technical knowledge and political organization; often, we speak of a civilization as having existed for a period in the hundreds, if not thousands, of years.

Club of Great Powers: A network of the great states of the Late Bronze Age that traded lavish gifts with each other; engaged in both warfare and diplomacy; and included Egypt, Mitanni, Babylon, and the Hittites.

Code of Hammurabi: A law code drafted by King Hammurabi of Babylon to help him govern his empire.

Commodity: Goods that are largely interchangeable with goods of the same kind.

Cuneiform: A Latin word meaning "wedge-shaped writing," cuneiform was a form of writing invented by the ancient Sumerians and made upon wet, clay tablets.

D

Dark Ages: A period in which there is relatively-little textual evidence that helps later historians understand the events of that era.

David: The second but far more successful king over a united Israel. Under David's reign, Israel becomes a more centralized state on par with the other kingdoms of the ancient Near East. Approximately, his reign was from 1010 to 970 BC.

Deshret: The Egyptian word for "Red Land," the desert region of Egypt

Division of Labor / Job Specialization: As communities grow in population, less people need to be directly engaged in farming and agriculture. More food means more people, and more people means more "activities" can be done that are not directly related to farming.

Domestication: A way of taking wild plants and animals and bringing them under human control to help with human flourishing.

E

Ecological Disasters: Events such as earthquakes, famines, and volcanic eruptions that often influence the course of human events.

Edict of Telepinu: This legal code was meant to provide a law code for the Hittite people and a plan for succession for new Hittite kings.

Egypt: One of the world's oldest civilizations, this is the Greek term for the land of the Nile River and the civilization that arose on its banks. The people of Israel spent 400 years as slaves in the land of Egypt.

Elam: A state to the southeast of Mesopotamia near the foothills of the Zagros Mountains.

Empire: One city or group of people who come to rule over many cities and many groups of people.

Enki: The Sumerian god of crafts, knowledge, and water, the equivalent of Loki or Prometheus.

Glossary of Terms

Eridu: The first Sumerian city, founded sometime around 5,400 BC.

Exodus: The word Exodus refers to the deliverance of the people of Israel from their slavery in Egypt; the word Exodus comes from two Greek words: *ex*, meaning "out of" and *odus*, meaning "way." Thus, Exodus refers to the Jewish people literally going out of their slavery in Egypt.

F

Fertile Crescent: A crescent moon-shaped region that includes the river valleys of the Tigris, the Euphrates, and the Nile where peoples first learned to practice intensive agriculture.

First Intermediate: A period marked by infighting between the various *nomes* of Egypt for control and influence over the rest of Egypt without a single, powerful pharaoh to maintain stability and order for the people of Egypt.

G

Genesis: The first book of the Hebrew and Christian Bible which was written by Moses, according to Jewish tradition.

Geography: The study and knowledge of natural, physical features such as mountains, rivers, oceans, and other natural features.

Greek Dark Ages: A period that lasted from approximately 1100 to 900 BC.

Guedena: The term *guedena* refers to the border region between Sumerian city-states, which contained resources those city-states fought over.

Gutians: A barbarian tribe from the Zagros Mountains that conquered large parts of the Tigris and Euphrates river valleys and put an end to the remnants of Sargon's empire.

H

Habiru: Groups of wandering nomads who may have composed part of the Sea Peoples and thus contributed to some, but not all, of the destruction. The name habiru also sounds eerily similar to Hebrew.

Hammurabi: A Babylonian king who turned Babylon into Lower Mesopotamia's most powerful state. He conquered much of the region, and he also drafted the famous Code of Hammurabi. He ruled Babylon from around 1792 to 1750 BC.

Hatshepsut: Hatshepsut was the queen of Egypt from 1479 to 1458, famous for trying to rule as a male pharaoh.

Hatti: The name given by the Hittites to their kingdom.

Hattusa: The capital of the Hittite kingdom, with its advantages including its location on a large hill with cliffs overlooking a plateau, abundant springs, and many nearby city-states to draw resources from.

Hattusili I: The founder of the Hittite kingdom who, circa 1650, conquered several small cities in the heartland of Anatolia, founded a new capital city at Hattusa, and knit together the region into an economically-integrated state.

Historiography: The study of historical writing and of the choices historians make in the presentation of their material.

History: Derived from the Greek word for story, "history" is the study of individuals who lived in the past,

Glossary of Terms

the challenges those individuals faced, and the choices they made to take on those challenges.

Hittite New Kingdom: Lasting from the reign of Suppiluliuma I to the end of the Late Bronze Age, this was a period in which the Egyptians and the Hittites struggle for dominance in Syria. The Hittite New Kingdom ended only with the collapse of the entire Mediterranean world at the end of the Late Bronze Age.

Hittites: The dominant kingdom in Anatolia (modern-day Turkey) and a powerful rival of New Kingdom Egypt. A significant player on the international scene during the Late Bronze Age.

Homer: A blind poet (according to tradition)credited with composing the epic poems Iliad and the Odyssey, both of which describe events that occurred during the Bronze Age. Homer lived during the 8th c. BC.

Hunter-Gatherers: The earliest groups of human beings migrated across vast distances in search of food and game.

Hunting and Gathering: A lifestyle, exercised by early human cultures, consisting of following animals and supplementing one's diet with crops found naturally in the wild.

Hyksos: A group of foreigners from Syria and Palestinian who invaded Egypt in the late 17th century BC and ruled the Nile River delta from their capital at Avaris.

I

Iliad* and the *Odyssey: Homer's *Iliad* and *Odyssey* are two epic poems which may be the most famous poems in the Western canon. These works were composed towards the end of the Dark Ages, but focus on events that happened around the end of the Bronze Age.

Imago Dei: Latin for in the image of God, this phrase refers to the special creation of human beings by a good and wise Creator.

Indo-European: A family of languages, including Italic, Greek, Germanic, and Celtic languages, spoken first in Europe and Asia.

Institution: A group of people working on the same task that helps improve the quality of life in a city, including markets, courts, guilds, etc

Iron: A metal that is stronger than bronze, can be sharpened and resharpened as needed, and is found practically everywhere on earth. As a result, iron would replace bronze at the end of the Bronze Age and thus usher in the Iron Age.

Israel: The Bible describes the patriarch Jacob wrestling with God and after the match, he is renamed "Israel," or "he who wrestles with God"; the name is one among many to refer to the descendants of Abraham, the Jewish people.

Israelites: The name given, collectively, to the descendants of Abraham, Isaac, and Jacob. In Hebrew, the name Israel means "one who strives with God" and is derived from an alternate name for Jacob, the grandson of Abraham. The names Hebrews, Israelites, and Jews may be used interchangeably with the term people of Israel.

J

Joseph:The great-grandson of Abraham who, despite being betrayed by his brothers and sold into slavery in Egypt, rescued his brothers and family from destruction during a famine.

Judges:A book in the Bible that describes the first few centuries when Israel lived in the land of Canaan.

Glossary of Terms

These judges were military leaders that led the Israelites into battle for short periods of time.

K

Kassites: A tribe that conquered Babylon in the 1500s BC, but continued, preserved, and even furthered Babylon's seminal literary and diplomatic culture.

Kemet: The word the Egyptians used called for their own country; the word means "Black Land" in ancient Egyptian and refers to the fertile soil of Egypt.

Ketuvim: From the Hebrew word for "Writings," this refers to books in the Bible that are neither prophetic in nature nor found in the Torah. They include works such as the book of Job, the Psalms, and Ecclesiastes.

King: A king is someone who has been given the right to rule over a group of people.

Kingdom of Nubia: The deserts to the south of Egypt and corresponding to modern-day Sudan; at times, Egyptian pharaohs would invade Nubia to obtain soldiers for its armies or to gain access to Nubia's considerable gold mines.

Late Bronze Age: The Late Bronze Age refers to the last thousand or so years of the Bronze Age, characterized by huge trading networks and international diplomacy. The Bronze Age lasted until approximately 1200 BC, when the period collapsed suddenly and without warning.

L

Lower Egypt: The northern region of Egypt that included the Nile River delta, whose ruler wore a red crown called the "Deshret," featuring an upreared cobra.

Lower Mesopotamia: The lower, southern region of the "land between the rivers." This region was largely ruled by the city of Babylon.

M

Ma'at: *Ma'at* was the ideal of truth, harmony, and balance in ancient Egyptian religion and culture. The pharaoh was responsible for upholding ma'at.

Material Culture: The physical artifacts that a people leave behind, which historians and archaeologists can later study.

Mediterranean Sea: From the Latin for "in the middle of the land," the Mediterranean Sea has long been the center of Western civilization and is surrounded by the coastlines of southern Europe, northern Africa, and western Asia.

Mentuhotep II: The Egyptian pharaoh who reunited Upper and Lower Egypt and founded Egypt's Middle Kingdom.

Mesopotamia: A Greek word meaning "the land between the rivers" of the Tigris and the Euphrates.

Mesopotamia: The Greek term for the "land between the rivers" of the Tigris and Euphrates; this word can be used in place of ancient Sumer or ancient Akkad.

Middle Kingdom Egypt: Egypt's Middle Kingdom was a golden age of Egyptian culture, one that lasted from 2040 to 1782 BC.

Mitanni: The name given by the Hittites to a large, powerful kingdom in western Syria.

Monotheism: Together, the Greek prefix *mono* and the Greek word *theos* means belief in only one God who, in Judaism and Christianity, is the creator of the world and everything in it.

Glossary of Terms

Moses: The leader of the Exodus, the author of the Torah, the first five books of the Bible, and a prophet who, in the book Exodus, spoke to and relayed God's instructions to Israel.

Murex Snail: A snail found off the coast of Phoenicia that produced a rare, valuable purple dye used for clothing and prized by the wealthy elites of the ancient world.

Mycenaean Greece: A period in Greek history that lasted from approximately the 18th century to the 11th century BC; Mycenaean Greece is so-named for the city of Mycenae, home of the famous Greek warrior Agamemnon.

N

Nefertiti: The wife of Akhenaten and the Queen of Egypt. She lived from 1370 to 1330 BC.

Neolithic: The word neolithic comes from the Greek words *neo*, meaning "new" and *lithos*, meaning "stone." The term *neolithic* means "new stone."

Neolithic Revolution: A point around 12,000 years ago when human beings discovered not only how to grow their own food, but also began living in cities and established communities.

Nevi'im: From the Hebrew word for "Prophets," this refers to the prophetic books in the Hebrew Bible and include the works of I and II Kings, Isaiah, Jeremiah, among others.

New Kingdom Egypt: Lasting from 1550-1069 BC, New Kingdom Egypt was the highpoint in Egyptian history in regards to its military and commercial power.

Nile River: One of the longest rives in the world, the Nile flows from sub-Saharan Africa northwards into the Mediterranean Sea; its regular, predictable annual flooding deposited nutrient-rich topsoil onto Egyptian farmland and enabled ancient Egyptian civilization to flourish.

Nomes: The word *nomes* refers to an administrative district in ancient Egypt.

Old Kingdom Assyria: The period of Assyrian history that begins with Shamshi-Adad's conquest of Assur but ends with his son's death in 1741, when Assyria would be superseded by the rising power of Old Kingdom Babylon, lasting from 1813-1741 BC.

P

Paleolithic Period: Derived from the Greek words for stone and old, the "Stone Age" was characterized by its use of stone tools.

Patriarchs: The name given to Abraham, Isaac, and Jacob, the "founders" of the nation of Israel.

Peninsula: A peninsula is literally almost an island, being surrounded on three sides by water.

Periodization: The process of dividing history into periods with certain beginning and end dates.

.Pharaoh: From the Egyptian for "great house," the title that refers to the king of Egypt. It is noteworthy that, in the Bible, Pharaoh is always unnamed.

Phoenicians: A seafaring, commercial people on the eastern coast of the Mediterranean; their commercial networks knit together the far flung civilizations of the Late Bronze Age.

Phonetic Alphabet: First developed by the Phoenicians, this was a writing system where symbols are attached to sounds, the symbols being what we know

Glossary of Terms

of as letters, and the sounds being combined together until they form words we can recognize.

Pogrom: A pogrom is an attempt to destroy an entire people, acts that are often directed against the people of Israel.

Polytheism: The belief in many (the Greek prefix, *poly*) gods (the Greek word, *theos*) who are often personified by, and in control of, the forces of nature.

Priests: Priests are relatively well-educated individuals who have a special relationship with the gods and know how to keep them happy.

Primary Sources: A primary source is an account of a past event written at or very near the time in which the event occurred; primary sources include diaries, journals, chronicles, and other similar types of source material.

Prophet: A figure who, in the Bible, would speak to and relay the instructions of God to the people of Israel.

R

Ramses II: Ramses II is perhaps the most famous of New Kingdom pharaohs. He built huge temples and monuments (to himself), and fought in the Battle of Qadesh. He reigned from 1279 to 1213 BC.

Ramses III: An Egyptian pharaoh who, in 1177, claims to have defeated the Sea Peoples and kept them from destroying Egypt. He reigned from 1186 to 1155 and is the last significant pharaoh of New Kingdom Egypt.

Rephidim: The location of the site called Rephidim is unknown but may be somewhere on the Sinai or the Arabian Peninsula.

Revolution: A period of immense, sometimes violent, but always significant changes taking place in a relatively short span of time.

S

Sargon of Akkad: Sargon of Akkad was the world's first empire builder and the conqueror of the whole of the Tigris and Euphrates river valleys.

Saul: The first king of a united Israel. Approximately, his reign lasted from 1037 to 1010 BC.

Sea Peoples: A mysterious group of marauders and invaders from (presumably) Greek islands in the Aegean and the western Mediterranean; they are often blamed for the collapse of the Late Bronze Age.

Second Intermediate: Lasting from 1786-1552, this period was characterized by the invasion and rule of the Hyksos, a race of chariot-driving, bow-shooting foreigners from Palestine and Syria.

Secondary Sources: These are sources of information created later by someone who did not experience first-hand or participate in the events or conditions of which they are writing; they are typically separated from these events by a long period of time.

Sedentary: A lifestyle marked by "sitting"; this is the period when human beings settled down, focused on farming and raising livestock, and lived in towns and villages that would eventually become cities.

Semitic People: Named for Shem, the father of Abraham, this was ethnic group from the ancient Near East that included the Hebrews, Phoenicians, Arabian tribes, and the Amorites, amongst other tribes and people-groups.

Glossary of Terms

Sexegesimal System: As developed by the Sumerians, the sexegesimal system was a counting system based on the number sixty.

Shadoof: A shadoof is a tool used for irrigating fields, first used in ancient Sumer and commonly used throughout the world today.

Shamshi-Adad: An Amorite warlord who conquered the city of Assur and founded Old Kingdom Assyria. He ruled from 1808-1776 BC.

Sinai: According to Jewish and Christian tradition, God gives the Ten Commandments to Moses on top of Mount Sinai, a small mountain on the Sinai Peninsula. The Sinai Peninsula is a relatively-small triangle-shaped piece of land connecting Africa to Asia.

Solomon: The son of David, who enriches the Kingdom of Israel through trade and diplomacy. While Solomon is fabled for his wisdom, he breaks many of the rule for kings, and the kingdom unravels after his death. Approximately, his reign was 970 to 931 BC.

Staple: A food like wheat or rice that forms a substantial part of the diet of a large group of people.

Strata: A layer at an archaeological site; lower stratas are typically from an earlier period than those strata closer to the top.

Stylus: An instrument used for writing; in ancient Sumer, that instrument was a reed.

Sumerians: A people known as "the black-hair kings"; they are credited with establishing the world's first civilization on the banks of the Tigris and the Euphrates.

Suppiluliuma I: Suppiluliuma I founded the Hittite New Kingdom and made the Hittites a great power once again. He reigned as king of the Hittites from 1344 to 1322.

T

TaNaK: A term to that refers to the division of the Hebrew Bible into the Torah, the Nevi'im, and the Ketuvim.

Telepinu: A Hittite king issued the Edict of Telepinu to provide the Hittites with both a law code and a clear, well-established plan of succession from one king to another, and thus save the Hittite kingdom from violent in-fighting between would-be rival kings; reigned from 1525 to 1500.

Ten Commandments: The Ten Commandments are the ten rules that God gave to Moses and the people of Israel. They included prohibitions against murder, theft, and idolatry. The Ten Commandments are also known as the Mosaic law.

Ten Plagues: A series of devastating natural events that God, through Moses, brought on Egypt that convinced Pharaoh to release the Israelites from their slavery in Egypt.

Territorial State: A small region comprising one dominant city (like Babylon or Assyria), several smaller towns, and the adjoining farmland integrated into one economic and political unit.

Testament: A binding agreement between two parties, often with one party being of greater power than the other.

Thutmosis III: A New Kingdom pharaoh famous for his military conquests, reigning from 1479 to 1428 BC.

Tigris and Euphrates: Two massive river systems that flow from the mountains of eastern, modern-day Turkey into the Persian Gulf and gave rise to the world's first civilization in ancient Sumer.

Glossary of Terms

Torah: The Hebrew term for "law" or "instruction," referring to the first five books of the Hebrew Bible that include the books of Genesis, Exodus, Leviticus, Numbers, and Deuteronomy. According to Jewish tradition, Moses wrote these books.

Trade: The commercial and intellectual interactions between people as individuals seek to obtain goods and services abundant in one area but lacking in their own.

Trojan War: A period in Greek history that lasted from approximately the 18th century to the 11th century BC; Mycenaean Greece is so-named for the city of Mycenae, home of the famous Greek warrior Agamemnon.

Tutankhamun: The son of Akhenaten and Nefertiti; his death at an early age may have been an accident or murder. The discovery of his tomb may be the most famous discoveries in ancient Egypt archaeology.

U

Ugarit: Along with Byblos, Ugarit was one of the principal cities of Bronze Age Phoenicia.

Upper Egypt: The southern region of Egypt down to the first cataract, whose ruler wore a white crown called the "Hedjet," adorned with a vulture.

Upper Mesopotamia: The upper, northern region of the "land between the rivers." This region was largely ruled by the city of Assyria.

Uruk: The world's first city with a population between 50 to 80,000 people. Uruk was located in southern Sumer on the Euphrates River and served as a convenient place for people nearby farmland, pastureland, and marshland to meet and trade goods.

V

Valley of the Kings: The burial site for New Kingdom's most powerful pharaohs and noblemen.

Vassal: The word vassal refers to someone who has taken an oath of obedience to a more powerful ruler.

Y

Yahweh: The name God uses to describe himself; the name derives from the Hebrew verb to be.

Z

Zagros Mountains: The mountains to the east of ancient Sumer, separating the Tigris and Euphrates rivers from the Iranian plateau.

Ziggurats: The step pyramids built by the ancient Sumerians that served as the "home" for the patron deity of a particular Sumerian city.

GLOSSARY OF TERMS

NEVER ✦ CEASE
LEARNING

Made in the USA
Columbia, SC
28 May 2023